ROUTLEDGE LIBRARY EDITIONS: RADIO

Volume 3

THE UNSEEN VOICE

THE UNSEEN VOICE
A cultural study of early Australian radio

LESLEY JOHNSON

LONDON AND NEW YORK

First published in 1988 by Routledge

This edition first published in 2017
by Routledge
2 Park Square, Milton Park, Abingdon, Oxon OX14 4RN

and by Routledge
711 Third Avenue, New York, NY 10017

Routledge is an imprint of the Taylor & Francis Group, an informa business

© 1988 Lesley Johnson

All rights reserved. No part of this book may be reprinted or reproduced or utilised in any form or by any electronic, mechanical, or other means, now known or hereafter invented, including photocopying and recording, or in any information storage or retrieval system, without permission in writing from the publishers.

Trademark notice: Product or corporate names may be trademarks or registered trademarks, and are used only for identification and explanation without intent to infringe.

British Library Cataloguing in Publication Data
A catalogue record for this book is available from the British Library

ISBN: 978-1-138-20918-3 (Set)
ISBN: 978-1-315-44344-7 (Set) (ebk)
ISBN: 978-1-138-20938-1 (Volume 3) (hbk)
ISBN: 978-1-138-20939-8 (Volume 3) (pbk)
ISBN: 978-1-315-45725-3 (Volume 3) (ebk)

Publisher's Note
The publisher has gone to great lengths to ensure the quality of this reprint but points out that some imperfections in the original copies may be apparent.

Disclaimer
The publisher has made every effort to trace copyright holders and would welcome correspondence from those they have been unable to trace.

THE UNSEEN VOICE

A cultural study of
early Australian radio

Lesley Johnson

ROUTLEDGE

First published in 1988 by
Routledge
11 New Fetter Lane, London EC4P 4EE

© 1988 Lesley Johnson

Typeset by Castlefield Press, Park Farm Estate, Wellingborough, Northants.
Printed in Great Britain by Richard Clay Ltd, Bungay, Suffolk

All rights reserved. No part of this book may be reprinted or reproduced or utilized in any form or by any electronic, mechanical or other means, now known or hereafter invented, including photocopying and recording, or in any information storage or retrieval system, without permission in writing from the publishers.

British Library Cataloguing in Publication Data

Johnson, Lesley
   The unseen voice: a cultural study of early Australian radio.
   1. Radio broadcasting—Australia—History
   I. Title
   384.54'0994   HE8699.A8

ISBN 0-415-02763-2

CONTENTS

LIST OF ILLUSTRATIONS	vii
PREFACE	viii
ACKNOWLEDGEMENTS	xi
INTRODUCTION: RADIO AS POPULAR CULTURE	1
Theoretical matters	4
Early Australian radio	9
1 A GIFT OF SCIENCE	11
Popular science versus a domestic commodity	11
The modern housewife	19
'Talk back' radio	25
2KY and the 'Babble Machines'	32
2 THE BEST SEAT IN THE HOUSE	38
Mike fright	38
The rivals	49
Varied tastes	62
3 THE INTIMATE VOICE	70
'Flesh and blood' radio	71
The everyday ordinary	82
What women have to listen to	100
4 THE WORLD OF RADIO	113
Popular personalities and programmes	113
Highbrow versus lowbrow	128
The problem of the 'B' class stations	145

vi CONTENTS

5 EAVESDROPPING ON THE OUTSIDE WORLD	163
As it happens	163
The basis of an opinion	176
The world tunes in	193
NOTES	207
BIBLIOGRAPHY	226
INDEX	234

LIST OF ILLUSTRATIONS

Women's domestic work made more enjoyable by the companionship of wireless — 20

Wireless creating a children's world — 24

Fetishizing the broadcasting microphone — 41

Women as both targets and symbols of advertising strategies — 67

The personality style of commercial radio — 75

Examples of radio design in the 1920s — 85

Examples of radio design in the 1930s — 86

Radio as the focus of family life — 92

The public face of a 1920s family – proud owners of a wireless set — 99

The contrasting styles of the different types of radio personalities: the popular — 119

The contrasting styles of the different types of radio personalities: the serious — 120

PREFACE

I began this project in 1978 as a study of the Australian Broadcasting Commission and Australian intellectuals in the 1930s and 1940s. I quickly became more interested in the beginnings of radio itself and the way in which its cultural tasks were determined for it. This topic raised a far broader range of questions than I began with. I had been interested initially in the role of intellectuals. Instead I turned to questions about the production of culture, the dynamics of popular culture, cultural hierarchies, the relationship between everyday life and the world of politics, and the changes wrought on women's lives, in particular in the two decades before World War II. This book uses those questions to analyse the first two decades of broadcasting in Australia. To do so I have drawn on a range of theoretical material from media studies, cultural studies, sociology, history and women's studies. In the introduction to the book I have discussed a selection of that material to indicate the starting points and framework for my analysis of early Australian radio. I also introduce explicitly theoretical material at times throughout the book. I have attempted to discuss the theoretical literature in such a way as to make that material comprehensible to readers who are not necessarily familiar with the theories.

Gathering material for this study was often difficult and disheartening. I knocked on countless doors and made many fruitless telephone calls, attempting to find material about the broadcasting stations of the 1920s and 1930s, as well as about programme production. Many recordings of programmes have now been rescued and preserved in the National Film and Sound Archives in Canberra, but I wanted to know about the decisions broadcasters made about programming, how they conceptualized the radio audience and how they defined the cultural tasks of radio. I could find little that was still held by the commercial stations themselves, the production companies or the advertising firms, and often the archival material on the Australian Broadcasting Commission was sketchy and poor. The few tentative attempts I made with oral history interviews of people connected with early Australian radio succeeded only in eliciting memories thoroughly contained in the form of reminiscences about 'the golden age of wireless'. I did use some of this material in its printed form; but I decided to forgo any project of oral history myself. But the private papers of F.W. Daniell, who had been a major figure in establishing the Macquarie Broadcasting Services, held in the National Library and the early radio magazines proved to be valuable and exciting sources. This material led me to ask additional questions, such as how both listeners and broadcasters were taught to adapt to radio as a domestic companion, the significance of the radio personality, and broadcasting's role in the defining of legitimate politics. These questions did not spring spontaneously from the material itself; they were a result of my theoretical framework, but I did often find myself adapting that framework to the material and returning to the theoretical literature to find ways of understanding the debates and discussions about broadcasting about which I was reading.

For several years I was involved in a slightly different version of this project. I contributed to the 1938 volume of the bicentennial history project, now to be published as a series called *The Australians*. For that work I was able to draw on the extensive oral history collection made of people's memories of the 1930s for the 1938 study. I found the project a stimulating exercise, offering opportunities of working at a high level of involvement with other people and of using a different type of material. Again, however, I remained sceptical about the usefulness of oral history for my purposes of understanding the impact of radio on everyday life or popular consciousness. Images of the golden age of wireless and of family life before the age of television have widespread currency today, promoted in particular by the media themselves. The dominance of these images raises fundamental questions about the extent to which people's memories of early radio and everyday life in the 1920s and 1930s are shaped and mediated by these public histories. Such considerations could be left aside for the 1938 essay because theoretical issues were to be submerged as much as possible in its writings. But for this more substantial work and one which does address questions about how the media form our sense of history and our sense of identity, I felt oral history sources posed too many problems. I am not suggesting that they could not be used (on the contrary), but their use would require the consideration of a wider set of theoretical tasks than I felt able to address in this study. I have provided a reference to my 1938 essay in the bibliography. As well, I have listed there my other publications about radio where I have tried out some of my ideas for this book and used some of the same material.

ACKNOWLEDGEMENTS

Throughout the process of doing this study and writing the book I have been assisted by many different people in many different ways. The two people who need the greatest credit for their work in collecting material for the study, for their exciting and insightful comments about that material, and for their continuing interest in and encouragement for my subsequent work are Pauline Johnson and Deborah Tyler. Their work as research assistants on the project demonstrated to me most forcefully the extent to which this category of work is not sufficiently appreciated or rewarded in universities. I have also been assisted by numerous librarians and archivists over the past seven years. I cannot mention them all by name, so will refer to most by their institutions only: archivists at the Australian Archives in Canberra, Melbourne and Sydney; Pat Kelly, Archivist (Documents) for the Australian Broadcasting Commission (now Corporation); archivists in the British Broadcasting Corporation's Written Archives; librarians in the manuscripts section of the National Library; librarians in the Mitchell Library; and Geoffrey Holden, Curator of Communications, Museum of Victoria.

Michael Counihan's Master of Arts thesis is a substantial and innovative study of Australian broadcasting in the 1920s. I have noted where I have specifically drawn on his study or where our analyses have overlapped, but I wish to acknowledge more generally the power and clarity of his analysis. I have benefited enormously from reading his thesis, reading his published work and from brief discussions with him.

I have also gained stimulation and encouragement from reading the work of and talking to the following people: Paddy Scannell and David Cardiff, John Potts, Stuart Hall, Ken Inglis and Judith Brett. Gwyneth Dow read the draft manuscript and gave me many useful suggestions. In

1980 I participated for two terms in the media working group of the Centre for Contemporary Cultural Studies at the University of Birmingham, England. Though the group was in the doldrums about their work for much of that time, I benefited from that contact and from reading their group presentation from the previous year. I thank most sincerely Richard Johnson for his warm welcome each time I have visited the Centre as well as for his interest in my work.

Two people have been crucial to my retaining the belief that my project was worth pursuing, particularly in the last few years. Geoff Swanton has constantly expressed enthusiasm for the project and quickly read the first draft of the manuscript. As the manager of 3CR radio he made me feel that the book could be of interest and value to a broad audience and that I should write the book with this in mind. But it is his continuing encouragement that has helped me most in the last two years. Similarly, I have appreciated Henry Mayer's constant interest in and support for my work. It has been of great assistance to know that he believed my efforts were worthwhile, and I was grateful to receive his comments on my work.

I received a grant from the Australian Research Grants Scheme over a period of two years in 1982 and 1983, for which I am grateful. I received research funds at various times from the Department of Education, University of Melbourne, to help me make my numerous visits to archives and libraries in Canberra and Sydney. I wish to acknowledge the work of Gloria Johnson, and in particular that of Dorothy Rowlands and Gita Grimaud in typing the many drafts, as well as the final version of this manuscript. I appreciate and thank them for their great skill, patience and constant readiness to assist. I also thank Gerard Lier, Chief Technical Officer in charge of the photography section of the Centre for the Study of Higher Education, University of Melbourne, who took the photographs of the wireless sets.

To friends and family I owe the warmest gratitude. Friends connected with the sociology research group at the University of Melbourne have been a great support: Helen Bannister, David McCallum, Gary Wickham and, again, Debbie Tyler and Geoff Swanton. They have been terrific companions, intellectually and emotionally. Others who have been helpful and encouraging are Marion Kosak, Michael Apple, Dick Selleck and Richard Teese. My family, Betty Johnson, Pauline Johnson, Terry Johnson, John Grumley and Martin Sullivan, have always been interested and sympathetic. Martin has given crucial editorial advice on various drafts and helped me in many other ways.

Introduction:
RADIO AS POPULAR CULTURE

In his inaugural address to listeners, Charles Lloyd Jones, the first chairman of the Australian Broadcasting Commission (ABC), described radio as 'this unseen voice'.[1] Broadcasting had been officially in operation for almost nine years, but he employed this image to create a sense of excitement and wonder about radio. The use of this rhetoric in 1932 reveals the extent to which people were not yet accustomed to the new cultural institution of broadcasting nor to this new phenomenon in their daily lives. This book examines the transition – the way in which people stopped treating radio as a marvellous if slightly mysterious piece of technology and became accustomed to the 'unseen voice' as domestic companion, a normal and necessary part of their daily lives.

The book studies the first two decades of broadcasting in Australia. During the 1920s, not everyone agreed that its potential as domestic companion was the best or only way to make use of this technology. Alternative ideas about its usage and social purpose were proposed in these early years, but by the end of the first decade, they had virtually disappeared from the field of public debate. The Australian population was being persuaded to accept radio into their homes and to make it central to the pattern of their daily lives. By the end of the 1930s it clearly played that role.

In the course of this transition, clear assumptions began to emerge about the type of broadcasting style and programme content appropriate to radio, many of them deriving from the definition of its use as domestic companion. Programmes such as the early family serials, women's sessions and music programmes relied upon and added to that understanding of its use, just as the intimate style of the radio personality, which began to be exploited in the 1930s, was predicated on the image of an audience ensconced in the comfort and privacy of their homes. News and information programmes were based on similar expectations and these broadcasts were celebrated as a means of bringing 'the outside world' to listeners in the context of their world – their domestic, everyday life.

As a means for the dissemination of mass messages from a central source to listeners in their private homes or domestic environments, radio both reflected and contributed to fundamental cultural changes occurring in the 1920s and 1930s. Radio, through its programmes and through the discussions that took place around it, promoted a specific image of people's daily lives. It glorified the everyday and the satisfactions to be found there. This world of the everyday was portrayed as separate from the world of work and the world of the political – the latter appeared as the domain only of politicians and public figures. The everyday revolved around the domestic, family life of individuals. Radio spoke to its listeners in this context as consumers, whose sense of themselves, or means of self-identification, was to be found through the exercise of individual choice in the market-place. But the history of the early years of radio also demonstrates the contested nature of social and cultural change. This study examines the gradual and at times contradictory development of these ideologies of the everyday, the political and the relationship between the individual and society.

In the late 1980s many of the assumptions and conventions about broadcasting established in the 1920s and 1930s may be challenged by the commercial success of video, cable and satellite technologies. Indeed many of them seem to have disappeared already or to have been transformed in the world of modern radio. For a time apparently usurped by television, radio has now once again overtaken television in popularity.[2] Talk-back programmes, music and news dominate the air, rather than the family serials of the 1930s. Official discussions of broadcasting over the past ten years have turned to questioning the viability and value of the Australian Broadcasting Commission (or Corporation as it has been called since 1983) as a public institution, or to the possibility of seeking commercial sponsorship for the ABC's programmes. The new system of public broadcasting stations introduced in 1974 has challenged the concept of the public previously embodied in the ABC, and encroached on its audience and territory of serious programming. The impact of the introduction of FM broadcasting in the 1970s continues as commercial concerns become increasingly interested in FM rather than AM licences as profitable investments. Finally, a trend begun in the 1950s and 1960s (assisted by the invention of transistor radios and portable record players) towards private and individual consumption of media products now appears to have reached its logical limit as young people, at home and in the streets, are cocooned in the private world of their 'Walkman' sets, listening to the throb of their favourite rock bands. This latter image seems to illustrate dramatically Baudrillard's warning that the most profound social and political effect of the modern media is that people are 'no longer speaking to each other'.[3]

This history examines the assumptions and conventions about radio programming and its significance in our daily lives established in the first two decades of Australian broadcasting. It thus provides a basis to assess the extent to which those assumptions still remain with us, but, more importantly, to assess their social value and political consequences in the past and the present. It offers, too, an insight into how such assumptions become established and are made to appear natural and necessary to the technology itself. This analysis is relevant not just to our understanding of broadcasting, but to a critical evaluation of current usages and understandings of new developments in communication and information technologies. This study does not enter contemporary debates explicitly, but has been conducted in the belief that an investigation of early radio will serve to highlight the profound cultural and political consequences involved in the development of these technologies and the way in which we can and should be far more aware of the steps involved.

Further, this history addresses contemporary discussions about popular culture. In Australia, as elsewhere, analyses of culture frequently resort either to celebratory accounts or moralistic condemnations of popular radio and television. An examination of early Australian radio raises crucial questions about the concept of popular culture. The history of the first two decades of radio is a history of the re-forming and re-working of the notion of the 'popular' and the setting up of and legitimating of distinctions between the culture of the élite and the culture of popular tastes. In Australian broadcasting, this opposition between high culture and popular culture may appear at first glance to have been institutionalized and arisen of necessity with the establishment of a dual system of broadcasting: the ABC, set up in 1932 to pursue cultural excellence, versus the commercially based radio stations of the 1930s, whose viability relies on the capturing of mass markets. This study suggests that the difference did not (and does not) lie here, but is a question of the fabrication of distinctions, the manufacture of cultural hierarchies and their legitimation through institutions like broadcasting.[4] Superior cultural tastes become the preserve of, and grounds for unity of, a limited social group, while the tastes and preferences of the masses are said to demonstrate their inferior intellectual and moral stature.

The celebratory approach to popular culture has dominated contemporary analyses in this field in Australia. In part it is a reaction to these traditional distinctions made on the basis of taste and superior moral worth, but it is also a reaction to radical critiques that have interpreted popular culture as the false consciousness of the masses.[5] Two commentators on Australian culture, Keith Windschuttle and John Docker, have in recent years analysed popular Australian television, or popular culture more generally, in terms of its providing an authentic reflection of people's daily lives. The popular media, says Windschuttle, sells Australian working people a culture they themselves have created – it is a matter of 'selling them themselves'.[6] To clarify the stance taken in this study on matters such as these and, more generally, the questions that organize this history, the following discussion examines a number of theoretical issues in cultural and media studies.

Theoretical matters[7]

Raymond Williams's approach in his seminal book *Television. Technology and Cultural Form* provided the starting point for this study. He argues that the technology of broadcasting was devised and developed with certain practices and purposes – certain social needs – already in mind. Decisions had already been made before the official development of wireless broadcasting was undertaken that directed the commercial and social exploitation of the technology.[8] This book examines, in the Australian context, the way in which broadcasting was defined as a means of one-way communication to a mass audience in the privacy of their homes. The material gathered in the course of this investigation elucidates the steps in this process, while also revealing that despite decisions already taken to develop the technology of wireless in this manner, this definition of broadcasting's social use was by no means guaranteed from the outset. Rather, it was a question of this definition becoming increasingly dominant during the first decade of Australian broadcasting.

By the mid-1920s, this social use of wireless had begun to appear inevitable and even necessary to its technology; but an important critique of broadcasting had emerged that attempted to keep alive the suggestion that its technology could be exploited for quite different social purposes. A section of the labour movement in Australia challenged the dominant understanding of and use to which wireless technology was being put (their political analysis of wireless and their suggested alternative ideas about communication form part of the material of this study), while in the international context, a number of critics also appeared whose similar attacks on the form and definition of radio broadcasting have achieved a more lasting recognition and have been incorporated into contemporary theoretical debates about the media and popular culture. The writings of Bertolt Brecht, Walter Benjamin, Max Horkheimer and Theodor Adorno remain pertinent today to discussions of the media, but it should be realized that the debates between them were first formed in the context of the early years of broadcasting. Their ideas and their disagreements will be discussed with this in mind.

Writing in the 1930s, Brecht argued that it should be possible to transform radio in the interests of 'proletarian communication': in the interests of working people communicating with each other and developing a sense of shared experiences and goals. This did not entail simply altering the content of the programmes sent out by radio, but changing the relationship set up between speaker and listener. Brecht attacked the form in which radio had developed, the one-sidedness of its communication; he saw radio's mode of operation at that time as purely an instrument of distribution of messages or content for which the listener was made a passive receiver. The listener, he declared, should be able to speak, not only to listen – to join in an active relationship with other listeners-speakers.[9]

The social and political context, Brecht acknowledged, would have to change if such an alternative social use of wireless technology was to become possible, but he remained committed to undermining its present functioning or social use. He sought to achieve this end by speaking publicly of his different conception of radio's potential, as well as by experimenting with programmes that attempted to break down the categories or boundaries placed between the roles of speaker/broadcaster and listener.[10] Brecht thus attributed a positive value to the technology of broadcasting, but he was hopeful too that, even within the restrictions that had already been placed on its social uses, wireless could be utilized for progressive social purposes.

Walter Benjamin echoed and extended Brecht's optimistic assessment of the possibilities of this new technology. In his essays on Brecht's work and, more generally, in his discussions of cultural production, Benjamin celebrated the potential held by such technology (though not necessarily its current social use) for breaking down the 'aura' of cultural objects, objects of 'art'. Through the new means of technical reproduction (whether photography, movie camera or broadcasting), the art object, Benjamin argued, is detached from its history and from the rituals that customarily attest to its authenticity, its unique existence. These processes of mechanical reproduction bring the art object into its listener's or viewer's own world, reactivating or renewing these cultural products and shattering their reliance on tradition or cultural heritage for their meanings. In *Ways of Seeing*, John Berger draws heavily on Benjamin's work and illustrates this point in his discussion of how the modern teenager covers the wall of his or her room with posters and prints of famous paintings. Juxtaposed with other items of personal significance, these reproductions of paintings acquire particular and private meanings for their owners that do not rely or depend on the history or traditions that surround the original objects of art.[11] Benjamin believed these new technologies of reproduction and dissemination, with their potential to change the social function of art, opened up the possibility of its use in political struggle or practice.[12]

Benjamin, like Brecht, warned of the forces that moved to obstruct this potential of the new means of cultural production. He pointed to the creation of movie stars and the building up of the cult of the personality by film studios as an attempt to replace the desiccated aura of the art object with the artificial aura of the commodity.[13] Such developments set out to create a distance between the new cultural products, in this instance films, and their consumers, thus mystifying their means of production. The role of the consumers was thereby contained or diminished. They were to be discouraged by the new aura being built up around films and movie stars from determining their own uses for and meanings to be given to these products. The mystique built up around a movie star suggests to the audience that there is only one set of meanings to be attributed to a film in which they appear: that determined by producers and agents. Similarly, the rituals and traditions surrounding an object of art imply that it has a unique value and authenticity whose meaning and significance can only be determined by the accredited few.

This history of early Australian radio examines the way in which a particular relationship between broadcaster and listener was eventually defined as necessary to broadcasting. Using the insights provided by Brecht and Benjamin, it does not assume that this development was inevitable, but rather seeks to elucidate the processes by which one particular concept of the relationship between the listener and the material broadcast came to dominate public discussions about radio as well as the practices of broadcasting stations. This course of events is shown to be complex and often confused. One articulate group within the labour movement resisted this definition of the social use of the technology of broadcasting; nor did purchasers of wireless equipment necessarily adopt the passive listening attitude required of them – the public had to be taught how to be 'listeners-in'; and throughout the 1920s considerable uncertainty existed about what the content of the broadcasting messages should be – there was no clear concept at first of programming.

Further, this study employs Benjamin's argument about art and cultural tradition to examine critically the distinction reasserted in the field of broadcasting between popular tastes and authentic culture. The attempts made by the ABC to create a sense of specialness and superiority for the traditional cultural items broadcast – classical music, plays by well-known dramatists, talks on scholarly subjects – mystified the differences between these programmes and those deemed 'popular'. The setting up of such distinctions between 'culture' and 'popular entertainment' discourages people from attributing their own meanings and significance to works of opera or serious drama. And lively debates exploring these issues frequently erupted in the popular radio magazines of the 1920s and 1930s.

Brecht and Benjamin formulated their views in opposition to the cultural pessimism of Adorno, and more generally of members of the Frankfurt School. Adorno and Horkheimer in their joint essays referred to the new mass media in derogatory terms as the 'culture industry'. The new means of cultural production, they argued, duped their consumers into becoming reliant on the marketplace for the goods and commodities provided for them. Adorno and Horkheimer developed some powerful criticisms of the functioning and social effects of the cultural industries; but they insisted upon the superiority of the traditional works of art compared with those of popular culture. The latter, they claimed, simply represented the manipulated consciousness of the masses.

Adorno and Horkheimer diagnosed the social effects of radio as derived from its form: 'the gigantic fact that the speech penetrates everywhere', they declared, 'replaces its content'.[14] They rejected all hopes of radio assuming any other form or of its technology being used in any other way than to manipulate the very manipulable masses. All popular art, popular music and popular literature, they claimed, is bad art. Listening to music on radio, Adorno added, whether classical music or jazz, is commodity listening: listeners respond to the music as quotations of itself, enjoying only what is comfortable, familiar.[15] The only point that Adorno and Horkheimer would concede in favour of popular culture was that it formed, they believed, the bad conscience of serious art. The existence of 'light art' and the very distinction itself arose only because there were those whose lives made it impossible to appreciate real art.[16]

Adorno in particular provides some valuable insights into the development of radio's cultural form that will be used and discussed in the body of this text. But this critique of broadcasting needs to be placed in the context of his writing during the early decades of broadcasting. In contemporary culture theory debates, the opposition between Brecht and Benjamin on one side and Adorno and the Frankfurt school on the other, is all too readily assumed to be recoverable in terms of contemporary stances. In the Australian context, this opposition has at times been reduced (and trivialized) to a question of being basically either for popular culture or against it: for Benjamin or for Adorno.[17]

This stance fails to acknowledge the extent to which Benjamin (and Brecht) believed popular culture to be a contradictory arena, a site of struggle.[18] The history of radio is the story of one important period in modern history in which we can trace the emergence of a new definition of the people. Radio and the publicity language that surrounded it presented its audience with a picture of themselves, of their daily lives and the social world, that excluded or marginalized such identifications as working class or working people. It spoke to its listeners as consumers, individuals, whose personal troubles – the realm of everyday life – were separate from public issues – the sphere of news and information programmes about the 'outside' world.[19] But this message was not clearly or consistently delivered at first, nor was it uncontested. Contradictory consequences would also emerge in the way in which radio spoke to different sections of its audience.

Radio, it will be argued, defined one section of its audience as more than a collection of individuals, as a group with shared fundamental experiences in common: women. In the 1930s, this message became crucial to the commercial stations, for women were seen as a major market by advertisers. Day-time programming set out to persuade women that they should understand themselves as having interests in common that would be satisfied by these programmes (and the items they advertised) and that they should think about their lives and experiences in terms of their being women. Thus, while at one level the radio audience was being taught to see personal troubles as private ones only, women's programmes were showing women that their troubles were shared by a vast, though as yet invisible, public. This defining of one section of the population as a group by institutions such as radio took on a new significance in the late 1960s when women began to mobilize this sense of being a group, of having fundamental experiences in common, to form a political movement.

Radio as an institution of popular culture further demonstrates the extent to which this is an arena of tensions and contradictions in its re-working of and re-creating distinctions between the popular and the serious. In the twentieth century, all culture has increasingly assumed the form of a commodity, produced and distributed by the minority for the majority.[20] Developments in early Australian radio demonstrate the way in which this process progressively undermines traditional distinctions of quality and merit. They also reveal the way in which those distinctions can be speedily re-drawn, as can the political function they play. Finally, it raises questions about how needs and desires for popular pleasures are produced.

Early Australian radio

Broadcasting was officially established in Australia in September 1923. In July 1924, the Postmaster General announced the setting up of two sets of broadcasting stations and the basis was laid for today's system of a combination of public and commercially operated stations. These stations, however, went through some major changes in the first two decades of Australian broadcasting. At first, the two sets of stations, designated 'A' and 'B' class stations, were differentiated primarily on the grounds that the former were to receive funding from licence fees collected from listeners. In 1929 the government decided to co-ordinate the activities of the 'A' class stations through a single national company. The Australian Broadcasting Company made the successful tender. But in July 1932 the running of these stations was again taken over; this time by the ABC established by act of parliament. The 'B' class stations remained on an uncertain footing throughout the 1920s, but at the end of the decade new and more powerful bodies began to acquire their licences. They changed from being small amateur operations to commercially based organizations relying on attracting advertisers for their financial success. Signalling this development, the new licensees sought official recognition for a change of name from 'B' class to commercial stations. Though this was granted a number of times in the early 1930s, they continued to be called 'B' class in many official documents as well as popular publications.

Though the history of these changes forms the background for this study, the book does not proceed by telling the story of radio's early years in straightforward, linear terms. The first two chapters deal with the 1920s. They examine the way in which broadcasting was discussed in these early years, how it was conducted, the confusions and debates that existed about what to do with this new means of communication and the way in which people had to be taught to be listeners-in (this attitude or relationship to wireless was not automatically accepted by its consumers as desirable or necessary, and the owners of broadcasting stations themselves did not necessarily understand their audiences in this way). The next three chapters examine the dominant understandings of radio and its audience that were beginning to prevail over all other alternatives by the late 1920s and early 1930s. This investigation discusses the emerging assumptions about what was appropriate content for radio programmes, what differences in style there should be between programmes, how broadcasters should speak and present themselves on radio, what the audience would like and why, how people should be divided into different audiences and what the relationship should be between the broadcasting stations and the state.

This history draws on an analysis of official statements such as those by politicians and public servants; statements or discussions of a more popular kind, such as those in newspapers, magazines and the popular radio journals; the actual practices of the broadcasting stations themselves (including the recordings of some programmes from this period) in so far as they reveal how conceptions about wireless broadcasting were developing or changing; and the private papers and official documents of various people and organizations involved in broadcasting in its early years in Australia.

1
A GIFT OF SCIENCE

Wireless was a wonder. Celebrated as a new science for the universal benefit of humanity, broadcasting officially began in Australia in September 1923. The magic, the marvel, the romance, and most frequently, the wonder of wireless were the terms in which the commercial beginnings of this culture industry were hailed. For the first few years this rhetoric was to dominate popular and official declamations about radio. It was claimed to be part of the exciting new age of modern electricity through whose bounty the everyday lives of the entire population would be made radiant. Opening the 1923 Radio and Electrical Exhibition in Sydney Town Hall, Dr Earle Page, the acting Prime Minister, was widely quoted as proclaiming 'the wonders of wireless' and expressing the belief that soon there would be 'wireless for all'.[1]

Popular science versus a domestic commodity

This language of excitement and wonder resembled in part a circus ringmaster announcing a thrilling new act. Audiences were shown the marvels of the new radio science at exhibition concerts or demonstration performances at the yearly electrical exhibitions. Newspapers and magazines kept their readers informed of recent advances, in Australia and overseas, of the successful transmission of concert performances from hundreds of miles away or of the new miracles of beam wireless. Wireless was a stunning trick: '"Broadcast music" is by way of being a simple and intelligible label for a magic as marvellous as any that could be imagined.'[2]

Yet this language also reflected the way in which wireless did function as a popular science in 1923. The images of excitement and wonder that surrounded wireless at this time were more than a publicity stunt for this new commodity: they celebrated the involvement of a broad range of people in its development and exploration as a new technology. Before the official beginnings of broadcasting, experimenters, or 'amateurs' as they were later called, were an exclusive group. Experimenting with wireless transmission and reception required considerable financial outlay for equipment not yet mass-produced and these activities were also heavily restricted by the Postmaster General's (PMG) department.[3] But in the early 1920s experimenters began to multiply. 'Wireless enthusiasts' built their own sets as wireless equipment parts began to be cheaper; they experimented with their equipment in the pursuit of better reception, and amateur clubs flourished. By the time broadcasting was established officially in September 1923, there were thirty-seven amateur clubs in New South Wales (NSW), with members exchanging information about set construction, exploring together the technical possibilities of wireless and logging the reception of amateur transmissions.

New radio journals and regular columns in the daily newspapers catered for and promoted this popular science. They provided endless information on the construction of crystal and valve sets and suggestions about how to improve reception. The *Daily Telegraph*, in its 'Radio Bureau' column, declared its intention 'to educate the public into understanding exactly what all this "wireless" and "radio" means'.[4] When the *Labor Daily* introduced a weekly section on how to make your own wireless set in 1924, queues formed outside distributing agents' shops and the paper quickly sold out. The same paper informed readers of 'a remarkable lad of 13, who has made a wireless crystal receiving set capable of cutting out unwanted stations and tuning in – completely contained in a match box'.[5] What was later to be depicted as predominantly the preserve of small boys – participation in the exciting developments of the science of wireless – was here portrayed as firing the imagination of everyone.

For many, however, it would be the imagination only that was fired. Although sets like that of the 'remarkable lad of 13' could be constructed for as little as two shillings, licence fees in Australia were prohibitive, thus limiting popular participation in the excitement surrounding this new technology. Broadcasting was officially introduced in 1923 under a sealed set scheme so that listeners had to pay for the station or stations to which they wished to listen. The wavelengths assigned to each station licensed by the PMG were treated as 'its own property for the purpose of providing its own service',[6] or in the words of the PMG, W.G. Gibson, 'a limited number of stations will be permitted to broadcast in each centre, and ... dealers will be able to supply receivers which will respond to the particular wavelength of each broadcasting station'.[7]

The licence fee to listen-in was an initial ten shillings per year to the PMG and broadcasting station licensees made their own charges in addition: these ranged from ten shillings a year for 2SB Sydney (later to become 2BL) to four guineas for 6WF Perth. Gibson envisaged broadcasting, not as a popular science, but as a 'competitive entertainment business' for which broadcasters (with the assistance of the government) should collect revenue for the maintenance of their stations and the provision of programmes.[8] This scheme devised by E.T. Fisk of Amalgamated Wireless (Australasia) Ltd (AWA) was, as Counihan suggests, effectively an attempt to set up a ticket box for listeners-in.[9]

With the introduction of this scheme, interest in radio slumped. The excitement and anticipation that newspapers and other popular publications had built up before September 1923 was not reflected in the number of licences taken out: in the period 1 August 1923 to 30 June 1924 only 1400 listeners were licensed. Traders protested bitterly, insisting that 'all the romance has been taken out of the wireless for the ordinary man'.[10] The scheme was denounced as a fiasco[11] and in July 1924 the PMG announced a new scheme:

> There will be two types of broadcasting licences. One will be for class 'A' stations, which will obtain revenue from licence fees, and the other for class 'B' stations, which will not receive any revenue from that source. Both types of stations will be allowed to broadcast advertisements, but class 'A' stations will be permitted to broadcast advertisements only for limited periods.[12]

Listeners now only paid one fee; and where there was more than one 'A' station in the state, licence fees were to be distributed by the government on a proportional basis: 70 per cent to one station, 30 per cent to the other.

But the licence fee remained prohibitive for many: thirty-five shillings per year. Though the 'open set' scheme was welcomed universally as preventing a monopoly of broadcasting by commercial interests, and as recognizing that broadcasting was a public utility, by October 1924 some dissenting voices could be heard. While newspapers such as the *Age* declared that the increase in wireless sales sought by traders would now depend on listening-in becoming a delight,[13] the *Labor Daily* began a campaign to abolish radio licences altogether. When Gibson had met with the wireless traders in April to devise a new licence scheme, this paper had greeted the new scheme as recognizing and serving the best interests of the public.[14] Now it attacked licences as providing enormous revenue to these 'advertising stunt firms': in NSW, Farmer and Co., who ran the 'A' station 2FC, and Broadcasters who ran the 'A' station 2BL. The federal government, declared the *Labor Daily*, 'should make listening-in either free or so cheap that every worker, in country or city, could receive from radio all that radio can contribute to the enjoyment, instruction, and education of mankind.'[15] This editorial, entitled 'Wireless for Workers', drew attention to the licence fee of only ten shillings in Britain. The expense of the licence fee in Australia, the editorial argued, restricted popular participation in the excitement of radio.

By 1924–5 crystal sets, including earphones, were advertised by department stores, such as Mark Foys in Sydney, for fifty-five shillings (when a yearly subscription to the *Labor Daily* cost thirty-two shillings), and they could be made far more cheaply. Valve sets, on the other hand, were being advertised for prices ranging from seven pounds to seventy-five pounds. These sets were a luxury item in the first years of broadcasting in Australia; the PMG noted in 1926 that only 20–30 per cent of listeners possessed valve sets.[16] But as a letter to the *Daily Telegraph* pointed out, the licence fee of thirty-five shillings applied equally to owners of all types of sets.[17] Though the number of licences soared in the first two years of the 'open set' scheme (by July 1926 there were 118,000 licences), owning a valve set and a licence was beyond most members of the population. But, for many, the cost of the licence itself continued to make radio a luxury they could not afford.

Despite this restriction on widespread participation in the excitement of wireless, official statements, advertisements for wireless equipment, newspapers, and the new radio journals insisted upon its democratic nature. Broadcasting's potential for popular participation in the exploration and development of its science was co-opted to promote sales of wireless equipment. Wireless was the concern of 'the man in the street', of 'everyman'. The first issue of the magazine *Radio in Australia and New Zealand* declared that 'the future of Wireless lies with "The Man in the Street"'.[18] The title of the *Daily Telegraph*'s regular column, 'Wireless for All', begun in October 1924, echoed Earle Page's speech of 1923. In 1926 this same paper instituted a radio supplement that became 'Radio for Everybody' in early 1927 (before being dropped later that year). And in 1927 advertisements appeared in the daily newspapers for an 'Everyman' receiver. Hailed as participants in the exciting new world of electricity and modern technology, this language addressed potential listeners-in and purchasers of wireless equipment not as a particular section of the population, but as 'everybody', you and me. Science was now accessible to all and a benefactor of all.

This was the image of science being exploited by publicity statements for radio, yet the actual involvement in the technology of wireless by listeners-in was shrinking, discouraged in particular by the new equipment being manufactured. Increasingly sets were designed as household furniture, with an emphasis on the simplicity of their operation rather than the need for technical intervention by listeners. Though the technical sections in radio magazines would remain important until the late 1920s, by 1925 the image of broadcasting as a popular science had become more what Stuart Ewen calls a cultural allegory than a reality.[19] Radio came to stand for modernity and universal progress. It symbolized the bounties of industrial capitalism with its endless production of new and existing commodities freely available to all in the marketplace. Wireless equipment was produced by a magical science for the benefit of all.

The profitable industry being established behind this market rhetoric was selling a tale about itself and its goods through images of modernity and progress. This allegory of wireless as democratic science did not include as participants the many workers employed by firms like AWA.[20] Science itself became the producer in the guise of 'electricity', the experimenters of the past, or, in the mid-1930s, as the mysterious scientists 'behind closed doors' of the advertisements for 'Bandmaster. A micro-sensitive radio'.[21] Science was something to marvel at, to wonder at, but increasingly to leave to others.

New innovations in the domestic apparatuses available in the marketplace now represented change, progress and the advancement of civilization: 'The latest marvel in the radio world is the 4 valve set, which is operated without aerial or earth wire. . . . One of the great factors is the simplicity of tuning.'[22] Publicity for the 1926 Radio and Electrical Exhibition in Sydney Town Hall advertised that visitors would be 'initiated into all the wonders of radio, and may see all the latest of the most wonderful apparatuses which the experts have to offer'.[23] At first the science of radio had symbolized the progress of civilization in appearing to open its doors to democratic participation. Now it became a sign or symbol of progress because of its endless munificence. Wireless for Everyman. And assuring this unbounded potential of science to bestow new pleasures on the world, whispers of the coming of television – wireless with pictures – were being heard in 1924 in the popular-style radio magazines and newspapers. Radio was one sign among many of the progressive, consumer orientation of western society.[24]

Radio and electrical exhibitions in this period conducted the most concerted campaigns to sell radio equipment through these images of science. Advertised as festivals for the general public to come and marvel at the new inventions of electricity, they were designed as massive promotion campaigns for electrical goods. Radio traders displayed their goods and demonstrated the capacities of their equipment. By 1933 broadcasting stations were setting up model studios as part of these exhibitions and conducting broadcast sessions on stage. To promote the sale of wireless equipment the exhibitions constantly found new strategies to enthrall the public.

Raymond Williams, in the British context, has drawn attention to the importance of radio traders and commercial interests in determining the direction of the early development of radio.[25] These interests had the most to gain by wireless being accepted as a piece of domestic equipment. The radio and electrical exhibitions in Australia attempted to persuade the public that every home should own at least one set. In the mid-1920s they exploited the image of a democratic science to attract prospective buyers, but the inclusion of radio in these exhibitions also ensured that it would be seen as part of an expanding manufacturing industry supplying electrical consumer goods for a domestic market.

Thus the major investment in radio at the outset was in the means of distribution, the domestic receivers, rather than in the content, the material to be heard on radio. This feature of the early development of radio is also reflected in the type of broadcasting stations established. A number of these were set up by radio traders as a means of advertising their companies and making the purchase of radio equipment attractive – by providing a service for their customers. Stations 2UE Sydney, 2UW Sydney, and 3UZ Melbourne were established for these purposes, as was the first station to go on the air in 1923, 2SB Sydney.[26] Usually broadcasting for only a few hours a day, their programmes were basic, even crude; sometimes as primitive as a piano played by a friend. The sheer event of transmitting anything was seen as sufficient. Though wireless was sold as domestic equipment, the excitement generated by its technology was satisfied by the success of tuning in or achieving reception; consumers of radio were not yet necessarily listeners-in.

The commercial interest in radio was not confined to radio traders and electrical goods manufacturers. The large department stores quickly moved into the market. Farmer and Co. in Sydney was there from the beginning; they established a broadcasting station and began selling wireless sets. Urged on by Fisk of AWA, they planned their radio station, 2FC Sydney, on an ambitious scale and secured an 'A' class licence. It began broadcasting in December 1923.[27] Advertisements appeared in a broad range of newspapers:

> Amalgamated Wireless (Australasia) Ltd have pleasure in announcing that, in view of the early inauguration of Broadcasting Services by Messrs. Farmer and Company Limited, they have designed a 'Radiola' especially to receive theatrical and other entertainments in every home.
>
> The design embodies the highest expression of the techniques of Radio Engineering as produced by the World's leading Wireless Engineers.... The Radiola will be unequalled in performance, simple in operation and reasonably priced.[28]

The public was advised that they would soon be able to purchase these sets from Farmer's. Other stores such as Mark Foys and Anthony Hordern were not so intensively involved in the radio business, but they vigorously advertised the ever-expanding range of wireless sets available from their shops.

In relying on the excitement of radio to create an expanding market, these commercial interests were assisted by the appearance of popular-style radio magazines. These magazines were preoccupied throughout the first three years of broadcasting with the sheer excitement of radio's existence. Technical sections dominated their content, providing information about improving reception and making wireless sets. Many of the feature pages were celebrations of the advances made by radio as a technology. The *Listener In*, established in Melbourne in 1925 and later to emerge as one of the major radio magazines, featured two regular sections: 'Wireless News from All Quarters' and 'What's New in Radio', both providing information about developments in wireless technology. Unlike its format in the 1930s, the programmes and personnel of radio stations formed a relatively minor section in the journal.

The content of these magazines perpetuated the image of radio as popular science, and no doubt facilitated the continuance of that interest among members of the public. But, just as the radio and electrical exhibitions recruited that excitement to the promotion of wireless as a piece of domestic equipment, so the radio journals attempted to establish these links. Front covers pictured wireless in a thousand contexts, bringing joy to people's lives and transforming their lives. Photographs or drawings showed adults and children wearing earphones, often presented in the style of family portraits. Radio brought bed-time stories to children, relaxing programmes to the busy housewife, companionship to the sick and entertainment to the family group. This visual imagery depicted wireless as renewing the private, domestic life of families. Eventually this rhetoric would displace the 'Everyman' popular science rhetoric about radio, but in the mid-1920s they co-existed.

The visual language used by the radio magazines about radio's domestic role represented it as coming to you, the listener-in, in your world and transforming it; radio gave your world an extra glow. By showing people in domestic settings such images made that world special, something pleasant and comforting to display on the front cover of your magazine; and the presence of radio appeared to be the additional quality that made this ordinary occasion extraordinary. Further, the photographic naturalism employed (in photos and drawings), where the subjects appeared to be caught unexpectedly in the normal activities of their everyday lives, portrayed them as universal, representative, in a world all listeners shared – your world and mine. Radio was a gift from science and, like all other such domestic commodities, was a symbol of progress and the democratic character of society. Everyone shared in a domestic life and all would benefit equally from these new inventions. Heath Robinson's cartoon character typified this view of radio: Mr Pimple lies in bed at night, dreaming of the joy and radiance of his family's life once he has made a wireless set for them.[29]

Readers of the popular radio magazines were simultaneously addressed (by different aspects of these journals) as participants in the world of science and consumers of radio as a new domestic commodity.

This apparent contradiction was mediated by constituting a gender differentiation of these two positions. Active participation was spoken about as the business of men; the visual images celebrating radio as a household friend represented this interest as the delight of women, children, and of men in the domestic setting of their families. Later, building radio sets would be the preoccupation of small boys only as radio became a piece of domestic furniture, needing and allowing little technical intervention. In the first few years, however, women were crucial to the radio traders and radio magazines in their efforts to domesticate radio.

The modern housewife

By 1925 advertisements for the radio and electrical exhibitions were encouraging women to attend with the suggestion that they had separate and special interests in the wireless. They should come to view the latest fashions in wireless sets. A writer for the *Daily Telegraph* noted this development in patronizing tones:

> Radio had made very good progress during the last few years and even in Australia has advanced to the stage where there are quite distinct fashions in radio equipment. Doubtless, this tendency has been created by the ever-present influence of women – bless their hearts – but it is there nevertheless. Perhaps it may come to this (although we hope not), that the radio set will not be so much a radio set as a piece of furniture.[30]

The representation of women's interest in radio as a piece of furniture continued to be a theme used by the exhibitions throughout the decade. But the choice of sets remained limited until 1926–7 despite the claims being made. Until 1926 cabinets were plain looking, rectangular wooden boxes with earphones or horn-shaped speakers. Choice was largely a matter of the type of wood used – a 'beautiful rosewood cabinet'. In addition, crystal sets were the most widely used and their technology resisted being neatly packed away in a box or furniture cabinet. Technical intervention was frequently demanded, the delicate cat's whisker causing most problems.

More pertinent to the lives of most women was the suggestion that radio held particular interest for them as a means of escaping household drudgery. The *Listener In* carried a front cover in 1925 showing a woman ironing wearing earphones; the caption read 'Brighter House-work'.[31] This photograph differed from the usual representations of domestic happiness in its recognition that not all members of the family were at their leisure in the home. The tedium and the isolation of women's work in the home were being acknowledged. A rare occasion where this work appeared enjoyable, more like leisure, was the front cover of one issue of *Radio in Australia and New Zealand*: two women were shown helping each other with sewing in a pleasant, airy room, but wireless interferes to issue a decree about fashion.[32] This image explored a theme that was to become increasingly important in later years, though it rarely appeared in these first years: radio as an intruder in the home.

This strategy to stimulate consumerism amongst women by speaking to them of the difficulty of their work in the home was exploited in the mid-1920s. It sought to sell radios by suggesting to women that this was

Women's domestic work made more enjoyable by the companionship of wireless (Photograph: courtesy of *Herald and Weekly Times*)

their realm, deemed so by nature and tradition: the drudgery was recognized and inevitable. Radio as a consumer item offered itself as a palliative. Thus radio joined the many new electrical inventions that promised to make the housewife's life less arduous: 'it will be demonstrated that electricity can be used for sweeping and cleaning floors, washing clothes and dishes, sewing and ironing, driving fans, and anything else in the way of saving "elbow grease"'.[33] All this and the 'wonders of radio' at the one exhibition. Unquestionably, the good life for women was close at hand.

These promises to housewives of miracles of efficiency effectively obscured the gradual decline in the status of housewives and their work.[34] Women were relinquishing their traditionally acquired knowledge about childbirth and child care as, increasingly, these practices were professionalized; the growth of food-processing industries undermined the need for traditional pre-industrial skills and the accumulated wisdom that accompanied them; and electrification of the home was accelerating the destruction of a range of skills and understandings. The process of deskilling domestic work was, as Braverman argues, part of a larger process through which all social life would be made dependent on the marketplace.[35] New electrical goods would alleviate some of the tedium of women's work (though often potentially creating more work than less and requiring new skills), but they would also ensure that women became increasingly reliant on the marketplace and the experts, their lives taken over by consumerism.

Although electrification of the suburbs proceeded throughout the 1920s, the extent to which people could afford to take advantage of this service varied considerably. Peter Spearritt suggests that electricity became an integral part of many Sydney households in the 1920s for lighting purposes and small appliances, but vacuum cleaners and refrigerators did not become widespread until after World War II.[36] Before the war, electrical appliances may have transformed the lives of some women; but for most, the image of the magic kitchen remained a dream.

It was, however, the selling of the dream that was central to business ideology in the 1920s and 1930s. While the ideology propagated by business interests sought, Stuart Ewen claims in the American context, to stimulate consumption among those who could afford to buy more goods, 'it also tried to provide a conception of the good life for those who [could] not'. New-style advertising set out to build on people's desires and discontentments and to create new ones. It redirected criticisms of their conditions of work and life into dreams of the good life to be attained from the marketplace. Social amelioration was promised through the images of a life made rosy by an abundance of consumer goods, rather than through collective political action. 'Only in the instance of an individual ad', says Ewen, 'was consumption a question of *what to buy*. In the broader context of a burgeoning commercial culture, the foremost political imperative was *what to dream*.'[37]

The selling of electrical goods through images of a woman's life made, if not beautiful at this stage of the campaign, then at least bearable, worked to create the same effects. Though many women would not enjoy the services offered by these new consumer goods, the advertisements and the general publicity campaign carried out by such means as the town hall exhibitions conspired to redirect their dissatisfactions with their position as women to dreams of the life just out of reach, but potentially open to all. Women were sold radio and the desire for its possession in the same manner: as something to bring them solace and entertainment and to make their labour less arduous.

To capture women's interest in radio as consumers or potential buyers of wireless sets, broadcasting stations began to provide special programmes for them and to conceive of them as a distinct or specific audience. The British Broadcasting Company had instituted women's sessions in 1923. Australian radio moved more slowly in this direction, but by mid-1925 this practice was established. 2FC Sydney provided Miss Gertrude Turnby, 'a well-known elocutionist, raconteur and lecturer' who gave talks on fashion and 'household matters'; and 2BL Sydney offered regular chats on 'Health and Physical Well-Being' interspersed with musical items.[38] The provision of these and similar programmes as regular items situated radio as having a part in the daily routines of women. They were a particular and important category of audience, at home during the day, and radio would cater for their interests. These programmes set out to attract women's interest in radio, to reassure them about the domestic role of this new piece of technology and to promote radio's domestic image.

For similar reasons children were also addressed as a special audience: as consumers of radio who would wish to hear particular types of programmes. To cater for their needs broadcasters assumed the personas of radio 'uncles' and 'aunts' and read children's stories or made them up spontaneously. 'Uncle George' (George Saunders) on 2BL was one of the most skilful at this practice of 'ad-libbing'. He attracted a wide following amongst children and adults, as did A.S. Cochrane, 'The Hello Man', on 2FC (known as such for his familiar opening call 'Hello, Hello, 2FC Sydney'). These broadcasters developed their personas to amuse their young audience, bewitching them with special voices and silly antics on air.

In many ways these children's programmes were the most innovative of the early forms of broadcasting. Broadcasters took on names (and personas) like Miss Kookaburra, Miss Mary Gumleaf and Billy Bunny and endeavoured to create a fantasy radio world for their audience. The emphasis on spontaneity, on the unrehearsed, on the relaxed and the friendly, and the invitation to young listeners to enter this imaginary world, exploited wireless broadcasting as a new medium more fully than did other early programmes. For an hour each day these sessions set out to enchant young listeners with such stories as 'Black Beauty', the 'Littlest Fairy', or Oscar Wilde's 'The House of Pomegranates'; accompanied by appropriate music, broadcasters read poems, sang songs and gave serious talks on educational matters. The sessions were a children's world, a 'children's corner', specially created by wireless.

American transcriptions such as *Tarzan* began to dominate children's broadcasting in the 1930s and fewer stations were to provide such children's sessions (though some significant programmes continued or were initiated in these later years, such as 3AW Melbourne's *Chatterbox Corner* and the ABC's *Children's Hour*). In the first years of Australian broadcasting, however, the majority of stations provided a variety of children's sessions, calling on this audience as a special category whose needs and interests could be catered for by radio. The interest of children in this new technology was a guarantee that it belonged in the domestic setting of the home. In 1925 3LO Melbourne held a children's party at the children's exhibition being held in the exhibition building. Characters from their children's programmes appeared and 'hundreds of children' and parents turned up.[39] Later in radio's development such occasions would be used by stations as evidence for potential advertisers of the success of a programme: they became a means of materializing the audience. In the 1920s they provided evidence of success for the stations themselves, and in this case the enthusiasm of the children furnished a public display that radio had been accepted into the heart of family life.

By appealing to women and children as special categories of audience, broadcasting stations were promoting a sense of the domesticity of wireless, an image of its natural place in the home as a commodity.[40] By the end of the 1920s, wireless as a domestic receiver in the private home would appear to be the obvious and eminently desirable use for this technology, arising as if by necessity from the requirements of the technology itself. But in the mid-1920s, the social uses of broadcasting technology were still a matter for debate.

Wireless creating a children's world – bringing radio into the heart of domestic life
(Photograph: *Listener In*, 1 August 1925)

'Talk back' radio

In 1925 2BL experimented with a new idea, allowing 'telephone users [to] ring up the studio and ask questions of the lecturer, both question and answer being heard by the listening-in public'. The *Labor Daily* welcomed the experiment as permitting the listening-in public to throw off its 'passive role' so that they '"talked back" at the broadcaster'. The experiment violated PMG regulations prohibiting conversations between individuals by wireless, and the writer of this article, E.R. Voigt, predicted that this 'impossible regulation' would soon be forgotten.[41] But Voigt was still fighting the regulation when he went before the 1927 Royal Commission on Wireless. He would continue to be unsuccessful.

The regulation existed to prevent wireless competing with other sections of the PMG's department: its postal and telegraphic services. The PMG's department exerted a crucial influence on the development of broadcasting through this non-competition policy.[42] It set out to define what broadcasting could and could not do by differentiating it from these other services: they were a means of point-to-point communication, thus broadcasting was restricted to acting as a medium for the public dissemination of messages from a central source.

The PMG's desire to limit the use of this technical medium complemented the attempts by the radio traders to define radio as a domestic receiver: broadcasting, according to these two interests, became a means of mass communication from a central source to privately owned receivers used in a domestic setting. But this conception of broadcasting was not accepted by all groups in this early period. Nor was it clear what the respective roles of broadcasters and listeners should be within the terms set down by this definition of radio. The process by which the social use of this technology was eventually confined to this one definition was a matter of the gradual elimination of alternative images and uses: there was no general or automatic agreement when broadcasting first began.

The early excitement about wireless as a popular science clashed with the PMG's concern to delineate a distinct social use for this technology. For the radio enthusiasts the technology itself was the interest and the excitement. They did not conceive of themselves as an audience for mass messages from a central source. Nor did they treat their equipment as a domestic commodity. Another source of opposition to the desires of the PMG and the radio traders to limit the social use of this technology came from people wanting to use it as a means of public communication and entertainment: wireless concerts, wireless dances, and wireless speeches were planned by various groups. In 1926, in north-western NSW, the Inverell Municipal Council contemplated installing a radio receiving set with a loudspeaker in the town hall and charging people an admission fee to take advantage of the information, music, and entertainment broadcast from stations all around Australia. The previous year, in the same town, a local radio dealer installed a loudspeaker so that a large crowd heard the leader of the opposition in the federal parliament, Matthew Charlton, make a speech.[43]

Nor was usage of domestic wireless equipment confined to individual, private listening-in. Letters to newspapers reported the enjoyment owners of radios had been able to give to their friends and neighbours; their friends listened with them to the broadcast of racing events, or they broadcast wireless music from their verandah for the entertainment of the neighbourhood. Neighbours would collect at the house in the street fortunate enough to own a set in order to hear the latest treat on wireless.

Wireless was welcomed in other contexts as 'annihilating distance'.[44] Radio, it was claimed, would bring country and city life closer together; it would keep migrants in touch with the 'old' world; and 'all countries and nations [would] become one under the wide internationalism of wireless'.[45] This theme of the creation of a new world by radio played on and extended the early excitement about the capacity of this new technology to broadcast speech and concert performances from many miles away. Now, however, this excitement was couched in a language about the public service benefits of broadcasting. But this image of wireless continued at first to sustain the possibility of its use as a means of point-to-point communication, rather than simply as mass communication. Wireless was commended as a means of calling doctors to distant places (not through a specialized service of the later shortwave flying doctor service, but through this public, general service); as a means of transacting business for country people; as a means of people sending urgent messages to each other; and as a means of passing on information between diverse communities. One newspaper reported enthusiastically on the 'infinite possibilities' of broadcasting for all countries of great distances,

> to keep isolated homesteads in touch with the centres from which they derive their supplies and news, and prospecting and surveying parties in contact with the base of operations . . . . It requires little

imagination to realise what value wireless may have in the detection of crime, and in rallying forces for the subjugation of forest and prairie fires.[46]

Radio magazines and other popular journals such as *New Idea* carried short stories throughout the 1920s of urgent messages being sent to women about their husbands being involved in accidents, or of radio 'saving the day' by passing on information to particular communities.[47] Broadcasting in these accounts was understood as a technology to serve interaction between individuals and communities.

Finally, the possibility of an alternative social use for broadcasting technology persisted with the existence of the 'B' stations. These stations did not receive financial support from the licence fees collected by the government and operated on shorter wavelengths than the 'A' stations. Until the establishment of 2KY Sydney in 1925 and 2GB Sydney in 1926 – 'B' stations of a more ambitious kind – these stations were conducted for research and experimental purposes or for the promotion of radio equipment sales. The 'B' licence had been introduced basically as a continuation of the experimenter's licence operating before the inauguration of wireless broadcasting in 1923. In the mid-1920s, these stations were subject to few restrictions and generally little official interest was shown in their operation. Indeed, throughout the 1927 Royal Commission on Wireless, the 'B' stations were rarely mentioned.[48] They were not considered part of official broadcasting in Australia: their existence was marginal and their role undefined by official language at this time.

Yet the absence of these stations from the field of official considerations about broadcasting did not result, for the most part, in their exploring alternative uses of the technology. E.R. Voigt, who had written so hopefully for the *Labor Daily* about the experiment in listeners 'talking back', would attempt to set up 2KY for these purposes. This would be a crucial experiment in Australian broadcasting. All other 'B' stations undertook to broadcast programmes to 'listeners-in': to transmit messages to a passive audience. In 1925 one station in NSW sought to find out how many people were listening-in by conducting a number-adding test; 230 replies were received.[49] There was no talk-back, no listener-supplied contribution to the communication process; rather, this experiment served as a stunt to materialize the audience.

The pressures directed against the exploration or contemplation of alternative uses of broadcasting technology came from a variety of sources, some more direct than others. The PMG regulations were the most direct force, though these did not prevent the discussion of alternatives and possibilities. Far less direct were the comments of people like T.W. Bearup, studio manager for 3LO at the time, who spoke of fascination with the science of broadcasting as a relic of the past. Writing in 1925 about the progress of wireless, he claimed that listeners were no longer enthralled simply by the experience of hearing speech and music through space. The official inauguration of broadcasting in Australia had occurred at a time when the technology was sufficiently developed for demands to be made about the quality of broadcasts and transmissions.[50] Such histories of radio by people working within the industry have always served to construct particular understandings of its contemporary operation and to direct those same listener demands that are represented as occurring spontaneously. In discussing the 'progress' of wireless, Bearup contributed to a process by which alternative notions about wireless technology were pushed to the margins. The popular science interest in broadcasting, as well as other ideas about its use, were dismissed as belonging to an earlier period when radio was immature: they were radio's past, and radio's future was about quality programmes for listeners-in.

Support for the radio traders and their interest in radio as a domestic commodity came from newspapers such as the *Age*. Throughout the 1920s it articulated demands on the traders' behalf. It had done so in the campaign against the sealed set system: in the mid-1920s it began to exert pressure on the broadcasting stations to improve the quality of their programmes and the quality of their transmission. It claimed to be representing listener demand: 'in the early stages . . . the most popular set was invariably the one which could tune in the far-off stations'. Now public interest, it suggested, had matured and the quality of programmes was its preoccupation.[51] Like the history provided by Bearup, these statements were banishing images of wireless as a means of communicating between people or of its capacity to 'annihilate distance' into history.

In the late 1920s the language about wireless and its power to annihilate distance was reworked into a different form. It became the dominant mode of representing radio's public service function: 'Radio is going to bring remote places within speaking distance of the big cities.' But the speaking would be done by wireless personnel and the communities would be spoken to by radio.

The broadcasting stations will carry to all parts of the country the news of the day, weather reports, entertainments from theatres and concerts, sermons, lectures from universities and other places of education so that isolation will no longer be so great a drawback to settlement.[52]

Wireless would make outback life more attractive and it would relieve the loneliness of migrants: not by facilitating communication between communities, nor by bringing people together in public situations to listen to wireless, but by bringing them programmes conceived as mass messages for a privatized audience.

Politicians argued over who should provide this service, but did not question that it should take this form. They talked of the musical and information programmes to be provided, and disagreed about whether it should be a service in the hands of government or private enterprise. They welcomed broadcasting as a means of bringing the same amusements, excitements and education enjoyed by city people to isolated rural communities.[53] Both types of communities were represented as collections of privatized individuals receiving the goods supplied. In parliamentary debates, the understanding of broadcasting as a medium for mass comunication had automatically been accepted by all parties.

The audience, or audiences, thus conceived in the dominant rhetoric about radio were constituted as having specific characteristics and needs existing separately from the world of broadcasting. Women, children, country people and, occasionally, migrants were spoken of as particular audiences. Their needs and interests stemmed from experiences – their worlds – which existed independent of radio. Women's housework was to be made tolerable; children's lives would be more enjoyable; the isolation and loneliness of rural people and migrants would be lessened. Later, radio would define audiences by tastes for the various programmes provided, thus representing their needs and characteristics as derived from and catered for within the world of radio. In these early years, however, no clear ideas existed about the radio audience nor about the activity of 'listening-in'.

In some quarters, there was a certain apprehension about the passivity of the audience being constituted for radio, though these were rarely expressed in such a form as to challenge the dominant social use of broadcasting technology. The *Labor Daily*'s enthusiastic reporting of the experiment in 'talk-back' radio expressed such misgivings and in other articles this same writer would articulate a forceful critique of radio. *Radio in Australia and New Zealand*, established as an enthusiasts' journal in 1924, lasted only four years, but in this time displayed some uneasiness about the course of radio's development. Editorials in this magazine insisted that the wonder of wireless did not lie in its ability to provide entertainment simply by pressing a key or lever, but on the contrary, lay in the constant progress of the science, of the technology itself.[54]

Other fears were also expressed about the development of broadcasting. Apprehensions about its social consequences, its impact on its audience in moral terms, began to be voiced by newspapers, but like most criticisms of the passivity of the audience, they did not arise in the context of the broader question about the social use of this technology. *Smith's Weekly* protested about the 'invasion of our mental processes' and the creation of the 'Mechanical Man'. This paper adopted a cynical attitude towards the advancements made by science from the beginning of broadcasting in Australia and warned its readers about the dangers of both wireless and the phonograph record.[55] Joining this attack, the *Daily Mail* (the *Labor Daily*'s predecessor) forewarned of radio's impact on the 'probing ears of youth' and declared that the 'mind of youth is plastic material'.[56] But these prophets formed a somewhat eccentric chorus. Later, such warnings would be articulated as part of a more powerful language about radio's intrusion in the home; the earlier expressions of misgivings about broadcasting drew on H.G. Wells-type images of the future that were ambivalent about the uses being made of science. It was a language of premonition, excited but wary:

> What a beautiful city ours will be when our quiet evening love or morning confidential talk with the wife is rudely broken by the raucous voice of the politicians delivering their election speeches, the greengrocers shouting their wares, and a thousand other chaps with goods to sell all piercing our ears in a medley of noise. It certainly will be exciting – but what a noisy world it will be to be sure.[57]

The dominant rhetoric about radio audiences conceived them as a variety of interests and needs to be pleased and satisfied by a variety of programmes. The experience of listening-in was not yet understood as qualitatively different.[58] The listening public were spoken about as 'silent spectators': they were the same as an audience at the theatre or the crowds at the Melbourne Cup.[59] This view was reflected in discussions about programming.

The dominance of the radio traders limited the extent to which the experience of listening-in or concepts of programming were discussed. For this group, programming was a matter of attracting potential buyers of radio equipment. Novelty, variety, and a general sense of excitement were seen as the best means of attracting consumers. Speaking on behalf of the radio traders, the *Age* claimed that the only way to attract and hold public interest was to provide a number of different broadcasting stations. The existence of over 500 stations in America, it declared, was a key factor in the 'wonderful boom in the American radio trade'.[60] These discussions did not conceive of the radio audience as a set of tastes in programmes, but as consumers of radio equipment.

The transformation in and of this language about listeners-in was not far off. Polls of the public taste for different types of programmes had already been conducted in the USA. An article in *Radio in Australia and New Zealand* noted this development and argued that soon the listening public would no longer be simply satisfied by the experience of radio as novelty. Consequently, 'popular opinion' would soon need to be known. The writer suggested that Australian amusement tastes may not exactly coincide with the American, but they would probably have much in common; the article listed the results of one poll recently conducted in the USA to consolidate this point.[61]

For the most part, early listener polls and plebiscites in Australia were conducted not to discern the preferences and characteristics of the listening-in public, but, on the one hand, to gather information about radio owners, and on the other, to promote a sense of excitement about radio. They formed part of the various tactics used by broadcasting stations to these same ends. Stations linked competitions with programmes like the first Australian serial, *The Green Diamond Mystery* (broadcast on 2FC in 1925), or band music concerts. These competitions attempted to materialize the audience in order to create the sense of endless novelty, as well as to provide an indication of how successful such programmes were in attracting interest in radio itself. The prize for winning *The Green Diamond Mystery* competition was a two-valve Marconi receiving set.[62] Similarly, stations invited people to come and see 'how it's done' to arouse their curiosity. In February 1925, 2BL broadcast a recital in front of an audience, rather than from its normal studio, 'in order to give the public a chance to see how broadcasting is done'. Later in the year, 2FC built a replica of a broadcasting studio on a theatre platform; shows were conducted and broadcast twice daily.[63]

One other mode of discussing the audience emerged in the mid-1920s; it prefigured later considerations of the experience of listening-in, but in this instance arose only in the context of references to the novelty of radio for artists and announcers.[64] Dame Clara Butt was quoted as finding the radio audience 'the best mannered audience I have ever sung to!', and she described the experience of a radio broadcast recital as singing 'from heart to heart'.[65] Interest in the techniques appropriate to the radio performance did not emerge until the late 1920s and early 1930s, but the question did arise in this form occasionally before this time. Radio would be understood by the mid-1930s as a particular experience for both performer and listener-in; it created a shared world for all who listened-in and radio performers must learn to adjust their art to this experience of listening-in.

These concerns would raise new questions about how a broadcaster reached or made contact with the audience. In the mid-1920s, the 'radio voice' had begun to be discussed: announcers, like A.S. Cochrane, 2FC's 'Hello Man', were praised for their ability to create 'an invisible link between thousands of listeners-in and the service of 2FC'. Similarly, the importance of the announcer's personality was noted in various contexts (the advent of the radio star was predicted) and announcers or performers reported on their experiences of broadcasting for the popular radio magazines.[66] But for the most part these early discussions of the performer's art were articulated within other languages or rhetoric about radio, particularly those that celebrated the thrill or the scientific wonder of the new technology: the skill of A.S. Cochrane as an announcer was one of 'the wonders of wireless . . . made more wonderful out of the sincerity of his labours'.[67]

2KY and the 'Babble Machines'

H.G. Wells in his book *When the Sleeper Wakes* (1899) had prophesied the invention of great speaking machines pouring out news and propaganda to the people. The *Labor Daily* delighted in quoting Wells and his predictions about the 'Babble Machines'.[68] During 1924–5 this paper carried a sustained critique of radio as a means of mass communication. Led by Voigt, secretary at that time of the Sydney Labor Research Bureau, the *Labor Daily* began an attack on the use of wireless for capitalist propaganda. Previously, in editorials such as

'Wireless for Workers', this paper had been preoccupied with the cost of the licence fee and the monopoly held over broadcasting in NSW by that 'drapery firm', Farmer and Co. But Voigt began to use the pages of the *Labor Daily* to advocate the establishment of a labour broadcasting station and to mount a remarkable cultural and political critique of wireless broadcasting.

In October 1924 Voigt sent a letter from North America (where he had been studying wireless developments) to the NSW Trades and Labor Council urging that a broadcasting station for the labour movement be established in each state. Voigt envisaged a broadcasting system that would be a tool for the unification of the working class, rather than a means of their mystification. A labour station would transmit material of benefit to this cause: labour movement news, strike news, information about meetings, and a programme of working-class education – all delivered to workers in the comfort of their homes. But the broadcasting system would be more than a means of one-way, mass communication. A series of smaller stations would be set up at union centres throughout the state so that communication between Sydney and these other sections of the union movement would be ensured.

Voigt shared Bertolt Brecht's optimism that radio's technology could have other, more progressive social uses than the one being allotted to it. Brecht complained that German radio was 'one-sided when it should have two sides'. Rather than being an instrument of distribution, he declared, 'radio would be the most wonderful communication system imaginable, a gigantic system of channels'.[69] Voigt sought this role for his proposed broadcasting stations, while also believing that the same system could send out news and information ensuring that 'capitalist lies could be nailed daily' for 'the workers sitting comfortably in their own homes'.[70]

Voigt's proposal was well received by the Labor Council and in February 1925 at his meeting with the Council, a wireless committee was established with Voigt as chairman. The Labor Council resolved to set up a broadcasting station to act as a counter-weight to the capitalist propaganda issued through the press, the schools and the pulpit. Voigt was adamant about the possibilities of radio. It could disseminate working-class education and news and break down the 'capitalist mentality' produced in the average worker through the power of these other institutions. On the acceptance of his proposal, he wrote enthusiastically for the *Labor Daily* about the future of broadcasting for the labour movement:

We can broadcast our news and views daily to scores of thousands inside and outside the Labor Movement. We can broadcast the mass of facts and figures concerning the work, wages, and conditions of workers in this and other countries, which is now lying useless in our Research Bureaux and in every union secretary's office.

Our lectures on economics, history, etc., from the working-class standpoint, in place of an audience of a score or so, could be broadcast to many thousands, who could never be reached by any other method than wireless.[71]

But, Voigt warned, the many advantages of broadcasting meant that it would not drop into the hands of the working class without a struggle.

Radio station 2KY Sydney was conceived within these terms. It was established under a 'B' class licence, a point insisted upon by Voigt so that the station would be free to devote its programmes solely 'to serious business rather than music, jazz and other entertainments'.[72] Voigt was critical of the Queensland Labor government's application for an 'A' class licence (4QG), for it committed them to the operation of an orthodox station as defined by the PMG's regulations. To avoid these differences in broadcasting strategies for the labour movement, Voigt called for a united Labor wireless policy. Such a common plan could shape broadcasting as the crux of working-class industrial and political activity and assist in the struggle to overcome restrictions placed in the way of such developments.[73]

Obstructions to Voigt's scheme had already appeared. PMG department regulations prevented the use of the proposed station as a means of communication between union centres. H.P. Brown, the Director of Posts and Telegraphs (DPT), publicly drew attention to the policy of non-competition, arguing that such a use of wireless technology would compete with the telegraphs section of his department. Voigt complained bitterly of this injunction to the 1927 Royal Commission on Wireless, with no success. Voigt's dream of a network communication system for the labour movement would never be fulfilled. The DPT had also announced that he intended to prohibit 2KY broadcasting for political purposes. But Voigt was victorious on this issue as the current regulations about broadcasting political propaganda were inapplicable to 'B' class stations. Brown was obliged to correct his statements publicly.[74]

2KY was to be established as a means of mass broadcasting; a means for the dissemination of news and information, a means of propagandizing. Voigt (and his colleague-to-be, A.C. Willis)[75] ridiculed the 'fiction of impartiality' and developed a critique of broadcasting as propaganda. They argued that the myth of impartial news reporting was used to suppress and distort the workers' case in any dispute between employers and workers. The difference between the proposed labour station and the 'A' class stations would be a matter of the former conducting its political propaganda frankly and openly; the existing stations transmitted propaganda in the guise of 'news'. 'Non-Labor is anti-Labor', said Voigt. It did not require much information, he suggested, 'to forecast fairly accurately the part such [anti-Labor] stations will play when there is a big industrial or political issue at stake'. Voigt drove home his point in a later article for the *Labor Daily* by reporting on the use made of wireless in America to break a New York pressmen's strike.[76]

The application from the NSW Trades and Labor Council for a 'B' class licence was finally granted and Voigt continued to predict a great forward march for labour. He still believed that the station would be a means of linking workers together. Voigt had sought the construction of a powerful transmitting station and he now enthused about its planned potential to be received throughout Australia, and, with the aid of the morse system, throughout the world. The station would transmit news and information, such as the latest NSW unemployment figures, to centres such as London, New York, Paris, Moscow and Tokyo: wireless could thus ensure that workers would not be kept ignorant of one another or of their struggles. All workers could be reached by broadcasting, not just the class-conscious minority who read the labour press.[77]

Further problems followed. The completion of labour's station was delayed by AWA's refusal to supply parts for its transmitter. Voigt set out to build the station as cheaply as possible by using Australian products, thus circumventing AWA and its expensive imported equipment. But when everything was almost complete, parts needed from AWA were refused. The situation was eventually resolved and wireless station 2KY Sydney was officially opened on 31 October 1925. It was broadcasting in time to be involved actively in the December 1925 federal elections and on 10 November the station announced that until the day of polling, its programmes would consist solely of musical items, interspersed with speeches from selected Labor candidates. Matthew Charlton's speech was broadcast live from Paddington Town Hall, deemed a considerable feat at the time.

One month after its opening, the *Labor Daily* declared that 2KY could claim responsibility for the 'huge increase' in licences (5299 for that month).[78] Once the elections were over the station settled into an evening programme format of news, musical items, talks and sporting information – with a considerable amount of the latter. This pattern continued into the late 1920s. In 1929 it was changed slightly by the introduction of a women's morning session with home hints and information (delivered by Mrs Grey who was to become one of the most popular women announcers in the 1930s) and a children's session in the early evening with the traditional 'uncles' and 'aunts'. In 1926, however, when a referendum was held to decide upon wider industrial powers for the federal government 2KY had been again fully involved.

By the late 1920s the general programme style of 2KY bore little indication of the station functioning as a means of working-class education. Talks were given that were different from those heard on other stations: broadcasts such as those given by the Militant Women's Group and Labor's Educational League. But talks were also given on such matters as medical problems, travel and gardening. By 1934 the manager of 2KY would proudly announce that his station 'has never made any attempt to lead the public taste, but has endeavoured to satisfy public demand'.[79] By the 1930s 2KY had become a popular entertainer, not a means of partisan education.

But Voigt's critique of impartiality and the presentation of news challenged an ideology that continues to be central to the power of the media. He declared all education and information to be partisan and argued it was essential that the labour movement not pretend to be otherwise. He did not appear to recognize, however, the central importance of his attempt to connect that critique to the argument for a different social use of broadcasting technology. He had hoped to develop an alternative system of radio stations that could be used for communication between groups; he had been critical too of the way in which the current use of this technology was making listeners-in passive; but he also believed it possible to exploit broadcasting within the terms laid down for it as a means of one-way communication. He did not acknowledge the political effects of the use to which broadcasting had been confined: in its very form, broadcasting addressed its audience as consumers – of the messages transmitted, be they labour or anti-labour. The radio audience became the subject of messages transmitted rather than active agents. Though the content of 2KY programmes may have spoken to its audience as members of a class, the mode in which those messages were conveyed addressed them in a different form. They were consumers of messages or content provided for them by others, not the collective agents of their own history.

Voigt's stance was not that of a lone individual. In arguing this particular line about propaganda and the possibility of exploiting broadcasting within the terms laid down for it, Voigt shared the commitment of the Labor Council in NSW and its executive of this period. 'Education of the workers on class lines', whether through wireless, the cinema, or a labour newspaper, was central to their agenda. The Executive Committee took a strong stance on the *Labor Daily*, for example, arguing that it must not attempt to 'vulgarise the tastes of the working class' by attempting to compete with the capitalist press by providing a '"bright and newsy" paper' nor should it shrink from using a distinctively class language of 'scabs' and 'bosses'. They threatened to withdraw financial support from the paper when an editor unsympathetic to this platform was appointed.[80]

The belief that wireless could be exploited in the interests of the labour movement reconciled Voigt (and the Labor Council) to the use of its technology as a 'Babble Machine'. One of the most developed conceptions of an alternative possible use of the medium would thence disappear from the public rhetoric about broadcasting. Voigt did argue once again for the establishment of different broadcasting systems by state governments – for the purposes of news and education only – before the 1927 Royal Commission. But such suggestions were defined as outside their frame of reference. The Royal Commission would seek to adjust, to smooth out problems, to satisfy some competing interests and to clarify the path already laid down for radio as a culture industry. 2KY in its mode of operating would not challenge the dominant understanding of radio; the content of its babble would for a time be different, but it would take part in constituting an audience necessary to broadcasting in this form. Propaganda and radio entertainment both accepted radio as a means of one-way communication and the audience as receptive consumers. The critique of propaganda and impartiality advanced by Voigt had failed to face these questions about the process involved in this habituating of people to the position of listeners-in. The necessity for 2KY to be entertaining and popular, rather than didactic and educational, in order to survive within the broadcasting system would be the consequence of this weakness in Voigt's analysis and the Labor Council's platform.

2
THE BEST SEAT IN THE HOUSE

A range of alternative images of radio and its social uses continued to be explored in the second half of the 1920s. Although the concept of wireless as a domestic receiver for mass messages from a central source had clearly begun to dominate official and popular discussions by 1926, the content of the messages to be transmitted and the mode in which they should be communicated had then to be decided. As Brecht observed, 'it was suddenly possible to say anything to everybody, but thinking about it, there was nothing to say'.[1]

For the radio traders, who had from the beginning sought to promote their equipment as domestic apparatuses, this question of the content of broadcasting was not initially a major problem. They relied on images of progress and the new exciting world to be created through modern science and invention as the central thrust of their sales promotion strategies. To have a radio in your home was, itself, a miracle; programmes were of secondary interest. But such a strategy for selling goods ran the risk of stagnation, of a diminution of excitement as people became accustomed to the idea of radio. As the sales of wireless equipment declined for a time in 1925, fears were expressed that this was already happening. New enthusiasm for wireless had to be created, or a new sales tactic found.

Mike fright

Radio became a performer of stunts. Listeners were to be thrilled by broadcasts from new and extraordinary places; radio would bring listeners the sounds and the voices of the-world-out-there. Stunt broadcasts were a deliberate strategy to rejuvenate popular excitement, but they involved too a new definition of certain existing broadcasting practices. The term 'radio stunt' drew attention to the capacity of its technology to make outside broadcasts. Though controversy about the extent to which radio stations should be involved in stunt broadcasting quickly flared, the development of such broadcasts would be crucial to the gradual delineation of the specificity of radio as a cultural institution.

Reported at first as broadcasting experiments, then as 'novel broadcasts' or stunts, radio stations transmitted programmes from the depths of the ocean, from down a coal mine and up in an aeroplane. In December 1925, 2FC announced its intention to make a feature of 'this novel type of broadcasting' after its successful transmission of a diver's description of the 'mighty drainage system' at the bottom of Sydney Harbour.[2] Another transmission was made by a parachutist in his descent to the ground. This specific genre of stunt broadcasts sought to create a general sense of excitement about the technology of broadcasting. Similarly, successful broadcasts between different countries and the early discussion of the possibility of an Empire Beam Wireless service were welcomed in the same terms: the extraordinary marvel, the wonders of radio broadcasting. These celebratory images contributed further to the mystification of the science of broadcasting; again its technology appeared in the guise of magic rather than as field of democratic participation.

A second genre of stunt broadcasts drew attention to one particular aspect of broadcasting technology: the station's microphone. This surprising piece of equipment can bring you, the listener-in, the most extraordinary range of noises and sounds from the-world-out-there. Early visual images of radio (such as those on the front covers of the popular radio magazines) had been preoccupied with showing wireless receivers in a range of domestic situations; now they frequently depicted a station microphone in a range of public situations. These visual representations of radio reflected and enhanced the sense of excitement about the broadcasting technology being created by the stunt broadcasts. The microphone brings you the noises of Flinders Street, Melbourne, at peak hour; the observations of a radio announcer (and the noises that surround him) standing in a busy shopping street; the public addresses of famous statesmen; or the sermon of a popular preacher from a city church. The *Listener In* hailed this new type of broadcasting with the introduction of a feature page of photographs, using captions such as 'Radio in Many Places' or 'What the Microphones Heard'.

Most significant for later developments in the content and presentation of radio magazines (but also more generally for the emergence of the notion of the radio personality) were the broadcasts by theatre stars talking from their dressing rooms before a show. These broadcasts began as stunts in 1925, and by mid-1926 became an important part of radio programming (for those stations that had links with the theatre world). The radio magazines welcomed this new type of programme with photographs of the stars as they broadcast, always with a station's microphone prominently displayed. A range of performers appeared, such as Marie Bremner, a popular musical comedy artist; Athol Tier, a vaudeville star later to become a popular radio personality; Walter Lindrum, speaking to the 3AR microphone while making a billiards shot; and various classical music performers.

Labelled as stunts, dressing room broadcasts and other 'novel' programmes did not differ markedly from the wide variety of outside broadcasts already being transmitted. These had been a feature of wireless stations' programming since late 1924; by mid-1925 items were being transmitted from theatres (large and small), halls, churches, hotels and sporting venues.[3] The naming of particular types of broadcasts – whether from a Tivoli star's dressing room or from down a coal mine – as stunts, drew attention to the technology of radio and created a sense of excitement about radio's capacity to provide these outside broadcasts. Specifically, it worked to highlight the source of the transmission – or rather one aspect of this equipment, the microphone – and the capacity of its technology to bring anything of the-world-out-there to you, the listener-in, in the privacy of your home. This language would be crucial to the construction of the specificity of radio. As eavesdropper on the world, the radio's microphone would be represented as setting up a new relationship between the listener, as the private individual, and the outside world of public events.

Other modes of discussing radio also made a tentative appearance with this image of the radio stunt. In the ensuing debate about the extent to which stations should rely on stunt broadcasts, a language about the need for variety to satisfy listeners and about 'what constitutes a popular service' began to take form.[4] It represented the listening audience or public as made up of diverse interests and needs constituted elsewhere; these interests were not derived from within the world of radio, but from worlds outside radio. Broadcasting programmes at this time sought to

Fetishizing the broadcasting microphone as part of the campaign by radio magazines to continue a sense of excitement and mystery about radio (Photograph: *Listener In*, 14 September 1927)

imitate, to reproduce the satisfactions provided by other means. Variety in programming, it was believed, would satisfy as many people as possible, thus ensuring popularity for radio. Stunts, then, were just one more means of pleasing listeners – as many listeners as possible – in the search for a means of broadening the market for wireless equipment. No concept yet existed of an audience for a particular type of programme, of interests and pleasures being created by radio itself; nor was there any notion as yet of one great audience constituted by and for radio.

There was, however, another major reason for the pursuit of stunt broadcasts. It was precisely as Brecht had said; no clear conception of radio broadcasting as a cultural institution had yet emerged. What was to be said or done with this means of transmitting messages simultaneously to vast numbers of people? Radio became a parasite. Landlines stretched across the cities in the search for people saying things, sending out music or performing in any way with sound. Outside broadcasts were a solution to filling the air for the period a station was open, and the radio stunt was one way of defining a broad range of sounds being heard out-there as legitimate material for transmission. In 1927 S.E. Wilson of Farmer and Co. of Sydney listed some of the broadcast stunts heard from their station, 2FC:

> We ... broadcast the arrival of the American Fleet at sea, the arrival of HMS 'Renown' with the Duke and Duchess of York, the HMS 'Otranto', the War Museum, the Jenolan Caves, a diver's descent under Sydney Harbour, a coal mine 3,000 feet under Sydney Harbour, an evening in the Municipal Market, popularly known as 'Paddy's Market', descriptions of the Cunard liners 'Franconica' and 'Carenthia' and a description of the Strasbourg Clock at the Technological Museum.[5]

Outside broadcasts, whether in the form of novelty items or regular programmes, provided a mainstay of broadcasting stations in the mid-1920s. Listeners-in could hear a wide variety of concerts and musical performances from theatres, from concert halls, from local operatic societies, and from performances in the open air (such as brass bands playing in parks or at the beach); the material to be heard ranged from grand opera to cinema organ. For talks and lectures, broadcasting stations turned to bodies such as the university, the Workers' Education Association (WEA), and the Royal Society. For news and information, announcers read summaries of the main bulletins from the major daily newspapers and their news agencies.[6] And of key importance, from the beginning of Australian radio, were the broadcast descriptions and reports of a wide range of sporting events.

Test cricket and the Melbourne Cup each year were seized upon by the radio stations as a means of creating excitement about radio. Initially in the form of stunts, these broadcasts were announced as bringing to the listener-in all the accompanying sounds of the events: the sounds of horses' hooves and the crowd cheering would be heard in the description of the 1926 Melbourne Cup; the bat striking the ball and other associated noises of a cricket match would be heard while the announcer explained every point of the January 1926 match between NSW and South Australia.[7] Cricket, in particular, became central to the sales of radio equipment as new advances in broadcast descriptions were hailed each year as promoting more and more widespread interest in the game. Radio traders broadcast the 1928 test matches between Australia and England, held in Australia, to large crowds inside and outside their shops.[8] By 1930 'ball-by-ball' descriptions of the test matches held in England would be given using cable facilities.

Such innovations were seen as important for creating a popular enthusiasm for wireless. So too were other major radio events such as the broadcasting of a whole opera season by the visiting Toti dal Monte in 1926 or the transmission of the sound-track of the new speaking movies. Included amongst these developments, as being devised for the same purposes, were three different modes of 'direct contact' between listeners and the broadcasting stations: radio plebiscites, radio clubs (such as children's birthday clubs) and public attendance at broadcasts. S.E. Wilson of Farmer and Co. was quizzed by a member of the 1927 Royal Commission about why 2FC had not been more vigorous, particularly in pursuing this third strategy, in the effort to 'popularize' wireless.[9] Later these strategies were to be seen as a means of materializing audiences for advertisers, and at the same time as creating a sense of participation in the world of radio, but here these three modes of 'direct contact' were represented as playing the same role as the latest stunt – to create an excitement about radio.

Stunts, outside broadcasts, a 'variety' of programmes', radio clubs and radio plebiscites were all pursued to create excitement about radio and to sell more sets and equipment; but they also contributed to the production of a new image for radio. Radio was no longer merely an exciting new invention, nor was it acceptable as simply a substitute 'gramophone record player'. A sense of radio as having a separate or specific sphere as a medium of communication had begun to evolve. In part this transformation appeared to respond to popular demand. Listeners-in, in letters to newspapers and magazines, voiced their objections to stations relying on the playing of gramophone records. Further complaints were registered in parliament, when the Sydney 'A' class stations amalgamated in 1928. Their programmes were said to consist mainly of gramophone records and advertisements. The protesters declared radio should be more than a 'glorified gramophone'.[10] These claims suggest a popular expectation that radio should provide something new, either in its content, or in the way in which it presented that content.

This demand was echoed in the popular radio magazines and mass circulation daily newspapers (and, no doubt, these bodies were as much responsible for producing the demand as being a reflection of it). To promote the sale of radios, they set out to convey the sense that radio did in fact have a sphere of its own, though the precise nature of the specific features claimed for radio were to change over a period of ten years. In the late 1920s, radio's distinctiveness as a medium was represented as residing in the variety of the content to be offered: 'as a means of entertainment for the house and as a household utility, the modern radio set is unrivalled'.[11] As both public entertainer and public service, radio offered a wide range of benefits for which no substitute could be found. A tribute by Eric Palmer, 'I Am a Radio', typified the form in which radio was being portrayed. Radio brings you, the listener-in, countless services and pleasures, everything to be heard in the-world-out-there, to you, 'right in your room'; 'All these am I and more.'[12]

I Am a Radio
I am a University, right in your room.
I am an Opera sung by your fireside.
I am an orchestra to set your feet a-dancing.
I am a band to enthuse your musical soul.
I am an orator, whose eloquence holds you still.
I am a violin recital, rendered by a master at your side.
I am a statesman, conferring with you on the nation's needs.
I am a diplomat, voicing a foreign friendliness.
I am a doctor, coming to your home without charge.
I am a banker, watching your laid-away pounds.
I am a leader of industry, analysing the economic trend.

I am a newspaper, describing events as they happen.
I am a drama, played in your parlor.
I am a debate, where you hear both sides of the day's problems.
I am a football game, with thrills by the score.
I am a boxing championship, with a seat at the ringside.
I am a governess, teaching your children each day.
I am a scientist, revealing wonders that you knew not of.
All these am I, and more.
I am a patriot, kindling anew your love of country.
I am a preacher, re-awakening your faith in human nature.
Yet, poor, foolish men just call me *RADIO*.
(Eric H. Palmer, *Daily Telegraph*, 30 September 1927)

Radio constituted all these services as a unity, a radio world, to be brought to listeners-in the privacy of their homes. Newspapers and magazines signalled radio's distinctiveness in these terms through features and columns such as the *Daily Telegraph*'s 'The Wireless World' (or 'The Radio World' as it became in 1926).

In the process of representing radio's particularity (the reason why every household should possess both a radio set and a gramophone player), a new language about broadcasting as a medium was being rehearsed. Radio was talked about as constituting a social relation, rather than being an object, a piece of furniture to be fetishized, or a scientific marvel: it was beginning to be discussed as establishing a relation between a set of messages transmitted (radio programmes) and an audience. Radio brought all these services, this variety of material, to the listener-in. The social relation represented by such images or language about radio was of the-world-out-there brought to listeners in a domestic, private life. Both worlds were portrayed as already constituted and separate, but brought together by radio. Listeners-in lived their private lives, but now radio brought the outside world of public events to them in the comfort of their homes. Without leaving their armchair, the listener-in could have the best seat in the house.[13] In the 1920s this language, however, was not clearly heard and was often articulated within other modes of discussing radio. Advertisements, for example, continued to represent the content of radio transmissions as the magic of radio: spirit-like violinists radiated out from the family wireless set.

As a medium between two worlds, of the social relation constituted by radio, the station microphone became a symbol of broadcasting technology. During the late 1920s this object was reified in much the same way as the radio set had been in the first three years of broadcasting. The radio magazines in particular took up the theme of the broadcasting microphone. Their front covers presented images drawing attention to the microphone: the *Listener In* photographed 3LO's large reproduction microphone over the doorway of their new studio and showed members of the Melbourne Concert Orchestra within the circle of a 3AR microphone. Two genres of radio stories appeared in the magazines, also drawing attention to the microphone: accounts of radio 'gaffs' made by announcers forgetting that their microphone was still switched on and tales about or advice to novices about 'mike fright'. Some of the radio 'gaffs' were more serious than others. Frank Brennan (Labor MP for Batman) made an indignant complaint to parliament: during an outside broadcast the *sotto voce* comment of a Nationalist supporter attending a public occasion had been heard over the air: 'These coves should be limited to five minutes.'[14] On the whole, however, no serious alarm was expressed about such radio 'gaffs'; their reporting by the radio magazines served as occasions to contemplate the wonder of the radio microphone. Later, 'forgetting' to turn the microphone off would become a deliberate part of the radio performance of announcers such as Clifford Niccola ('Nicky') Whitta. In this earlier period, the stories served to highlight the social relation facilitated by this piece of equipment and by this new medium.

Stories about 'mike fright' were precursors of a new feature of radio magazines. By the end of the 1920s articles on radio announcers and their work would become vital to the promotion of a new image of radio by these journals. In 1928, the *Listener In* ran a series of articles by 'leading broadcasters'. Other magazines ran features on the qualities necessary for a good announcer, and photographs and cartoon representations of various 'popular' announcers began to appear regularly. Some public interest in announcers had always been promoted through the presentation of the various 'uncles' and 'aunts' of children's programmes. Figures such as 'Uncle George' and the 'Hello Man' did appear to have a genuine following among adult and child audiences alike. The change in the late 1920s was the promotion of interest in the radio announcer for all types of radio programmes and the tentative exploring of the notion of a radio art or skill in the work of announcing.

'Mike fright' provided a means of discussing techniques of radio performance and a means of suggesting that there was something different about performing on radio. Many recommended an 'informal', 'friendly' style as the appropriate 'microphone voice'. The 'friendly' performance had been exploited from the commencement of radio broadcasting in children's programmes; the success of these broadcasts provided evidence that this was the required style of performance. But this notion of the radio style was not automatically accepted as proper and desirable in broadcasting. A number of broadcasters appear to have been trained in elocutionary techniques, and advertisements for new programmes occasionally mentioned that the announcer was a 'fine elocutionist',[15] suggesting that this continued to be thought the appropriate training and style for radio performers throughout the 1920s. But others rejected this view, denying the need for a 'formal style of correct speech and pronunciation for radio'.[16] In the 1930s it would be agreed that the intimate, friendly voice met the requirements of a good radio performance. In the late 1920s this question continued to be debated, though discussions of 'mike fright' and the radio 'gaff' were ensuring that the microphone would be identified as requiring a particular style of performance – whatever that may be.

The reification of the station microphone reached its apogee with the advent of 'Mike', a new wireless stunt. The 'novel broadcasts' had been one of the first ways in which popular attention had been directed to the microphone. 'Mike' was a rather different stunt; it was a 'mysterious voice' on 2FC, heard without warning, whispering to listeners between programme items. Announcing himself as 'Mike speaking' or 'Hush, it's Mike speaking', the announcer would provide information about the artists appearing in the programme or would respond to requests for information from listeners. Newspapers and magazines added to the mystique by reporting the whispering as coming from the radio microphone itself and they published letters from listeners (particularly from women) describing their surprise at hearing this intimate, whispering voice. The stunt lasted approximately one year, during 1927 and 1928, and the announcer remained anonymous.

In this period discussions about the microphone voice or radio performance were not identified as central to radio's development. The whispering 'Mike' illustrated how this issue largely emerged and was articulated within the context of the continuing promotion of radio through images of popular science and the mystery of wireless. In the late 1920s the microphone was a symbol of radio's capacity to establish a relationship between the-world-out-there, gathered together and transmitted to the listeners-in, and the listeners-in in their domestic worlds. Radio was characterized as special because of the extent to which the-world-out-there was brought to listeners through this magical technology, and by the variety of pleasures the microphone could capture for the listeners' benefit.

This rhetoric depicted radio not only as constituting a social relation between individual listeners and the outside world, but as creating a whole network of social relations. Radio brought all the peoples of the world together, breaking down isolation: 'A Radio wave circles the Globe seven and one-half times in a second.'[17] People in England could listen to programmes broadcast in North America; people in the country could listen to the same programmes as people in the city. This was the theme most frequently used in parliamentary debates about the public utility value of radio. Broadcasting was welcomed as a means of bringing city amusements to country listeners as an incentive to stay working on the land. Farmers were said to be increasingly reliant on the broadcasting of market reports and weather forecasts, while also enjoying the entertainment items. Billy Hughes, MP for North Sydney and a former Prime Minister, proclaimed to parliament in 1927 the progress brought about by wireless broadcasting:

> No step has been taken that is more calculated to bring about not only progress and happiness among mankind, but also the peace of the world. Wireless brings the whole world in touch, it banishes isolation, it annihilates distance, it brings races sundered through the ages by fathomless oceans into close touch with one another.[18]

The reappearance of the theme 'radio annihilates distance'[19] in the late 1920s hailed a sense of community of an abstract nature; the unity created by radio, it was claimed, would arise from a generalized orientation to a central source of information and entertainment. Radio kept listeners 'in touch' with the world, with civilization, as something already constituted, separate from them. They were kept 'in touch' with each other, not by direct communication, but by sharing an orientation; they were unified, part of the nation and the Empire, as provided for them by radio.

> Broadcasting is accomplishing for the whole listening-in world what formerly travel and letter writing alone were mainly responsible for – and all the while the tea kettle is singing on the hob and the baby sleeps in the cradle.[20]

Now you could have the 'best seat in the house', the news of the world, information about other people and their lives, the feeling of being part of a community, without moving from your domestic setting. The listener-in became the 'fireside tourist'.[21]

Alternative images of the communication facilitated by radio continued to be promoted by Voigt and the *Labor Daily*. Wireless, they still insisted, would link the workers of the world. Wireless as the product of the labour of workers should also serve workers, keeping workers in all countries informed of the conditions and struggles of their fellows: 'the ether waves . . . will spread their message of hope, brotherhood and working-class activity over the entire surface of the earth'.[22] This vision of a rather different network of social relations, created by radio, however, had been contained by the PMG's regulations preventing broadcasting from competing with other means of telegraphic communication. Workers were to receive information about each other, rather than to inform others directly of their struggles and achievements.

The alternative vision for radio sustained, albeit in limited form by the late 1920s, by Voigt and others made no impact on the dominant discourse of parliamentary debates and official statements about radio, nor on the popular imagery being created by the mass circulation newspapers and radio journals. A sign of the future was the *Listener In*'s report of the success of the catch-cry 'Everybody Happy? That's the Idea'. Used by Rupert Hazell in the introduction to his various wireless entertainments on 5CL Adelaide, the magazine declared it to be on everybody's lips. During a maudlin film showing in Melbourne, a member of the audience was said to have called out 'Everybody Happy?', and half the audience to have shouted back, 'That's the Idea'.[23] The sense of unity being promoted by such tales hailed members of the listening public as privatized individuals brought together as an abstract community by catch-cries, common amusements, and interpellations such as 'everybody'.

The rivals

The discussion of radio's distinctiveness as a medium, as a new addition to the entertainment and information industries, was formed as part of the sales rhetoric of the radio merchants, but it was important too as a dress rehearsal for a more developed language about radio as a cultural institution in the 1930s. Cutting across these earlier representations of radio was another set of debates about the operation and control of wireless broadcasting. Terms such as 'monopoly', 'copyright', 'competing interests', 'government control' constituted a different field of representations about radio that were more concerned with constructing an object of governmental policy than marking out its social domain as a new technology. Nevertheless the two fields of debate did intersect and each contributed to the form and terrain of the other.

Parliamentary debates about wireless focused for some time on the monopoly given to AWA. Under an agreement with the government, AWA undertook in 1922 to erect a station in Australia for direct communication with Great Britain, an 'Empire Wireless'. As part of this agreement, the government purchased 500,001 one-pound shares in the company (giving it a controlling interest of one share). The government represented this enterprise as a matter of securing a means of official communication between countries and the states of Australia, rejecting the suggestion that it was supporting a commercial venture into a competitive retail trade. But AWA, under the control of its managing director, E.T. Fisk, moved rapidly beyond this conception of the company's role. As an offshoot of the powerful, British-based Marconi Co., it acquired 'the present and future patent rights, the good will, and the right to the technical knowledge and experience of the principal wireless systems of the world',[24] belonging at that time to Marconi and the German Telefunken company. It charged royalties on all Australian-made sets, and charged royalties at a higher rate on sets made elsewhere in the Empire; and still higher rates on 'foreign-made' sets. It charged broadcasting companies a royalty fee and a royalty of five shillings on each listener's licence. The New Zealand government successfully challenged AWA's right to charge such fees; in Australia, the government assisted in their collection.

Members of the Labor Party attacked AWA as a 'huge monopoly', evincing no conception of wireless broadcasting as a national service and demonstrating an 'insatiable appetite for making extortionate demands upon every branch of the industry'. Brennan, in this same onslaught, declared that even private enterprise, 'the spoiled darling of this Government', was being impeded by the government's marriage to this particular company. Traders, manufacturers and listeners-in were victims of its stranglehold.[25] Further, it was objected, the government was allowing (and even assisting) a foreign-based company to dominate an Australian industry. Similarly, the *Labor Daily* protested against the existence of this wireless monopoly and the exorbitant licence fee collected to put money in the pocket of the 'monopolistic . . . Marconi combine'.[26]

The National Party retaliated with eulogies to the initiative of AWA, the widespread popular interest in radio fostered by AWA's activities, and the infinite possibilities for wireless's progress stemming from the system of co-operation between the Commonwealth and private enterprise.[27] But complaints about AWA's monopoly were to be a major factor in the establishment of the 1927 Royal Commission on Wireless. In 1926 a meeting of the Association for the Development of Wireless, held in Sydney, called for a Royal Commission to inquire into AWA's monopoly, licence fees, copyright fees and the advisability of government control of broadcasting.[28]

Accusations of monopoly were levelled at other sections of the broadcasting world. J.C. Williamson Ltd, a powerful Australian theatrical entrepreneur, acquired a significant position in the broadcasting industry during the early years. In Britain, theatrical interests remained hostile to broadcasting, but in Australia the large companies, like J.C. Williamson and J. and N. Tait, sought a controlling interest in broadcasting and wanted to use it to promote their activities. J.C. Williamson held the major interest in the company that controlled 3LO and this station was affiliated with 2FC (though the latter was wholly owned by Farmer and Co.). Both stations made reciprocal arrangements with other musical and theatrical companies.

These arrangements ensured that particular stations had exclusive rights to most of the popular performers in Australia and to most of the artists visiting Australia from overseas. A witness before the 1927 Royal Commission listed the sources in Sydney for 2FC's musical and theatrical programmes: by arrangement with J.C. Williamson – Her Majesty's Theatre Royal, the Criterion Theatre, the Palace Theatre; by arrangement with J. and N. Tait – Musgrave's Tivoli Theatre, Union Theatre, the Haymarket Theatre, the Prince Edward Theatre; and as well, the Sydney Madrigal Society, the Royal Apollo Club, and the Sydney Harmonic Society. Another witness appearing before the Royal Commission provided a rather different perspective on these arrangements when he complained that since he had had a disagreement with J.C. Williamson, he had been unable to get any work on radio.[29]

Newspaper companies were also eager to move into the broadcasting business in the 1930s. But at first they were more concerned to maintain their ownership of the news collected by them or associated agencies and insisted upon 'the principle of private property'.[30] Arrangements were made by the various broadcasting stations with the daily newspapers; 2FC, for example, took their news from the *Sydney Morning Herald* and the *Evening News*. But by the time of the establishment of the ABC in 1932, the situation had become more complex. As radio grew more successful and a possible threat to the newspapers, their insistence on a private property right over the news collected by them became increasingly a claim to a prior right to collect and disseminate all news.

In 1929 the Herald and Weekly Times Ltd took over 3DB Melbourne, signalling the beginning of a new era; in the 1930s newspaper companies and religious bodies would become the main licensees of the 'B' class stations, whereas in the 1920s their licensees were predominantly radio traders. In 1932, the newspapers used their political power to ensure that the ABC was not permitted to set up its own news-gathering department, and, more important in the long term, to remove from the act establishing the ABC the provision that would have allowed the ABC to seek sponsors for its programmes. But the only accusations of monopoly or of burgeoning power made against the newspapers in the 1920s came from one main source – the labour movement. The NSW Trades and Labor Council had already attacked the capitalist press for its dishonest propaganda; Labor politicians constantly complained of the power of the press and the manner in which, as Senator Grant declared in 1927, it 'arrogates to itself the right to manufacture and disseminate public opinion'.[31]

Radio was also viewed as a threat by racing clubs. Racing broadcasts became a feature of many stations' programmes in 1926. By 1927 some stations (like 2KY) had begun to build up an image of themselves as racing stations. But in 1930 racing broadcasts were seriously threatened as individual clubs began to ban broadcasters from their courses.[32] Racing clubs feared the broadcasting of races would damage attendance at their events. Moreover, the PMG's department did not wish its revenue, collected from the use of telephone and telegraph in the transmission of racing results, to decrease; and police spokesmen predicted a dramatic increase in illegal starting price (SP) betting. Listeners, for their part, wrote protesting letters about the mobilization of those forces against what, to many, was central to their interest in radio:

A little while ago we read of the gramophone people trying to prevent their records being broadcasted, then the Stadium fights, and now – the races. It only wants the newspaper proprietors to object to their news being put over the air, and we in the country will get very little for our 24/–.[33]

Racing broadcasts continued to be a controversial issue. They began as stunt broadcasts; by 1927 they had become important to radio traders as a means of selling their equipment and to radio stations as a way to attract a listening public; by 1930 they were a site of a struggle that raised new issues about the wireless audience and the uses made of broadcasting programmes. Evidence was sought of the impact radio had on other public events. Broadcast descriptions were credited with increasing public interest in and attendance at cricket and wrestling. The *Wireless Weekly* declared that it was country listeners who benefited and that the racing clubs were displaying a selfishness detrimental to the national interest.[34] But racing clubs insisted that attendances declined at those fixtures where races were broadcast.

In England theatrical interests were making similar claims about the threat to attendances as those made by the racing clubs in Australia. But the issue had wider implications in Australia because of the attendant struggle over the question of SP betting. Police constantly undertook surveillance activities of local communities as they attempted to control this popular practice among one section of the population – working-class men. This group welcomed radio as facilitating their enjoyment of this favourite pastime and sets were installed in many hotel bars for their benefit, despite protests from police and other organizations. Racing broadcasts and the manner of their use continued to be a controversial issue in the 1930s.

A further issue about private property rights emerged in 1926 with the establishment of the Australian Performing Rights Association (APRA). This body, formed by Allan and Co., a large musical company with interests already in the broadcasting business, in association with other music companies, began to charge exorbitant royalties on all music broadcast. Critics of this body argued that the claims of copyright were not made on behalf of the artists writing or performing the works,[35] but were an attempt by one section of the industry to make as much money as possible. A rival body was established, an amalgam of three record companies – Associated Record Manufacturers (ARM) – in the attempt to prevent this encroachment on their domain. A Royal Commission into Performing Rights was set up in 1932 to adjudicate on the issue, just as the 1927 Royal Commission on Wireless was established to consider this matter of copyright as well as other claims of private property being made by competing interests in the broadcasting field.

At one level, then, radio's connection with the various sectors of the entertainment and information industries was celebrated as radio's capacity to bring the whole world into listeners' living rooms. This publicity language sought to foster popular enthusiasm about wireless broadcasting and to sell more radio equipment. At another level, however, wireless was being discussed in terms of exclusive rights, private property claims and monopoly. Clearly, the world being transmitted to listeners-in was a world manufactured, framed and owned by the different media or culture industries, but this connection was rarely made. For the most part the two sets of representations or discourses about radio did not overlap or intersect. They were produced and developed in different settings so that it was possible to define and discuss radio as a cultural institution in quite contrary ways. Hence, in the late 1920s, the popular magazines, newspapers and radio traders' advertisements defined radio as constituting a social relation – between the-world-out-there and the listener-in. Public servants and non-Labor politicians spoke of radio as re-constructing the world as a new unity, an abstract community. The rival culture industries proclaimed territories and agreements. The labour movement decried monopolies and defined radio as a national service (though with a different image of nationhood than that supported by non-Labor forces), although different sections of the labour movement disagreed about whether or not wireless broadcasting should be state controlled.

These competing claims and notions about broadcasting served to constitute radio as an object for governmental intervention and governmental policy; radio became a matter for the neutral state to clarify and organize. As such the language of national service provided a positive guise for the government's involvement in the future direction of broadcasting. The state appeared not merely as an adjudicator between competing interests; it represented the national benefit, the public interest. Yet disagreements existed between the political parties about the extent of that involvement: the Prime Minister, Stanley Bruce, was to ask in 1929 whether the Labor Party was seriously suggesting that 'the Government should provide musical and other programmes'.[36]

Governmental intervention had directed the development of wireless from the beginning, but the scope of its concerns had largely been set by the 1905 Wireless Telegraph Act, vesting in the PMG control over the technology of wireless transmission – over who might broadcast and under what conditions.[37] This had had profound repercussions in the form of the PMG's non-competition policy, through which a particular social definition of broadcasting technology had been made to prevail. But it was not until the 1927 Royal Commission, and the subsequent demands by the PMG that the 'A' stations in each city co-ordinate their activities, that programming began to appear on the agenda of public policy. The content of radio as well as the use of its technology was to become the object of governmental intervention.

The issue of radio programming, however, was not constructed by the 1927 Royal Commission as central to its domain. It had been established initially in response to charges of monopoly against AWA and to the increasingly vociferous complaints about copyright demands and the high price of the listeners' licence fees. The Royal Commission made only two recommendations about programmes, one about the fostering of educational work by radio and the second about advertising on 'A' stations. Nevertheless, questions about programming did arise throughout the process of the commission, in particular through the submissions made by witnesses. Listeners made submissions to the Commission about there being too many racing broadcasts, that advertising should be banned altogether, that there was too much dance music, or too little variety. Newspapers such as the *Daily Telegraph* urged listeners to make these submissions. Other groups also made submissions on programmes: broadcasters, such as Dorothy Jordan who advocated an increase in women's programmes; various sections of the community argued on behalf of their particular interests, like Bernard Heinze who talked of the need for musical 'up-lift'; and broadcasting personnel, such as W.T. Conder of 3LO, appeared to sing the praises of their stations and programmes. Finally, the Commissioners themselves pursued questions about programmes with some witnesses, generally in terms of whether better programmes would make radio more popular.

These discussions about radio programming involved particular ways of talking about radio. New to the definition of wireless were the references to its intrusion into the privacy of the home. Though images of radio's place in the private home had been employed from the beginning, no indication that this might provoke some tension had previously been registered. A number of listeners-in, however, spoke before the Commission of broadcasting as unwelcome in the home – of its bringing horse-racing, poor English pronunciation and jazz into the sanctity of the home.[38] Here the image of radio as an intruder was only a shadow; later it became central to the debate about censorship.

More important to the 1927 Royal Commission was the pursuit of the question of what was popular. Commissioners questioned witnesses about what programmes would make wireless more popular. The chairman of the Commission (J.H. Hammond, KC) probed further, asking whether the lighter programmes were more popular and hence would create widespread enthusiasm about wireless. Questioning S.E. Wilson of 2FC, he suggested that there should be two classes of stations: 'One class would contain the sporting programmes, the jazz music, and the things which would appeal to certain people. On the other side, you would have heavier things, such as classical music.'[39] This differentiation of programmes according to particular images of taste would be crucial in the 1930s in the construction of a radio audience for different types of programmes. Nevertheless, these categories – the heavy and the light, the serious and the popular – did already play a role in this earlier period. They were drawn upon in the context of the Royal Commission's considerations as part of its search for ways to create a sense of excitement, of variety, to foster widespread interest in radio.

Central to the 1927 Royal Commission's concerns were the accusations about monopoly and the competing claims for copyright. In pursuing these issues, the Commission listened to and questioned Fisk, appearing for AWA, for several days. It heard calls for complete government control of broadcasting; for less advertising or no advertising at all; and for better-quality transmissions. It listened to representatives of newspaper companies argue against government control of broadcasting, to representatives of education departments generally antagonistic to any full-scale development of school broadcasts, to broadcasting personnel promoting their particular stations and causes, to listeners claiming to speak for their neighbourhood or various listeners' leagues, to E.R. Voigt putting his case for broadcasting as a means of class education and class communication, and to R.G. Menzies appearing for Victorian and South Australian radio interests. The Commission was set up to examine existing practices of certain bodies – AWA in particular – but it became an extensive review of Australian broadcasting.

No dramatic changes were proposed. The Commission recommended a reduction in the listener-in fee from 27s 6d a year to a uniform 24 shillings. It issued 'an extended series of severe strictures'[40] against AWA. And it recommended that the control of broadcasting stations should remain with the PMG, subject to the administration of an Australian Wireless Committee (controlled by three officers from the PMG's department). Voigt characterized this move as similar to 'placing the development of motor traffic in the hands of the Railway Department'.[41] The government used the Commission's censorious remarks about AWA to force it into an agreement where the government would pay it three shillings from every licence fee in return for its releasing broadcasters, manufacturers and traders from all royalty obligations for five years.[42] Very little else changed directly as a result of the Commission.

Significant developments in the organization of Australian broadcasting did, however, occur in the following eighteen months. In 1928, W.G. Gibson, the PMG, instructed 'A' class stations in Melbourne and Sydney to co-ordinate and improve their programmes; in 1929, he announced that the government would take over all 'A' class licences and arrange for their programmes through a single contracting company. Tenders were called for, the PMG supplying a description of the type and format of programmes to be required from the proposed Australian Broadcasting Company thus to be formed. The language used in the tender forms for this national broadcasting service marks a significant break in the official ways of talking about radio; good taste, good education, 'high class' music were to be the business of this organization: 'The successful tenderer shall do all in his power to cultivate a public desire for transmissions of educational items, musical items of merit, and generally for all items and subjects which tend to elevate the mind'.[43] The content of radio broadcasting now appeared firmly on the agenda of government policy and positions on a hierarchical ladder of cultural merit were being defined. 'A' class stations were to concern themselves only with material of 'high standing'; the nature of the ladder was assumed, not explicitly stated.

The successful tenderers, a joint submission from Union Theatres Ltd, Fullers' Theatres and J. Albert and Son (a music company), were all major companies in the 'amusement industry' (a term they used in their tender). They drew attention to their considerable experience as evidence of their suitability and stressed that the success of their businesses attested to the abilities of the directors of each company to 'interpret public opinion'. But, in accordance with the tender schedule drawn up for the Australian Broadcasting Company, they declared their commitment to the ideals of a national service, education, programmes of outstanding merit and the elevation of the public mind.[44] These avowals suggest contradictory commitments towards the claims of cultural merit and public or popular taste, but, as the *Wireless Weekly* pointed out, these were not of their own making. In its review of the tender requirements, this magazine characterized the specifications for the Australian Broadcasting Company as making more than taxing demands. The successful tenderer was required to 'elevate the mind', but they would also be asked to 'cater for the reasonable tastes of the community as a whole'.[45] The ABC, established three years later, would similarly be asked to juggle these two demands. A hierarchy of tastes was affirmed as part of the specifications for the conduct of the new broadcasting company; it would, as a government-sponsored body, naturally cultivate the top grade, but concomitantly, the company would be required to tend to other interests and tastes.

The language of national service and the elevation of the public mind provided a suitable guise for governmental intervention to make the content of radio broadcasting an object of public policy. The liberal state, as representative of the public interest, held positive powers in these spheres. Governmental intervention was legitimate to ensure that this 'public utility' was equally available to all members of the community, whether they lived in the country or the city. And, by 1928–9, governmental intervention was being justified in the area of programming on the basis of the state's obligation to serve the 'best self' of the nation. It was responsible for ensuring the general education of the community, as well as its cultural and moral uplift. Three years later when the ABC took over the role (and the stations) of the Australian Broadcasting Company, the positive powers of the liberal state would be elaborated further to represent the 'A' class stations as central to its educative work.

As Stuart Hood points out, talking about the British situation, the effect of such policies of government intervention in the area of radio programming was to relieve radio traders of the need to produce and finance the programmes necessary to attract interest in and the sale of their equipment.[46] The *Age*, lobbying on behalf of the radio traders from the beginning, began to argue for government intervention in programming as early as 1924. Initially, it had called on the PMG to use his powers to insist on better programmes from 3LO and 3AR – the two

'A' class stations in Melbourne. It claimed listener dissatisfaction with the lack of any control over the programmes provided by these stations. By 1928, the *Age* was insisting the government should assume complete control of broadcasting. Through editorials and reports (including eulogies about the wonderful success of the British Broadcasting Corporation – the BBC – established in 1926), it declared broadcasting services to be of a 'unique' character. The usual claim for private enterprise, it explained, did not hold for such a service: 'broadcasting, which is at once an entertainment, a service and a medium for education is not suitable for exploitation for profit'.[47] State intervention in the case of a medium for entertainment, for people's pleasure, would appear authoritarian; in the case of a public utility and a medium for education, it was a duty and the legitimate sphere of the state.

The 'A' class stations were gradually brought under governmental control, their programmes being provided by the new broadcasting company. The 'B' class stations, on the other hand, remained untouched and apparently outside government concern throughout the 1920s. Although a number of witnesses appeared before the 1927 Royal Commission on behalf of 'B' stations, and despite its wide-ranging review of broadcasting in Australia, it confined its deliberations about and recommendations for these stations to two questions: the interference to transmissions by 'A' stations caused by 'B' stations; and the use made of advertising by 'A' and 'B' stations. It recommended that the number of 'B' stations in any state be controlled according to the population size and that their wavelength be limited to avoid the problem of interference. Second, it argued that all forms of advertising (direct and indirect) should be prohibited on 'A' class stations in those states where both 'A' and 'B' class stations operated. It framed this recommendation as a response to the complaints made to the Commission about advertising on 'A' class stations, but it acknowledged also that 'A' stations received revenue from licence fees, unlike the 'B' stations.[48] Effectively, the latter recommendation constructed the 'B' stations as commercially based organizations. But, as Counihan suggests, it was formulated in response to complaints about advertising on the 'A' stations, not as an explicit decision to improve the viability of the 'B' stations or to determine their financial basis.[49]

In the mid-1920s, the 'B' class stations remained essentially extensions of the experimenters' or enthusiasts' licence; the 1924 PMG regulations were mainly concerned with designating which stations would receive licence revenue, not with the differences in the type of broadcasting to be undertaken by these two systems of broadcasting stations. Few demands were made of the 'B' stations in official and popular debates about broadcasting. The 1924 PMG regulations, under which these licences were issued, assumed that such broadcasters would remain restricted to providing for a particular and limited audience; it carried this assumption in its specifications about wavelengths. With the granting of licences to 2KY in 1925 and 2GB in 1926, however, the notion of a limited audience acquired a new dimension. 2KY was to broadcast to a particular political constituency; 2GB to a particular religious body. But in neither case did those organizing and operating these new stations accept that their broadcasts would in fact be confined to an audience limited in size, or indeed to only one section of the public.

2GB was established as an organ of the NSW branch of the Theosophical Society. Like 2KY, it was conceived of as a means of education and public appeal. A.E. Bennett, appearing before the 1927 Royal Commission on behalf of 2GB, proclaimed the purposes of the station to be the general education of the population and the spread of culture. He also spoke ardently of 2GB's concern to cultivate an 'intense patriotism in the hearts of Australians' and an 'all-Australian' attitude. The language wore the appearance of non-partisanship, mobilizing the terms 'nationhood', 'citizenship', 'a unity of interests', 'culture', 'education' and 'Australian motherhood'.[50] They remained silent on their private hopes to 'Theosophise' Australia.[51] Not so silent, but still not explicit, was the political conservatism articulated through these images of nationhood, motherhood and the 'All-Australian' attitude. In the actual broadcasting practices of 2GB, their political position was more clearly identifiable: in broadcasts like Arundel Nixon's 'Advance Australia News Service' and in their providing ready access to broadcasting facilities for conservative politicians.

With the 1927 Royal Commission pending the PMG did not issue any further 'B' class licences. Indeed he did not do so until 1930, by which time a number of 'B' licences were up for renewal and the PMG was forced to address himself to the question of the role and place of the 'B' stations.[52] Apart from the licences granted to 2KY and 2GB, then, the main development in the organization of the 'B' stations in the late 1920s was confined to some important changes in ownership. In 1927, 3DB Ltd took over that station as a company solely concerned with broadcasting. In 1929 the station was again taken over, this time by the

Herald newspaper. In 1928 2UW Sydney was taken over by Farmer and Co. and Palings, the music company; and the *Sun* newspapers in Sydney acquired an interest in 2UE (to be consolidated in the early 1930s).

For these new owners, the restricted wavelengths of the 'B' stations posed a particular problem. They were concerned to place the stations on a commercial basis through the use of advertising, and attracting advertisers depended on the acquisition of a large audience. 3DB Ltd had been the first to seek such a financial basis for their station, though in 1927 they had no particular preference for this source of income (they argued before the Royal Commission that they should be given an 'A' class licence). The interest in advertising among 'B' class stations in the 1920s was a matter of expediency, of financial viability. It was not until the 1930s that the 'B' stations began to represent their difference through a rhetoric of independence, separation from the state, and freedom, and to argue that advertising, commercially based operations, served this purpose. (They also began to insist in this latter period that they should be called commercial stations rather than 'B' class stations.) Meanwhile, these stations were becoming more interested as a group in the size of their audience, in the potential reach of their transmissions. Just as 2KY and 2GB envisaged their broadcasts as seeking out a broad audience, so the new type of owners were interested in a wider listening public.

In official and popular representations of the 'B' stations, however, their role continued to be discussed as operating for limited or sectional audiences, rather than the 'general body of listeners' who were the responsibility of the 'A' stations. The 'A' stations, as beneficiaries of licence fees, were under an obligation to satisfy all listeners, to provide a comprehensive service; the 'B' stations were subject to no such demands. At this stage, whether serving a particular type of audience or offering a limited service only, the 'B' stations remained unfettered by notions of the public interest or national service. In the 1930s this distinction would be reworked in crucial ways. The 'B' stations, playing on the notions of 'popular' and 'what the public wants', would represent themselves as serving the real interests and desires of the general public, as servicing the 'real' nation. It would be a populist language, feeding off its opposition to the images of nationhood, the public interest, embodied in the 'A' stations as expectations imposed, expressions of domination, rather than true reflections of the people's desires.

Varied tastes

In a statement to the *Listener In* at the end of 1929, Stuart Doyle, the chairman of the newly established ABC, announced: 'Radio has become part and parcel of the everyday life of the community, and as such the whole of its potentialities should be exploited and brought into the service of all classes.'[53] The statement combined two important images of wireless. The first – radio's necessity to everyday life – was evoked only intermittently in the 1920s. It would become a dominant image in the 1930s as radio was talked about less as an invention of science, a toy, a magical relation between two worlds, and more in terms of its domesticity. The second – radio serving all classes – was a theme of the late 1920s, a way of talking about radio, largely eclipsed by different images in the 1930s.

Doyle identified those sections of the community, 'classes' or groups, whom he saw as being served by wireless. They included those who required classical programmes, those who preferred entertainment of a lighter nature, talks and lectures, or sport. They were country listeners or city folk, those who wanted religious programmes or those who did not. They were definite groups and they appeared, in the context of this type of discussion about broadcasting, as already constituted. They possessed certain characteristics, needs, preferences, not in relation to the world of pleasures or services to be offered by radio, but in relation to their lives as already defined. Radio was depicted as addressing all their needs and desires.

This mode of representing the radio audience (or audiences) differed from the way in which they had been discussed in the first few years of broadcasting in Australia. In the earlier period, radio had been depicted as transforming the lives of everyone by the simple fact of its existence. Radio entered all the different worlds – that of the country listener, the city listener, the housewife, or the child – and made them more exciting. Now all those worlds meant that listeners had varied specific tastes, needs or desires that radio programmes could satisfy.

The demand that radio please all tastes grew more strident throughout the late 1920s. All were agreed about the existence of a broad range of tastes; disagreements only arose over whether every station should provide a varied programme or whether variety should be provided by the different stations. The *Age* and the *Argus* advocated the co-ordination of radio programming so that two stations would not broadcast the same type of programme at any one time. Listeners should have a choice. Others argued that the 'A' stations, paid for by the general public, should attempt to please all sections of that public by each providing a varied programme. Thus, witnesses before the 1927 Royal Commission sometimes complained of stations such as 3LO transmitting 'too much of the one thing'.[54]

Themes of choices, of what the public really wants, were being mobilized. The introduction of plebiscites played a significant role in this process. They provided a sense of people's tastes being taken into account, of the stations investigating what people really wanted, as well as appearing to affirm the notion that those wants were varied and broad ranging. A major plebiscite conducted by the *Argus* (in conjunction with 3LO) placed Sunday church services at the top of the poll, hard evidence, it was proclaimed, of how little was yet known of the listening public.[55] Tastes were varied and unpredictable; listeners must be allowed to exercise and gratify their choices.

At times the licence fee was evoked as good reason why listeners should be able to make a choice. It gave listeners a right to insist on their demands. W.T. Conder of 3LO argued that listeners 'are paying the piper, and I think they are entitled to call the tune to some extent'.[56] Similarly, the *Daily Telegraph* urged listeners to make submissions to the 1927 Royal Commission claiming that the radio industry existed only for the listener. As the one who pays, the listener should have a '"say" in the conduct of the system'.[57] Listeners too took up this theme pointing out in letters to the editor of the newspapers and radio journals that it was the listening public who provided the revenue for stations such as 3LO. They debated with one another whether particular stations did or did not serve the public well or whether listeners were receiving the full value of their licence fee from the 'A' stations as a whole.

These letters indicate the way in which listeners were adapting to radio as a cultural institution, but more importantly, they reveal an ambivalence towards or a certain sense of contradiction in the experience of wireless for listeners-in. As contributors to the revenue of the 'A' stations, listeners insisted they had a right to influence or at least be served by those stations. Plebiscites affirmed that belief, as did the catch-cries 'Wireless for All', and the constant repetition of claims about radio as the democratic cultural institution (either through the earlier representations of its science, or later by references to what the public wants). Radio was a public institution over which the public had a say. Yet the letters suggest an anxiety and a frustration through their frequent acknowledgement that a 'letter to the editor' represented only one individual talking about his or her privatized pleasures. Signing themselves as 'Fed Up', 'John Citizen', or 'Listener In', listeners indicated their search for a collective statement – from a position of isolation. They argued for their case as part of a community of listeners, but had only the experience of listening-in as isolated individuals to draw on. Letter writers reminded one another that they were each only one voice, only 'one small sum of 27/6d per year out of £60,000', but then would simultaneously retreat to notions of 'the public', what is 'popular', or to claim that 'no doubt many would agree' to support their criticism of others.[58]

Listeners were adapting to radio as a public institution and learning to speak of themselves as part of a general public or listening public. The ideology of radio exploited these images or representations of the radio audience to construct a sense of community, a nation unified by wireless: 'wireless keeps the whole world in touch'. Listeners were members of that abstract community, the listening public, and could 'have their say' through letters to the radio stations, letters to the editor of newspapers or journals, or through the new radio plebiscites. Their power, their right to be heard, was no more than votes in a referendum; each one was merely a single voice among many – listeners could either accept or reject the material proffered, but their opinions would disappear into the clamour made by the variety of tastes and needs to be heard. Their letters of the late 1920s did not question the non-reciprocity of radio, the social relation of consumer to the marketplace now being represented and established as natural to the technology of wireless. But they did articulate a certain unease or anxiety about the isolation and anonymity of the individual simultaneouly being assumed; their letters suggest an awareness of being isolated individuals whose social role was being confined to the sphere of cultural consumption.

Just as women had been one of the first groups to be made a specific target for advertising campaigns to sell wireless sets as domestic equipment, so were they speedily designated as a group with particular needs and interests to be satisfied by the provision of special programmes. Radio magazines and daily newspapers began to include special feature pages in 1926 identifying this interest among women. With titles such as 'What's in the Air for us Women', 'A Page for Women' and 'Mainly for Women', articles instructed women about using radio, finding programmes pertinent to their needs, and ensuring too that the whole family did so. The *Listener In*, the first magazine to move in this direction, presented a feature page that bore the subtitle 'A department to help our readers to a better knowledge and appreciation of their share in the programmes'. Women were endlessly reminded of their good fortune; of how radio brought them cookery and household hints, it brought them knowledge and information so they could become 'good conversationalists', and the latest scientific theories about bringing up children. They were advised to regard the radio set as a friend, a companion in the house, but to be discriminating – to switch from one station to another to find the programme that suited their individual tastes.

These pages utilized the language of choice, of listeners as tastes and needs to be served, and of the variety of pleasures on offer. The *Listener In* informed its female readers:

> wireless has really done more for women than any other class. It instructs and entertains. If we like a certain thing, we can write and ask for more, and if a talk or musical interlude does not please us – well, we merely pull out the plug, or switch on to another station, and there we are![59]

Wireless was munificent. Women's lives were no longer represented as drudgery and toil, but as normal domesticity. Radio responded to their interests, ensuring that their everyday life was made full by its companionship and variety. Addressed as the fortunate consumers of programmes made specially for them, women were 'very lucky creatures'.

The interests and needs of women were specified as domestic. Household hints, cookery hints, beauty hints, child care hints: knowledge represented as easily assimilated or consumed, and all of a domestic character. Knowledge of the 'outside world' too was represented in these same terms, of effortlessly acquired information. Wireless took women on a 'magic carpet' tour of the world, satisfying their curiosity and keeping them in touch with the world outside. They could listen in to that world while doing the ironing or shelling the peas. They were addressed as consumers, of the information purveyed and the programmes provided. The magazines worked hard to produce this image of women and the central role radio should play in their lives. They proclaimed a 'feminine radio world' catering exclusively for women's needs – a world of 'feminine fashions, fads and fancies'.[60]

Representing radio as surrogate companion and friendly adviser, this publicity language simultaneously articulated and denied the reality of many women's isolation and alienation in the home. The feature pages of the radio magazines and of the newspapers gave words to that experience in order to open up a space for – a need for – radio in women's lives. Women's work in the home was becoming increasingly privatized and solitary. Many now lacked social contacts in their work and daily lives and were unable to share their problems or seek advice from companions or their extended family. Radio filled this need. But once acknowledged, given voice, the problem was covered over, disguised. The reasons why women might seek advice and companionship from outside, rather than from each other, from their mother or friends, were not discussed.

The feature articles for women worked to produce a particular orientation to radio programmes, but they continued, too, to attempt to promote an interest in wireless among women. Proclaiming the number of items of interest to women, the articles depicted wireless as essential to the lives of all women. So too did other articles and other journals. *New Idea*, a well-established women's magazine, advised its readers to include a radio set in planning their home furnishing, 'In the modern trend towards dainty and artistic furnishings, radio is playing an increasingly important part. Wireless cabinets are nowadays beautifully in keeping, and the housewife is keenly appreciative of Australian timbers for Australian homes.'[61] Women, thus, appeared to become a central target of all marketing strategies for wireless, a trend most clearly indicated in the radio and electrical exhibitions. In 1928 the Sydney exhibition introduced a series of competitions and displays of women's cooking and handiwork, organized by 2BL's women's session announcer, Dorothy Jordan.

Advertisements depicted women reclining in armchairs with a wireless set beside them or being presented with a set for Christmas. 'Ladies! The Excellazone may be had in a choice of Oak, Blackwood, Rosewood or Antique to Match your Furniture.'[62] Occasionally a flapper appeared activating an image of femininity discordant with that of the domestic woman, but for the most part women were represented as doing domestic chores or relaxing in a domestic setting. All advertisements underlined the simplicity of operation of their sets. Harrington's store declared of the latest 'Popular' receiver that 'A child can work it'. The new Astor Aladdin in 1929 banished 'radio muddle' for ever. The advertisements thus stressed the lack of technical intervention necessary and portrayed a casualness about the contact between the listener and the radio set. Images of radio as a symbol of

Harmonious *alike* to Eye and Ear

No. 501 Receiver, Treasure Chest, 8-tube; coils shielded; operates from AC house lighting circuit or batteries.
Price less accessories $65/17/6

No. 5-A Cone Speaker. Violin wood sounding board. Licensed under Lektophone patents 1271527 and 1271528. Other patents pending.
Sold only with Stromberg-Carlson Receivers.

Complete power supply equipment for Stromberg-Carlson Receivers. Left to right:

No. 3906 "A" Socket-Power Unit. £16/16/-
No. 201 Power-Switching Relay. £1/10/-
No. 401 "B" Socket-Power Unit with U.X.-213 tube £18/18/-

"WHY, Edith, it's beautiful! When I heard that John had given you a Radio, I couldn't quite see it in this perfect room of yours. But, it makes it all the prettier."

"Yes, isn't it good-looking. But wait till you hear it. It's a Stromberg-Carlson, you know, and the tone is the clearest, purest thing I've ever heard."

Stromberg-Carlson receivers do combine beauty of tone with beauty of appearance. Throughout the whole receiver every precaution is taken to preserve the naturalness and beauty which a program possesses when it leaves the broadcasting station. Total shielding protects it as it enters the receiver and is amplified. A truly remarkable audio system insures that the program leaving it is a natural reproduction of the original.

Combined with these features is a beauty that is stately, yet simple, elegant, yet conservative. The lines of the Stromberg-Carlson blend harmoniously with the furnishings of any home. It is a pleasure to see a Stromberg-Carlson. It is also a pleasure to hear one.

Stromberg-Carlson (Australasia) Ltd.
Sydney: Berk House, 76 William Street.
Melbourne: Hardware House, 386 Post-office Place (F3278).

Authorised Stromberg-Carlson Dealers:
Henry G. Small & Co., 357 Post-office Place, Melbourne.
Suttons Pty. Ltd., 290 Bourke St., Melbourne, and at Geelong.
Let your dealer arrange a Stromberg-Carlson demonstration for you and try it yourself.

Stromberg-Carlson
Makers of voice transmission and voice reception apparatus for more than 30 years

Women as both targets and symbols of advertising strategies that set out to produce a domestic image for radio (Photograph: *Argus*, 18 June 1927) science were absent in this context; the wireless set was to be secured a place in the domestic setting. Women were both targets of this marketing strategy and its symbol. In portraying women as users of wireless sets, the advertisements placed both in the home as integral to the everyday life of the family. Radio was a beautiful piece of furniture, and even 'A Child Can Work It' – a female child. Men appeared in advertisements as father figures of the nuclear family; they were seated comfortably in a lounge room, often with pipe in mouth. Men and boys, pictured on their own, were employed to activate echoes of the earlier excitement about radio as a new technology, as science.

The radio magazines throughout the 1920s continued to be as much for radio enthusiasts as for listeners-in. The *Listener In* and the *Wireless Weekly*, among the most substantial and successful radio journals in this period, carried central features on the technology of wireless sets, including advice to enthusiasts, instructions about building the latest sets and recommendations about better reception. Other features too, such as regular sections on radio's success around the world and advances in the technology of broadcasting, continued a sense of excitement about the technical side of radio. For the listeners, on the other hand, these magazines now provided radio programme details; news about future radio programmes; discussions about the politics of radio – the latest government manoeuvres; plus features on studio gossip, radio personalities, and articles on radio techniques that were in some ways the precursors of the radio magazine of the 1930s. Studio pages such as the *Wireless Weekly*'s 'Between You and Me and the Microphone' which drew attention to this component of the technology of the broadcasting was characteristic of the late 1920s. Stories were often of radio gaffs or descriptions of chaos behind the scenes, but, like the pages on radio personalities, these features created a sense of a 'radio world'. Later, that world would become a world of glamour and stardom; in the late 1920s it provided a sense of excitement about the technology of broadcasting and its capacity to bring these voices to you, the listener-in.

Readers of the popular radio magazines were simultaneously addressed as participants in the technological advances of broadcasting, and as consumers of radio programmes and radio itself. The magazines continued to circumvent any possible tension or contradiction between these two positions, as they had done within the first few years of broadcasting, by implying gender differences in these two interests.

Advertisements for radio and electrical exhibitions were indicative of the differentiations being drawn. They pursued the interest of women through accounts of the displays of listeners' craft and cookery skills, the presence of women announcers, and the range of furniture styles in wireless sets to be viewed. Men were accosted with the displays of broadcasting technology to be viewed and the presence of experts to be talked to: 'No Radio Man Can Miss It'.[63] In the 1930s the technical sections of the radio magazines would disappear or be drastically reduced. Other journals which had concentrated on the technology of wireless and the radio enthusiast market would collapse, and new magazines such as the *Radio Times* and *Broadcasting Business* would appear in the mid-1930s. Radio's cultural forms, its mode of operation, its social and political functions, and its place among the culture industries would be clearly delineated in this period.

3
THE INTIMATE VOICE

In the 1930s radio would no longer be celebrated as a magical invention of modern science, nor spoken of as a gadget or toy; preoccupation with its technology was replaced by a preoccupation with its content and audience. Similarly, alternative images of radio's possible use – as a means of communication between groups, a means of class education or of public entertainment – largely disappeared from official and popular discourses about broadcasting. These changes, foreshadowed in the late 1920s, signalled the delimiting of radio's social usage: radio was now clearly defined as a means of communicating messages from a central source to a mass, albeit privatized and passive, audience.

The definition of radio in this manner established a particular relationship between radio message and audience to which both broadcasters and listeners had to learn to adapt. In the 1930s a radio style or mode of radio performance evolved as broadcasters sought to provide a 'viewpoint', a position from which the audience would listen in. The audience reached by radio was a mass audience; the radio performance set out to make each listener feel as if radio personnel were speaking to him or her in particular, to each of them as individuals, rather than the crowd. Simultaneously, listeners were taught how to be listeners. Radio magazines and the radio feature sections of the daily press provided information about the broadcast programmes available each week, but they also instructed listeners about the best way to listen to radio and informed them of its significance in their daily lives.

'Flesh and blood' radio[1]

In the 1920s a number of broadcasters had begun to explore a style of presentation in which they 'personalized' their performance. These were the announcers who had been so successful in establishing children's programmes as a feature of early radio broadcasts, though they had also been more extensively involved in the work of various stations. Announcers such as A.S. Cochrane (2FC's 'Hello Man') and G.A. Saunders (2BL's 'Uncle George') established a means of presenting their personalities. Cochrane, for example, made himself 'friend and counsellor of countless hundreds'.[2] But criticisms were levelled at announcers who sought to be too friendly, too 'chummy'. Discussions of radio techniques in this earlier period were largely confined to the importance of elocutionary training for the right style of voice for broadcasting. Presenting the announcer's personality was not yet considered as the art, the technique, to be mastered as appropriate to broadcasting.

The first analyses of good radio technique appeared in the form of stories by popular announcers about what it was like to work at the radio microphone. These stories contributed to and were formed by the mystique surrounding the radio 'mike' in the late 1920s, but were also a crucial sign of shifts occurring in the way in which radio's relationship to its audience was to be represented. Frank Russell, a 3DB announcer, wrote the 'inside story' for the *Listener In* about cricket broadcasts:

> The secret of successful broadcasting is absence of effort. To 'make a speech' to a microphone is fatal. The pomposity of self-importance is 'amplified' a hundred-fold and strikes the ear with an effect of deadly boredom. To speak as quietly, as naturally, with as little desire to impress as though one were speaking to a friend in the room, is the only way to broadcast, whether it is an advertisement or a great national message.[3]

Here, the argument for a special style of radio performance was couched in terms of the radio microphone and its effects; later, discussions of techniques would proceed from an understanding of radio as constituting a social relation between broadcaster and audience within the world of radio. But the themes of intimacy, ordinariness (versus pomposity) and speaking 'as if' to a friend sketched in here by Russell would become the fundamental taken-for-granteds for radio personnel.

In the 1930s it would no longer be regarded as appropriate that announcers talk at their unseen audience, lecture at them or simply read the newspaper to them. Announcers wrote of the moments when, caught without a script, they had had to speak spontaneously, ad-lib in their descriptions of a wrestling match; all reported a favourable response by listeners to the more relaxed, friendly style they had discovered through such mishaps. Such tales served to affirm the appropriateness of the friendly versus the formal performance, while also creating a further sense of intimacy between listener and broadcaster: the listener was taken behind the scenes, told the broadcasters' private stories. But perhaps of greater significance would be the suggestion that the appropriate style of radio performance was a performance that was not a performance. These tales conveyed the message that broadcasters had discovered, as if by accident, that they were most successful when they spoke directly to listeners – spontaneously and as equals.

As the competition for audiences intensified, discussions of the 'art' of radio broadcasting became more serious. In public and in private, broadcasting organizations and other groups dissected the radio performance style. They claimed that announcers provided an invisible link between the audience and the radio programmes, provided a point of identification for listeners. Here was a friend talking to each listener in the intimacy of their homes: Vernon Sellars, said the *Labor Daily*, 'seems to have a happy knack of speaking to listeners individually'.[4] Common to all discussions was the conviction that radio was most successful when 'intimate', 'human', 'personal'.[5] Techniques to create an intimate world of radio had to be devised and learnt by announcers, lecturers, playwrights, interviewers and the various artists performing or broadcasting.

The intimate, human mode of address or performance continued to be discussed explicitly throughout the 1930s, rather than to become an automatic assumption about what was necessary to good radio. One source of unease or uncertainty that sustained periodic debates about the issue was the newly formed ABC. Officially opened on 1 July 1932, this organization took over the operation of the 'A' class stations from the Australian Broadcasting Company and was modelled on the BBC. Throughout the 1930s, officials and broadcasting personnel within the ABC frequently turned nervously to the example of the BBC, anxious that they were failing to emulate it and the cultural mission being forged for it by the towering figure of its first director-general, John Reith. The ABC was to shy away from the intimate, human style of radio performance repeatedly throughout the 1930s, fearing that such a personal mode might threaten the aura of culture it sought to present. Yet, it could not achieve an unequivocal stance on this question and contradictory statements were often made by different people within the organization. In 1933, the first chairman of the ABC, Charles Lloyd Jones, declared that particular attention would be devoted to 'humanizing' its broadcast programmes by 'the continual inclusion of items which represent ordinary thought and action, laughter, and the real things of life, by the encouragement of artists and speakers who have the happy gift of preserving their personality over the air'.[6] But ABC announcers, particularly in its evening programmes, would be required throughout the 1930s to retain a formal, distanced manner.

The 'B' class stations, or commercial stations as they sought to be called in the 1930s, on the other hand, adopted the informal, friendly mode of radio performance with increasing enthusiasm and no signs of ambivalence. The new types of owners beginning to appear in the late 1920s, concerned to place these stations on a commercial basis, were most interested in ways of attracting and holding audiences. Broadcasters and announcers for the 'B' class stations rapidly developed techniques they believed would serve these purposes. They began to learn to exploit the technology to produce personalities for themselves. Themes of the performance that is not a performance, the natural, friendly style, and the ordinary, fellow-next-door personality dominated their discussions and practice of the broadcasting art. Norman Banks of 3KZ Melbourne, consistently voted one of the most popular male radio announcers in Victoria in the 1930s, was a pioneer of its skills and techniques. He set himself up as a friendly adviser, full of commonsense wisdom in programmes such as *Help Thy Neighbour* and *Husbands and Wives*. He was just another member of the family, the ordinary man with no pretensions – leaning over the backyard fence, chatting. His populist style worked to produce an image of a programme that simply held up a mirror to listeners' lives.

Similarly, Nicky (Clifford Niccola Whitta), one of the most successful innovators for 1930s commercial radio, created a world of everydayness through his persona and programme formats. Nicky's world was one of 'chums', of an intimate domesticity, and he addressed his listeners with an easy familiarity. In the 1920s, forgetting that the radio microphone was switched on had been a source of amusing stories for radio magazines; Nicky, on the other hand, pretended he did not realize the microphone was there or that it was switched on to exploit techniques of ad-libbing. The earlier stories destroyed the aura of radio for an instant and produced a sense that listeners would enter the secret life of the broadcasting station's studio. It was this sense Nicky manipulated to draw listeners into his programmes. His world was a self-enclosing, secure world in which the listener joined in with his foolishness and antics. Listeners became part of his everyday world of domestic troubles and pleasures; it was a fantasy world of simple fun and forgetfulness.

Nicky first explored these radio techniques on 3AW Melbourne, in the children's show, *Chatterbox Corner*, and in his breakfast programme with Tuppy (Fred Tupper) in the early 1930s. Nancy Lee (Kathleen Whitta), Nicky's wife, who also worked on *Chatterbox Corner* for a number of years as one of the 'chums', claims that the 'homeliness', 'guilelessness' and a sense of the ordinary guaranteed the success of the show. Her own popularity she attributed to her image of 'the girl-next-door'. She was no moralist, or slightly prudish aunt of the ABC; she was 'one of us'. Nicky developed his 'ordinary' image on this programme as he did his characteristic acting the fool while on air. He adopted the persona of the Ginger Meggs cartoon character (a classic 'ordinary Australian bloke' figure), appearing on public occasions in appropriate clothes of short shorts and braces, and he greeted his listeners-in with the line 'Ar there, Fellars'. A little later in his career, Nicky modified his persona for day-time programmes to become a cheeky, but warm-hearted tease. He now called his listeners 'Mum' and 'Darl' as he encouraged them to buy his sponsors' products ('friendly advice' it had been called on *Chatterbox Corner*). As an announcer, he exploited his 'homely' style, treated listeners to (usually fabricated) stories of his daily life, and then would apparently forget about his audience as he leant out of the window to talk to the 'garbos', the garbage men. The world of the 'chums' of *Chatterbox Corner* and of Nicky's day-time programmes was a world where daily life, the ordinary person, common sense, the family, were celebrated.[7]

Thus broadcasters were developing techniques so that radio spoke to 'you and you alone';[8] it entered listeners' lives, their ordinary lives, and spoke directly and personally to each one. The image developed of radio offering itself as a friend – speaking intimately and personally to each listener – worked to produce a sense that both companionship and individuality could be provided by this product of the marketplace. As a means of direct and personalized communication, it insisted that the individuality of each listener was affirmed without their having to do anything.

The personality style of commercial radio (Photograph: *Listener In*, 3 February 1934)

Each and every one of you is special, is someone; radio speaks to you, directly to you, in your life. Denying that radio was a means of mass communication, a part of the mass society, the broadcasting performance style (and the celebratory statements about its practice and practitioners being made in the print media) represented radio as both symbol of the primacy of the individual and vendor-cum-guarantor of the listener's individuality. 'Radio has a big but intimate audience.'[9]

The intimate, human performance began to dominate all fields of radio programming. This mode was discussed explicitly during the 1930s as a means of drawing the listener into the programme, as a means of capturing and holding audiences to prevent them turning the dial. The listener was to be addressed or placed as a friend, as one of the family, or as an eavesdropper, within the programme. The techniques required for each programme type were discussed in these terms, and new radio forms were devised to suit these purposes.

The interview was a major innovation, often seen as replacing the talk for particular categories of audience, or for specific subject matter. Dorothy Vautier, a successful women's session broadcaster for 2GB, claimed that interviews were most suitable for female audiences, catering for their interests in the personality of the speaker rather than their ideas. The interview was designed to draw the listener into the programme, either as eavesdropper or as represented by the interviewer.

The BBC had given its imprimatur to this innovation as a legitimate means of dealing with certain topics. Thus the ABC followed suit in the mid-1930s as it sought to deal with controversial issues and educational matters. They experimented with staged conversations (between two actors) in the attempt to deal with educational material in a more entertaining, more 'human' manner. In handling subjects defined as 'controversial', they preferred to employ an interview-style presentation, in which the interviewer was said to represent the listener and the 'man-in-the street'.[10] But the ABC's experimentation was far more haphazard and uncertain compared to the work done at the BBC to establish specific categories of topics and the corresponding styles of presentation deemed appropriate to each category.[11]

Family serials, an important radio innovation of the 1930s for the 'B' class stations, addressed listeners in an intimate manner through both their style of presentation and their content. Listeners became eavesdroppers on the lives of these fictitious characters, spoken to as 'one of the family' by the programmes and the publicity material that appeared in vast quantities. Advertisements for shows such as *Those Happy Gilmans* or *Digger Hale's Daughter* called out to listeners as sharing the problems and the joys of the radio family – both by listening to the programme, and in their own lives. *Dad and Dave*, the best known of these serials, was introduced in its first episode by an announcer inviting listeners into its world: 'This is a human story of two typical Australians, their families, their lives, their hopes, their doubts, their fears, and their triumphs. . . . Perhaps their troubles will remind you of your own, and perhaps their courage will inspire you.' The direct, intimate mode of address set out to capture listeners within the viewpoint of the programme and to tie them to the station and its broadcasts. These techniques were self-consciously discussed as officials and personnel connected with this new culture industry explored and clarified the cultural tasks being determined for it.

Playwrights had to be educated to adjust their art to this new medium. Broadcasting, it was claimed, requires 'a quieter and less strident approach'.[12] A radio play, suggested one writer, was a theatre performance 'with the curtain down'[13] – a phenomenon to which both audience and playwright would have to adjust. Recommendations to the playwright included: the number of characters must be kept small and clearly distinguishable from each other, the action of the play should be kept simple and changes of scene to a minimum. To the actors: voices should be conversational in tone; rather than acting for an audience, actors should speak to each other; the unseen and unseeing audience should be treated as an 'eavesdropper' – both by actors and playwrights. This advice did not consider the radio play as a totally new form, but looked only to adjust the art to the demands of the microphone and the needs of the listener-in.

Plays were deemed successful that conveyed a sense of realism. Sound effects, developed at first as stunts to create further excitement about the technology of radio broadcasting, now became crucial to conveying or creating realism. The calculated unrealism – the 'as if' – of crackling paper in front of the microphone to represent the sound of fire or knocking coconut shells together to represent the sound of horses' hooves became the serious business of broadcasters as they sought to represent 'the real things of life'. The ABC had no doubts about the style required for this specific genre of radio performance. Plays were already defined as legitimate art and they sought merely the best radio techniques to draw the invisible audience into the action and meanings of its theatre. They led the way with their collection of sound recordings. In 1934 the ABC Sydney studios were reported to have a sound library of two hundred records 'representing street crowds, cats fighting, the rushing of fire engines, the crying of a baby, the noise of naval bombardment, and the crash of motor cars in collision'.[14] The commercial stations, on the other hand, relied less on recorded sound effects and tended to produce them in the studio when needed; but by the end of the 1930s, 2GB would boast of 25,000 records and hundreds of sound effects in their library to be used in the production of plays. 'Radio realism', it was claimed, was both a question of dramatic presentation and of the 'commonsense qualities' of the play.[15] Listeners were to be drawn in, their attention held as if eavesdropping on a slice of real life. Realism entailed both a certain style of presentation – the use of 'human', conversational voices and the use of sound effects as points of recognition – and characteristic preoccupations – plays 'representing ... the real things of life'.[16]

The 'as if' style assumed by radio plays characterized the way in which all broadcasting programmes would address audiences and attempt to place them or provide them with a point of view. Radio worked to produce a sense of the announcer or personality speaking personally to each listener; 'as if' the music was being played in your own home; 'as if' you were a member of the radio family whose life was being unfolded to you day by day in serial form; 'as if' this too were your everyday life; 'as if' the world of radio and your world were one and the same. Listeners were to be drawn into the programmes, into their point of view, their representations of social life, by this mode of address. The suspended disbelief of the 'as if' employed by radio plays suggested a shared orientation, a recognition of the world of reality being portrayed, just as did the techniques – the 'as if' talking to you and you alone – employed by radio personalities.

But listeners' acceptance of the positions designated for them by these techniques was by no means guaranteed. They had to be taught how to 'listen-in'. In 1926 the *Daily Telegraph* had run a competition to find a name for people engaged in this activity:

> The man who drives a car is known as a motorist, the player of a piano is a pianist, and the airman who flies is an aviator. Surely some equally effective and practical name could be evolved to describe the individual who tunes his radio set and listens to broadcasting.[17]

The analogous examples used in this call for a description of the person who listens to the wireless all referred to activities controlling or managing a piece of technology. Similarly, the listener-in was represented as needing to be able to control the equipment involved, to tune the radio set to achieve adequate reception. The term 'radio catcher', at times advocated by the *Daily Telegraph* and elsewhere, illustrates the extent to which 'listening-in' in the late 1920s was still as much a question of striving for good reception as of being interested in the content of programmes.

With the change to radio as intimate friend, the listener was represented as passive consumer – of the entertainment, education, companionship, individuality, provided. Radio itself was no longer the fun, the excitement: owning a wireless set was no longer a question of learning to adjust the dials in the search for good reception of as many stations as possible. Radio was now the medium for amusements, transmitted to the listener-in in the intimacy and privacy of the home. Admonished previously for not adjusting their sets properly, for not understanding the techniques necessary to acquire the best reception from the equipment, in the 1930s listeners were to be delivered exhortatory statements about how to be good listeners-in.

In an editorial entitled 'Intelligent Listening', the *Wireless Weekly* informed listeners in 1931 that they must consult radio programme guides and take the trouble to turn the tuning dial, rather than just simply switching the radio on and listening to whatever was to be heard on a particular station.[18] This advice reflected three aspects of the transformation occurring in radio. Radio magazines were shifting from being predominantly interested in a radio enthusiast's market to a major concern with the listener market. Technical sections in magazines were reduced and collected together as a special feature, rather than as a central theme of the publications. Second, the advice formed part of the thrust to interest wireless owners or potential purchasers in the content of the radio programmes, no longer simply relying on the novelty of this new gadget to recruit buyers of wireless equipment. Third, a major shift had occurred in the concept of the radio audience. Listeners-in were now represented as well as catered for by radio programmes. Intelligent listening was a matter of making choices, selecting programmes appropriate to one's needs or desires. Radio was a bountiful medium, providing for all tastes and moods, and the listener must be responsible in choosing from the array of goods offered.

Listeners were admonished too for dial-twisting. They should select their programmes, not fiddle or play with their wireless set. Radio was no longer a toy, a piece of technology; it was to be treated as a normal part of daily life, or rather, radio programmes were to take on this function. Advertisements for radio cabinets in the late 1920s had begun to promote a casual approach to the technology of wireless. The stress on ease of control, on radio as household furniture, sought to create a sense of radio's ordinariness, its everydayness. The 1930s advice on the 'art of listening' similarly stressed the ordinariness of radio, its integral part in daily life. Some articles cautioned that listeners would find radio boring or an intrusion because they had not yet learnt its proper use. This advice, at times, acknowledged that radio had previously been promoted through images of magic and the wonderful gifts of science, but declared listeners at fault in failing to adjust to the new techniques of listening-in. All articles, however, were an implicit recognition that the listening-in attitude did not come naturally; it had to be learnt.

'Background listening' posed problems. Much of the advice proffered suggested that any listener dissatisfaction with radio programmes was their fault. Grumbles and complaints were caused by listeners failing to use their wireless set wisely. Simply switching on the radio and expecting to be pleased was the problem, not the lack of good programmes. Listeners had to select their radio stations, to be aware of what was on offer and to be attentive to the content of a programme, once chosen. Listening to programmes, to music in particular, in the background placed different demands on programming and did not appear to require the same techniques, or art, generally being promoted as necessary to listening in. Though reluctant to concede this style of listening as being legitimate, articles acknowledged that radio was being used in this way. Apocryphal tales were told of neighbours shooting each other because of a radio set's constant noise.[19] Listeners were warned that if they wished to use the wireless as background, they should turn the set down low and not expect top-class musicians to play for such programmes.

At times these articles appeared to recognize that the position being defined for the listener was passive and powerless. The *Daily Telegraph* carried a vehement editorial in 1937 calling for intelligent listening. Blaming the use of radio as background noise, it declared a need for the return to a sense of wonder and excitement about radio. Radio was dulling our perceptions and stifling our curiosity; only the development of 'a faculty for intelligent listening' would rescue us.[20] This outburst harnessed its protest to a criticism of listeners, of the failure to listen with the right approach, to make selections and to concentrate on the programmes heard. It did not extend its critique to the medium, to the way in which radio technology was now being employed. Other articles trivialized the issue by telling quaint stories about how this 'unseen audience' was making itself known through funny letters and telephone calls to radio stations and their personnel. Yet some recognized a problem, only to couch it in terms of the need to ensure that a variety of opinions must be heard on any particular topic to be discussed or debated. The listening public is unseen and silent, said the *Age*, and hence it is imperative that issues be dealt with fairly and impartially.[21] For the most part, however, the listener's position was declared to be that of the consumer of programmes provided: someone who listens-in. The position was represented as arising from the very nature of radio as technology. Any problems listeners had adjusting to their passive role was simply because of the newness of the medium.

The radio play appeared to be one radio form that would pose particular problems for the listener-in. At first listeners were counselled to switch off the light and close their eyes to achieve proper concentration: 'The distraction of company, of features of the room, are thus minimised and it is possible to enjoy the radio play at its true worth.'[22] They were instructed to let their imagination go to work, rather than relying on the actors and sound effects to convey all the details of a story. By the end of the 1930s, commentators were declaring the listening audience to be 'radio educated' or 'radio minded'. The audience had now adapted to radio as a medium, showing themselves to be able and willing to follow longer and unfamiliar plays without complaint.

The techniques of the radio performance and these instructions about how to be a good listener-in all sought to place the radio audience. The problem was two-fold: first, the public had to be accustomed to assuming the position of consumers of material provided, to becoming listeners-in rather than participants in the world of radio; and second, having created this listening public, the 'unseen audience', broadcasters wished to pin their audiences down, to control how they listened-in. This latter preoccupation would become increasingly important to the 'B' class stations as they became reliant on advertising. They needed to persuade advertisers that a reliable and predictable audience could be expected for their programmes. But, more fundamentally, this preoccupation arose out of the very social usage established for radio. As a means of disseminating messages from a central source to a mass audience, broadcasting had become a question of capturing and holding consumers for the programmes, the cultural products, provided. It was this central feature of broadcasting that created the ABC's ambivalence and frequently inconsistent stance on the friendly, informal performance increasingly understood as necessary to 'good broadcasting'. On the one hand, its personnel wished to control both the way listeners used their programmes and the meanings they attributed to them by the techniques understood as necessary to good radio; yet, on the other, the friendly, intimate relationship scarcely appeared appropriate to the aura traditionally associated with objects of legitimate culture – deemed by act of parliament as well as by general understanding to be its special preserve. In the years ahead, this dilemma would continue to create problems for the ABC that it could never resolve.

The everyday ordinary

By 1938 the PMG was claiming that two in every three homes of the Commonwealth owned a wireless set.[23] Australians were said not only to be well served by the number of stations and the extended hours of broadcasting available to them, but to be keen listeners.[24] W.A. McNair's study of radio advertising and techniques of audience research, published in 1937, similarly suggested that this enthusiasm was widespread and further, that it was 'spread fairly evenly throughout all economic groups'; a 1936 survey in Sydney showed that 12½ per cent of radio sets belonged to the upper 10 per cent of the population and 45 per cent belonged to the lower 50 per cent of the population.[25] At the beginning of the 1930s, the popular radio magazines had shaped a rhetoric about radio as an everyday necessity; these figures of the apparent eager embrace of radio by the populace were now employed as its vindication.

The rhetoric began as a new twist in the advertising strategies to sell wireless sets. Insisting that radio was no longer a gadget or a novelty, claims were made about its necessity to daily life. At times radio's guise would be of emergency aid: declarations about radio's essential role in daily life would turn to examples of SOS messages transmitted. But the dominant image was one of radio being part of the daily routine of home life: 'Radio has now definitely left the ranks of the novelties, or even the musical instruments. It is a vital factor in modern home life and the home which has no radio is not a home in the full sense of the word.'[26]

This editorial in the *Wireless Weekly* exhorted its readers to buy a wireless set for Christmas, just as had the *Listener In*'s front cover a few years previously. Radio's significance in people's daily lives was to be its constancy and its companionship.

From the simplest equipment (still with separate speakers or earphones at the beginning of the 1930s) to the most elaborate pieces of furniture, the image constantly evoked by advertisements for wireless sets throughout this decade was of a nuclear family in a domestic, home setting – mother, father and usually one or two children. Their faces radiant, the wireless claimed the devoted attention of this family grouping. More than simply a companion in the home, radio re-created the home – it was the new heart, the surrogate centre of the family. The elimination or marginalization of alternative images of radio in the 1920s had ensured that its place in the private home would assume a natural, inevitable aspect in the following decade; this publicity language was working to create more than just a place in the home – it sought to insinuate the wireless into a central position in people's daily existence.

A series of equations between the everyday, home life and family life formed the basis of this selling strategy. A similar series of equations was fabricated in a range of different popular and official representations of wireless. Emerging clearly from the imbrication of these discourses was the construction of a particular concept of the 'everyday'. Daily life as home life, as family life, was the shared-in-common of all members of society: radio was both symbol and restorer of this 'everyday'. The design of sets, the more general publicity language for radio produced by magazines and newspapers, and the content of programmes themselves all established a specific representation of the 'everyday'.

The designs of equipment and the publicity language that surrounded them proclaimed a central place for radio listening in people's daily lives. In 1926 a writer for the *Daily Telegraph* had complained in mock tones that if women had their way radio would be treated solely as a piece of furniture and its magic forgotten. Ten years later the same paper would declare, 'radio stopped being a curiosity years ago and became an article of furniture – nearly as essential as a bath'.[27] Readers of newspapers, radio magazines and women's magazines were advised to purchase sets in keeping with the other furniture in their homes. *New Idea* informed its female readership that '[i]n the modern trend towards dainty and artistic furnishings, radio is playing an increasingly important part'.[28] The colour of the wood, the shape of the set and its size all should be considered to ensure an artistic and modern home. And, of course, there was a set to suit every taste and every purse.

> In choosing a radio, there are several points to consider. First, it is advisable to buy the receiver housed in a cabinet that is unobtrusive in design, so that it will fit in perfectly with the general character of the room . . . . There are sets to meet all purses. It is a wise investment to choose a set that is good, but . . . moderately priced.[29]

The sets were specifically designed as pieces of furniture to enhance modern home life, to be a symbol of its modernity, and thus to declare radio's natural place in the centre of that life. Throughout the 1930s, in shape and decoration, they reflected contemporary preoccupations and assumptions about domestic furniture. Some of the earlier furniture-style sets of the late 1920s and early 1930s were referred to as 'Jacobean' with finely turned wooden legs and late Edwardian decorations; Stromberg-Carlson, Astor and Radiola (AWA) all proudly announced their elegant sets of this design. But by the mid-1930s the dominant style emphasized a 'modern' form, with patterns of decoration now celebrating straight, geometrical lines. These characteristics symbolized a concern with functional design, a rejection of trivial ornamentation.

Stuart Ewen notes that streamlined design was used for many mechanical products in the USA at approximately this time. 'In physics', he says, 'streamlining was a design that was a "graphical representation of movement".'[30] It celebrated nature, and the science that discovered it, by clean lines, the appearance of form following function and the appearance of simplicity. The movement represented by the lines of shape and of decoration was one that seemed, says Ewen, to happen by itself – by virtue of itself. Science and nature represented progress, modernity, rationality and the inevitable. The 'modern' designs of wireless sets with their straight lines and apparently no-nonsense shapes mystified the science of broadcasting: reducing the technical intervention and hence technical knowledge required of listeners (the listener had only to turn a few knobs and know no more), broadcasting technology was concealed behind rather than revealed by these cabinets.

Whether it was Stromberg-Carlson's 'Concert Grand' model or Airzone's 'Popular Entertainer', the radio cabinets were 'streamlined', 'modern' and 'smart'. Occasionally a new set would introduce a design feature evoking the Jacobean style of curls and twists of ornamentation

Examples of radio design in the 1920s
Top left: 1929 AWA Radiola, six valve set, wooden box, battery operated, to be used with a speaker or earphones
Top right: Amplion horn-shaped speaker, 1927 or 1928
Bottom left: Atwater Kent speaker, 1927 or 1928
Bottom right: 1929 RCA Radiola, model 44, with separate speaker (tapestry cover), wooden box, valve set, mains operated, period furniture style

Examples of radio design in the 1930s
Top left: 1934 or 1935 Astor, wood veneer, mains operated, neo-classical furniture style
Top right: 1938 a 'Fisk Radiola', dark brown bakelite, five valve, mains operated, modern design
Bottom left: 1932 AWA set, dark brown bakelite, mains operated, 'cathedral' style
Bottom right: 1936 AWA set, plastic case, battery operated, modern design with marbling effect around the speaker

(usually the fretwork covering the speaker) – the language of advertising in such instances would include terms such as 'classic', 'traditional' or 'refined', while insisting on the science, the engineering skill involved in the sets' production. These representations of science in the design features of the radio cabinets and the language of the advertisements stood as symbols of the progress of civilization now benefiting every home. They were comforting, not futuristic images of science; they emphasized the sense in which radio as science's supreme product adapted to – perhaps even recovered or re-created – home life, but was by no means a threat to its existence. Science was not an intruder, but a provider, if necessary a healer; it facilitated the continuing strength and revitalization of the home.

These images and symbols assembled a powerful alibi for the new consumer society. To achieve change in one's daily life one had but to turn to the market to be provided. Discontent could arise only because of the absence of a wireless set or other items in the home. Radio was now 'an everyday necessity, rather than a luxury'.[31] As Ewen remarks of the ideology being mobilized to sell consumer goods more generally in the USA, change appeared as 'something which took place on the commodity market' to be then 'mirrored in people's lives'.[32] The everyday, the life being transformed by the possession of a wireless, was home life. The wireless set belonged in the home – as did all such wonderful, new consumer goods produced by the market – and it was here a better life was to be achieved. It would bring pleasure and fulfilment both in its programmes, its content, and in itself as symbol of the new advancements made in daily life.

The depression was not permitted to contradict this representation of radio's role. On the contrary, it was seized on as a further reason for insisting that radio in the home was essential to people's daily lives. Publicity campaigns for wireless from the beginning of 1930 mobilized the theme 'stay home and be entertained'.[33] Though people may be out of work and have less money to spend, wireless, it was claimed, ensured that they had some domestic comfort and that they could keep in touch with past interests. A listener, said a *Wireless Weekly* editorial, 'may justly claim that he has a front seat at all entertainments, and the foremost place at every important event'.[34] Home life became a place of escape, of solace, and a source of optimism. Wireless was evidence that the market could still provide despite economic difficulties, and further, that security, if not change, could be achieved in one's home life with the aid of that market.

The representations of radio's role in the depression constantly rendered a separation between unemployment – defined as the personal hardships of daily life in these 'bad times' – and the depression as a feature of the outside world. The front cover of the first *Listener In* for 1930 showed a smiling girl and the caption read 'Start 1930 with a Smile'. In an editorial-type page, rarely used by this magazine, readers – listeners-in – were adjured to pull together, help each other, and smile in the face of the present economic malady. The depression was to be scarcely mentioned again in this magazine throughout the 1930s, but here listeners were advised 'to tune out the gloom', to listen in to 'music which knows no country, class or creed, is available to the multitude'.[35] The market could still provide, and change was possible in one's daily life ... at home.

Further constructing a sense of the depression as something distanced from people's daily lives was the establishment of various radio clubs as a means of keeping spirits high. These included 3DB's *'Smile Away' Club*, the Australian Broadcasting Company's *Optimist's League*, and 2GB's *Happiness Club*, perhaps the most successful of all. 3DB's club set out to link 'lonely people into one happy family together with those who are suffering from the effects of depression'. It conducted bright, 'cheery' programmes and organized parties, excursions and sporting tournaments for its members.[36] Despite similar aims, the Australian Broadcasting Company's league was a dismal failure; it succeeded, it was claimed, only in being boring and solemn.[37] But the 2GB club continued to operate throughout the 1930s, providing day programmes, outings and club rooms for a predominantly female membership. In 1939, its founder and president, Mrs Stelzer, claimed the club had more than 16,000 members.[38]

The clubs, like the call to 'stay home and be entertained', worked to suggest that private remedies should be sought for private troubles. The problems an individual faced were thus couched in terms of gloom, despair, lack of faith in the future. Cheery programmes or even outings organized by the radio clubs proffered private solutions to the private problems of daily life – means of holding on, escape, lifting the gloom. The depression, the economic troubles, on the other hand, were thus defined as of a different order and beyond the control of private individuals. These problems belonged to the world of government action, economic measures and international affairs. Radio, however, brought the additional solace of the Prime Minister, James Scullin, speaking to listeners 'heart to heart' of his solutions and of theirs.[39]

The 1933 Radio and Electrical Exhibition was billed as a moment for great confidence and optimism, for the depression appeared not to exist in the wireless industry. Essential to the success of the industry had been a prohibition on wireless imports, introduced by the Scullin government in 1930 as part of its depression measures; but the growth in licence numbers in the early 1930s also suggested that the market for wireless equipment was rapidly expanding. In 1930 the *Listener In* had declared that 'despite what is commonly known as the depression, which pessimists would have us believe is going to overwhelm us, wireless licences in the Commonwealth continue to increase'.[40] Between 1930 and 1934 licence numbers grew from 312,192 to 599,150 providing substance to this claim. Wireless stood as 'evidence' that the market had not failed, that it could continue to be the source for change in people's daily lives and that it was indeed being used in this way.

This rhetoric was central to the publicity campaign to create an ever-expanding domestic market for wireless equipment. The design of wireless sets, the advertising language about radio in the home and the representation of radio's role in the depression, all worked to constitute a vital link between daily life and home life. Wireless belonged in the home as a means of entertainment and information, speaking individually, intimately, to each member of the radio audience. And home life was the source of true fulfilment, the place where change and progress – modernity – were to be achieved. It was 'the real' of daily life, where despite economic problems or hard times, control over one's own life was to be exerted, and all with the assistance of the market. Wireless was an everyday necessity because it made daily life – home life – radiant.

Some difficult manoeuvres were required in placing wireless at the centre of family life. Most advertisements, when seeking to portray radio's centrality to home life, employed the apparently simple image of a nuclear family. Yet showing the family as happy because of the presence of an object, that is, as happy because of something external to it, risked undermining the power of the familial ideology relied upon in such publicity. An image of the family was being mobilized that represented the family as central to daily life, central to people's existence, but it was a notion that relied for its justification on the intrinsic value of the family and its naturalness as a social form.

Barrett and McIntosh, in their analysis of the ideology of familialism, argue that appeals to naturalness and to the socio-moral character of the family are nowhere more constantly evoked and confused than in this realm:

The prevailing form of family is seen as inevitable, as naturally given and biologically determined. As such, however, it is imbued with a unique social and moral force, since it is seen as the embodiment of general human values rather than the conventions of a particular society. The image of the family in contemporary society relies heavily on this combination of the natural and the moral.[41]

The nuclear family, characterized by a clear division of labour between male and female members, by its focus on having and raising children, and by its functioning as a privatized unit, appears as the natural, universal and most desirable social form. The ideology upon which the legitimacy of the nuclear family relies claims universality of this form, which in turn stands as evidence for the intrinsic moral value of the family; all other forms of domestic organization are made deviant, differing from the norm.

Representations of wireless assumed the nuclear family as the natural social form. Listeners were spoken of as members of a family unit with two sets of needs: those dictated by the rhythm of family life and those dictated by the particular position occupied in the family. The family was portrayed as having specific rituals that wireless was said to serve. Most frequently mentioned was the period between the time when father came home from work and the dishes were washed after dinner. Referred to as 'family talk times' by one commentator,[42] wireless provided background music or family entertainment as an added dimension to this particular pattern of life. Similarly, other rituals were spoken about as part of family life: Sunday as the day when the family shared in various tasks and pleasures, or the time after dinner when the family relaxed together in the lounge room. Wireless provided additional companionship to the family as it carried out these rituals or it ensured that these rituals were enjoyable, meaningful.

This representation of wireless appeared in a variety of contexts. Discussions of new programmes or new programme styles emphasized their appropriateness for the family. Fisk of AWA announced that in taking over the station 2CH Sydney, his company intended 'to give listeners the best form of entertainment, particularly music, and to provide a service that would appeal to the whole family'.[43] Analyses of the success of particular announcers or personalities argued that their art lay in their capacity to address the whole family, to make their programmes a 'family concern'.[44] More generally, newspapers and radio magazines made statements about wireless and the family in various types of discussions about programmes, the state of the broadcasting business or as part of other issues they were busy constructing about radio, such as the debate about highbrow programmes. The image always evoked was that of the nuclear family in a privatized, domestic setting where each member had clearly defined roles according to their position in the family.

Advertisements for wireless sets worked upon this theme. By the mid-1920s sets were being advertised as the focus of family life. Pictures of a nuclear family gathered around a set became a means of visually representing radio as part of everyday life (while men gathered around the set represented its science, its novelty, its status as extra-ordinary). Harrington's, for example, frequently advertised its sets with the assistance of a drawing of the happy family: readers of the *Labor Daily*, as early as November 1925, were told 'You owe it to your Family – Install a Harrington Popular Wireless Set'.[45] Such advertisements in the 1920s and 1930s depicted the addition of the wireless set to the home as guaranteeing the unity of the family and the stability of each member's role. Father provided for the home which then became his 'haven in the heartless world' where he could smoke his pipe, in his chair, with his family gathered around him (or at least gathered around the wireless). Mother sat on the arm of the chair, or in her own chair, her daily tasks in the home now finished; and children sat with their parents. The value of wireless being central to this scene was described in terms such as, 'to induce pleasant and lulling harmonies into office-jaded minds, and as the music comes over the air one reads and chats and works in an easy domestic way.'[46]

Stuart Ewen speaks of a growing tension in the USA during the 1920s between the 'home and hearth ideal' and the reality of the home almost totally dependent on industrial production – a source outside itself. Representations of wireless convey some sense of that tension as being created by radio. Much of the celebratory language surrounding radio worked to place it at the centre of family life, but at times questions were raised about the impact this new presence in the home would have on 'family life'. In the official discourse of politicians, policy documents and parliamentary reports recognition that the promotion of wireless as central to family life cut across representations of the intrinsic value and internal coherence of the family was articulated as part of the language about censorship and vulnerable audiences.[47] In the popular discourse of radio magazines and newspapers, this problem appeared to be more

Radio as the focus of family life (Photograph: *Listener In*, 8 February 1928)

clearly enunciated as a problem in itself. It was posed in two related forms: the first suggested that radio was creating dissension in the home, the second that radio was displacing the real centre of the home.

Stories and articles about radio depicted it as causing family squabbles. Disagreements between husband and wife or between all members of the family about which programmes were to be heard were the subject of a number of cautionary and humorous short stories in radio and other types of magazines. Similarly, radio magazines warned readers of such dangers:

> Radio has been the means of engendering a certain amount of disruption in families. For instance, Mother wants to listen in to a classical concert being put on by, say, 3LO. Father is interested in a novel broadcast to be transmitted by, say 5CL. Sister and brother have a stand-up fight whether they will listen to the wrestling from 3UZ, or enjoy the whimsicalities of 'Charlie' from 3DB.[48]

While recognizing superficially that radio could be a problem for the coherence of family life, this statement served both to affirm the 'naturalness' of different roles, and hence different interests in the family, and to provide evidence for the 'need' in every family for more than one wireless set. The problem took a more serious form in debates such as those in the *Women's Weekly*, sometimes between letter writers, at other times conducted in the 'point of view' type columns. On one side, it was argued that wireless was the cause of a new harmony in the home – it kept husbands at home, it gave family life a focus – but, on the other side, it was claimed that wireless caused disharmony and contributed to a shift in people's orientation away from the home. Wireless conspired in the 'Americanization' of the young people in particular, hence creating loyalties to a non-traditional, less worthy culture, rather than to the family and its ways.[49]

Themes such as 'radio does not know its place' articulated the fear that radio would displace the real centre of family life. Similarly, complaints of the demise of certain family rituals suggested radio had appropriated this role. Evenings where members of the family gathered around the piano, played cards or read stories to one another were evoked with nostalgia, as were such images as: 'Mother is no longer the wonderfully wise being who knew such frightening, lovely tales. There is nothing but a voice from the formless void to sing you to sleep.'[50] The centre usurped by radio was that of parental authority; but more than this, radio disturbed the rituals and practices that symbolized the family's intrinsic unity and value. The family may be formally together – sitting around the wireless – but wireless was now the *raison d'être* for these rituals, not the family itself. Similarly, the roles ascribed to each member by the nature of the family, and their ritualistic affirmation such as in the telling of bed-time stories, were being overturned by radio.

Although these discussions and debates about wireless suggest some tension in representations about its role in family life, they served as much to affirm the ideology of family life being articulated in the more celebratory language about radio as they did to explore the evils of radio. The stability and universality of the family as a social form were called into question by such debates, but the voicing of fears about radio as a threat to the family provided the occasion for the reassertion of its intrinsic value and the naturalness of the positions ascribed to members of that unit. Rituals of family life stood as symbols of an authentic existence, vulnerable to outside influences, yet still somehow 'natural'.

For the most part, however, radio was portrayed as serving the rituals of family life, or re-creating them. The ideology of family life brought into focus by these representations of wireless spoke of the family as the natural social form, as possessing intrinsic moral value and as the place where meaning was bestowed on the individual's daily life: here one was truly 'at home'.

This language of radio shaped a particular definition of the everyday. It represented people's lives as primarily about their domestic social relations and practices and these, in turn, were equated with the activities of a nuclear family in a private home or household. The radio audience was addressed as if all shared such an orientation, as if all occupied a position in a family unit. And in doing so, this language, in its verbal and visual modes,[51] worked to constitute all members of its audience as, precisely, occupying such a position. The everyday was home life and the private world of the family its horizons. Only the depression appeared to present a challenge to those horizons, to place them in jeopardy. But the differentiation between private troubles and the public sphere of politicians and economic strategies reasserted the naturalness and stability of those horizons.

Underlying this definition of the everyday ran the further theme of everyday life as the life of everybody, the life shared-in-common by all members of society. 'Radio is an everyday necessity' intimated a pattern of existence shared by all. As Henri Lefebvre suggests more generally of the methods of publicity, it 'insinuate[s] into each reader's daily life all possible daily lives'.[52] A common denominator linked the lives of all members of the listening-in audience in the sphere of the everyday: radio 'knows no country, class or creed' – radio was evidence and symbol of the shared-in-common of the everyday.

This definition of the everyday was constructed by the publicity language about radio as it sought to persuade people of the central significance of radio in their daily lives. Similarly, the programmes themselves – in the way in which they addressed the listening audience and in the themes they explored – formulated a powerful definition of the everyday within the same fundamental parameters. The emphasis on announcers chatting informally to listeners – as if sitting together in the same room – which developed in the 1930s as appropriate to radio, worked to produce a sense of the ordinariness of radio. The performance that was not a performance: listeners and broadcasters were represented as operating as equals and at the level of the everyday-ordinary. Similarly, programme styles, such as the variety shows, radio vaudeville and the family serials that emerged in the 1930s, set out to create a 'one of the family' atmosphere to draw listeners into the programmes through a sense of 'humanness' and the shared preoccupation of the everyday-ordinary of life.

Programmes such as Athol Tier's *Mrs 'Arris and Mrs 'Iggs* and Norman Banks's *Grocer and Madam* drew on theatre traditions of vaudeville comedy. They created a world of the everyday, a world of 'over the backyard fence',[53] in which the situation portrayed appeared to be the familiar daily routines of your life and mine. Similarly, the humour of such programmes, like that of Nicky's *Chatterbox Corner* and his other shows, worked to catch listeners through complicity, to draw them into the world of the programmes by a sense of shared orientation. The jokes, the playing the fool, worked to provide a position of recognition, of inside information so that listeners could join in the everyday-ordinary of this world of radio. The antics of these broadcasters formed an effective set of strategies in which the use of informal, ordinary language fabricated a sense-in-common. Broadcasters such as Nicky and Nancy Lee celebrated the language of everyday domesticity, the rituals of home life, as the source of all truly human values. Broadcasters and listeners lived together in this world of common sense and edgy optimism.

The two themes of this concept of the everyday – its private, family domesticity and its world-shared-in-common – were played upon most powerfully in the form of radio family serials. At first there was some scepticism about serials as a radio genre; listeners had to be accustomed to this form of listening-in and adjustments were made to the length and frequency of the episodes.[54] But by the mid-1930s they were a dominant feature of broadcasting, and 'family' serials were among the most popular. These programmes, written about one family for the family, focused on the domestic life and practices of the household unit. With titles such as *People Like Us*, *One Man's Family*, *Fred and Maggie Everybody*, *Those We Love*, their preoccupation with the everyday-ordinary as a shared-in-common of broadcaster and listeners was explicit; but programmes such as *Martin's Corner*, *Digger Hale's Daughter* and *Dad and Dave* were similarly structured along these lines.

The publicity language for these programmes celebrated their qualities of being 'homely', 'intensely human', or being about 'people like us', about 'you and me', about 'the typical Australian family'. A writer for the *Wireless Weekly*, in analysing the popularity of family serials such as *Martin's Corner*, claimed them to be about 'ordinary people' and to be all very believable 'because Pop Martin is a bloke very much like myself'.[55] One of the first programmes to be successful in these terms was *Fred and Maggie Everybody*, featured three nights a week, which began on ABC radio, was moved to commercial broadcasting on a morning session and then to an evening time. First heard in March 1936, it continued (in various evening time slots and with changes in name) to run for twenty-one years. Domestic incidents 'which can and do happen in the homes of everybody in most parts of the world' formed the apparently simple focus of this family programme: 'They live in the type of suburban home that you and I might be paying off in instalments; they have a mother-in-law, and next door neighbours.'[56] This was the life of everybody, every day.

The programme that was to set the style for many of the family serials in the 1930s and 1940s was *One Man's Family*. An Australian adaptation of American scripts, this serial lasted for just over two years – finishing in 1938 only because the American author refused to provide further scripts. Thereafter various programmes were publicized, for listeners and advertisers, as being in the *One Man's Family* style, likely to be its successor, or having much in common with this serial. The popularity of this programme in both America and Australia, declared the *Listener In*, lay in its focus on 'human interests and domestic tangles; so many people have been through the same things'.[57] Publicity photographs often showed 'the family' sitting in the living room in much the same pose as advertisements for radio equipment depicted a listening-in family: 'the family at home' of this publicity was both the Barbour family of *One Man's Family* and your family, listening-in.[58]

One Man's Family was commended in newspapers and journals for the quality of its Australian production and the excellence of its actors. Previously, American serials had been condemned. The excessiveness of the American accent and the poor acting of American transcriptions in particular had been blamed for the decline in popularity of serial plays in 1935. The *Radio Times* conducted a plebiscite in September that showed serials as only sixteenth in a list of twenty programme categories.[59] But six months later *One Man's Family* was being proclaimed as the 'Radio Drama that is enthralling the World' and the family serial in particular was being sold to advertisers as a means of capturing a large and receptive audience.[60] In 1937 Charles Moses, general manager of the ABC, was to complain of the popularity of these programmes: despite the triviality of their material, he declared, 'these familiar characters, discussing either everyday happenings or fantastic adventures, have perhaps a wider following than any other type of programme, even among people who would never be expected to listen to them at all.'[61] Despite such protestations the ABC was soon to follow suit with Gwen Meredith's *The Lawson Family*, to be renamed *Blue Hills* in 1945.

The radio version of *Dad and Dave* began in 1937, presented by George Edwards and sponsored by an American company, the manufacturers of Wrigley's chewing gum. Edwards, in an article for the *Wireless Weekly*, spoke of the sponsor's desire for a programme that would last for five years, achieving the same success in Australia as *Amos and Andy* had achieved in America.[62] He did not explain that the reason Wrigley's wanted a long-running programme was to ensure that the Australian audience would make the serial and the product it advertised part of their daily lives. The characters of this programme were devised to represent the quintessential Australian in order to sell the habit which, as John Potts suggests, was repugnant to them: the American habit of chewing gum.[63]

Potts analyses the way in which this serial set out to align itself with listeners' daily lives. It did so through its frequency (four episodes a week) so that it was in fact (nearly) broadcast every day; listeners were encouraged by its regularity to see it as a normal ritual of daily life. The promise, and actuality of, its longevity similarly promoted a sense in which listeners could adjust their daily habits to this programme without then being let down by its sudden disappearance. The representation of the characters as the quintessential Australians invited identification with their lives, problems, and pleasures, as well as suggesting that there was a shared-in-common of Australian life at this level of the everyday. Listeners were addressed as identifying with these characters, as well as sharing part of their daily lives with them. George Edwards wrote of the success of the programme in these terms, telling stories of listeners writing in to the characters, Dad, Dave, Mum and Mabel, as if real. Finally, each episode focused on the daily 'experience and escapades' of this family; they were anecdotal in form as if told by way of gossip. The special events of the 'everyday life' of the nation, which by their sense of occasion emphasized their integralness to domestic rituals, were timed to appear in the programme at the same time as in the 'real' life of the population: the Melbourne Cup coincided with the running of the Snake Gully Cup; Christmas was celebrated in Snake Gully; and the birthdays of members of the family, particularly Mum and Mabel, were major occasions.

Whether in this comic form or in the straighter versions of *One Man's Family*, the representation of the family in these programmes was similar. Though *Dad and Dave* was placed in a rural setting, it was a modern family, as Potts points out, oriented to the consumer goods of modern society. Cars, house mortgages, new domestic appliances, gadgets, clothes, all formed part of the plots of these serials. The family functioned as a consumer unit, and the mother in particular played a crucial role in organizing – managing – the consumption activities of the household as she pushed or cajoled her family in this direction. Maggie argued with Fred Everybody about a bank loan for a holiday house; Dad and Dave secretly plotted to buy Mother a car; people's clothes were the subject for female gossip in *Martin's Corner*; and Ethel Gilman, 'an everyday mother' from *Those Happy Gilmans*, fussed about her husband's clothes.

In these representations of the family, its identity was organized through its consumption activities: the type of house, car and domestic commodities possessed; the type of clothes worn by different members of the family. These preoccupations ensured that members of the family turned inwards to one another. The happy families as portrayed in the publicity language for radio equipment and in the family serials were made happy by their shared, private activities as consumers and family members. The visual images of the family, in advertisements or portraits of the casts of various programmes, showed its members in this private mode, usually sitting together informally in a living room setting. These were quite different images to the stiff, formal photographs of Edwardian families in which the patriarchal authority of the father was clearly depicted as the family posed looking outward (towards the photographer) for their representation to the public world. The family of the new, modern age of the wireless was a private entity, defined by its internal relations and practices (of consumption), not by its patriarch and his public practices.[64]

The public face of a 1920s family – proud owners of a wireless set. This image contrasts with the representation of the private family depicted in the *Listener In* advertisement (see page 92) (Photograph: courtesy of *Herald and Weekly Times*)

The constant repetition of these images of the everyday and family life by radio programmes and the publicity language that surrounded them worked to produce what Adorno referred to as 'standardized enthusiasm'. He analysed audience mail to a rural, American radio station in the 1940s to show how letters revealed that listeners' enjoyment of programmes was formed by announcers' publicity statements about the musical items played. The exuberant letters merely repeated the rubber-stamped phrases of the radio programme rather than exhibiting an authentic response to the music itself: 'listeners were strongly under the spell of the announcer as the personified voice of radio'.[65] Listeners' letters about family serials conformed to this pattern. Indeed, when the continuance of *One Man's Family* seemed threatened, listeners wrote vigorously in support of its popularity, using precisely the terms in which it had been advertised: 'that touch of humanness', 'it is so intensely human', 'the laughter and tears of real life', 'the players are the most natural'. In the same manner, *Dad and Dave* was praised as 'human' and the characters as 'natural', 'humanly weak', 'lovable'.[66]

Yet what these letters reveal is not that listeners' enjoyment became standardized, but that their ways of articulating their experiences took a standardized form when expressed through 'letters to the editor'. Such letters operate like a referendum where only specific and limited representations of popular responses are permitted. In this instance, the letters about family serials adopted the conventions and the language understood to be appropriate to the expression of a 'point of view', the public statement of a private experience or response. It was a language given currency and legitimacy precisely by its constant repetition by the radio stations and print media promotion of these programmes. The role of these letters in the contemporary radio magazines and newspapers was not to provide an authentic indication of listener response, but to close the circle. They supplemented the publicity language, working to produce a powerful sense of – an 'as if' – listeners, broadcasters and the families of radio serials all shared the same orientation – of the 'human', the everyday-ordinary and the centrality of family.

What women have to listen to

Henri Lefebvre suggests that 'everyday life weighs heaviest on women'.[67] The images of everyday life produced by radio in these various contexts all worked to place women as organizers of the everyday and as confined to, but fulfilled in, this realm. These images depicted the sphere of domestic relations and practices as their special place – by necessity – but further held out a promise of an alternative social basis of power for women as a result of their dominance in this sphere. Here women were defined and affirmed as woman, as feminine; and here women were in charge: their family's happiness depended on them. Men had a separate existence, an existence apart from the world of domesticity – of everydayness – from which they derived alternative definitions of themselves and their existence; women were represented in this language of radio as totally defined by their existence within the sphere of the everyday.

Epitomizing this definition of women by radio was the development of the women's sessions which had appeared early in the history of broadcast programming. By designating certain programmes as women's, radio worked to produce the sense in which all women were commonly defined by one thing: their relationship to the private, domestic sphere of family life. Men, on the other hand, were not so defined; they were variously referenced in broadcast programmes by their relationship to a range of public activities, of work and non-work interests. The radio magazines were crucial in constructing these differences and persuading listeners of their pertinence to their lives and experiences. They set out to teach women that they had a particular interest in radio programmes, that radio provided special services for them, as women. Though men were specifically addressed as a group through the ever-diminishing technical sections of the radio journals as concerned with science and technological advances, they were rarely spoken to as having particular programme interests or as having common experiences and needs as men. Their interests and concerns were not those of a group, but of the general, the universal and the norm.

Articles in the radio magazines of the 1920s had already begun to specify the interests and needs of women as operating in the domestic sphere: they were depicted as preoccupied with housework, child care and fashion. These articles and the women's programmes were permeated by the ideology of modern housewifery through which women were addressed as efficient organizers of the home, as thrifty and wise purchasers for the household needs and as scientifically minded parents, concerned with the latest theories about child-rearing. By the 1930s, the radio magazines were a little less moralistic in tone and less didactic. They no longer worked so hard to teach women to listen to radio nor to remind them of their special needs and concerns to be served by wireless. Women's sessions were now conducted by most stations and the ideology upon which they were based required less securing. None the less, the ideology of separate spheres continued to be promulgated by these magazines as they kept women informed of the latest new women's session and provided the added service of cooking recipes or fashion news for their female readers through columns variously called 'What Women Have to Listen to', 'What's on the Air for

Women', 'A Women's Page' and 'Mainly for Women'.

Stuart Ewen argues that mass advertising in the 1920s and 1930s in the USA sought to create a reliance among women on the outside world of commodities. They were being taught that solutions to all the family's needs were to be found in the marketplace and, further, that through goods purchased they could construct a sexual identity for themselves to elicit affection and secure their domestic relationships. 'Corporate America', he says, 'had begun to define itself as *the father of us all.*'[68] Radio programmes for women in the Australian context formed part of a similar thrust to redefine the nature of women's work and to create a reliance on the market. Detailed cookery information, fashion talks, health programmes, the promotion of electricity and/or gas in the home, talks on efficient housework, all worked to produce an orientation to the market or to a source outside the family. Women were being taught to be efficient managers of the consumption activities of the home.

The radio magazines spoke of the good fortune of modern housewives for whom the new advances in 'labour-saving' devices in the home made their work no longer a drudgery: 'Whereas a few years back the girl who married became a slave to her home, in these days she introduces the latest hygienic labor-saving devices'.[69] The modern housewife, it was suggested, should organize her day efficiently with the aid of these devices. Radio would assist her by providing companionship while she did her tasks; but, more importantly, she could take breaks from her work to listen to a programme built round her special interests: this truly was rational efficiency. To ensure that she was an efficient and thrifty household manager, the programmes provided handy hints about cooking, cleaning problems, sewing, fashion, shopping, organizing your day, and entertaining visitors: 'Perhaps you forgot the salt or spilt the milk? However, when little nagging difficulties crop up, don't wrinkle your brows and worry, just take your troubles to this energetic and well-informed lady, and she'll do the rest.'[70]

This publicity for the women's programmes represented them as providing a surrogate mother and neighbour for their listeners. The women who conducted the sessions were praised for their ability to identify themselves with the problems and concerns of their 'unseen audience'. And the knowledge and information imparted was depicted as friendly advice, handy hints – provided as one woman to another. The modern housewife was being taught to rely on the world of commodities, and to seek her information from experts, from institutional sources. But she was to be reassured by the form of this advice: though the radio women's sessions encouraged her to shift her orientation away from the traditional knowledge of her mother, from the culture and common-sense wisdom of the women of her family, she was to be reassured of its similar character and concerns by its presentation in the form of 'hints', practical wisdom and by its 'woman to woman' style.

Most clearly reflecting this attempt to change women's orientation were the radio talks on child care. Here too women were being taught to be scientific and 'rational' in their child-rearing practices through a language couched in common-sense concerns. 3AW Melbourne had a twice-weekly child psychology session provided by the 'Answer Man', sponsored by London Stores Ltd and the Australian Child Psychology Society. For the first quarter hour of his session, Gwen Varley, a successful woman announcer, interviewed the 'Answer Man' as he presented a topic 'more in the line of parent aid than children's problems'; for the second quarter hour, the 'Answer Man' responded to questions sent to him by listeners.[71] Similarly, the Mothercraft Society provided talks for 2GB as early as 1926 on the care of babies (under the auspices of the 'Advance Australia Radio Club'). The problems dealt with might be teething, bed-wetting, fear of the dark or talkative children. Though they were cast in these common-sense terms, these sessions served to teach women to turn to expert advice, while providing the opportunity to promulgate the 'scientific methods' of the new professionals in the fields of child care and education. Women thus were advised that their past ways were not 'modern', were based on 'old wives' tales', and that they no longer needed to waste time chatting over the backyard fence – radio could provide them with all the entertainment and companionship they needed, while permitting them to get on with their work.[72] But just in case they were beginning to feel that their labour was being devalued, deskilled or alienated, an alternative means of satisfaction was offered: beauty, glamour and the fashionable presentation of their physical appearance.

Though the radio programmes offered less scope than the increasingly important women's magazines for the presentation of images of glamour, they nevertheless included sessions on beauty hints, make-up advice, exercises, diet advice, and fashion notes. The radio magazines supplemented the work of the programmes with pictures of models or film stars wearing the latest clothes, as well as by carrying pictures of radio personalities which themselves conveyed images of beauty and glamour. Women's work, organizing and managing the consumption activities and domestic relations of the home, was added to by this further consumption work. Through the construction of herself with the aid of a tool-box – by the use of commodities – she was being taught to present herself as a commodity and required to lead, as ads for the *Women's Weekly* acknowledged, a double life. The busy woman of today, said these advertisements, needs to be 'efficient, capable, interesting, charming, smart'.[73] As Game and Pringle show, this sexualization of the woman's identity so that she was expected to be both a good household manager and physically appealing to a husband was to be a major aspect of the construction of femininity in the years after the second world war.[74] In the feminine world of radio in the years before the war, the major preoccupation lay with the woman's role as manager, efficient organizer of consumption, household tasks and child care; but the theme of a woman as defined, valued, through her sexual identity played an important, though secondary role.

The growing interest of advertisers in radio by the mid-1930s was to ensure that commercial radio stations in particular conspired in this redefinition of women's work and daily lives (though both 'A' and 'B' class stations appeared to use basically the same format for their women's sessions). Women were sold to advertisers as a captive audience. In the new radio journals, such as *Broadcasting Business*, directed largely at the advertising and business world, and in station advertising brochures, women were depicted as alone in the home all day with only the radio for companionship. Radio programmes were sold to advertisers as an integral part of the daily rituals shared by all women: 'Day-Time Radio has become the Housewife's Friend – While she Works – and Plans — and Lives through Busy Days.'[75] Women were portrayed as powerful because they controlled the family's finance and directed all its buying activities: 'the very colours of a man's shirt, in fact, the clothes he wears and the food he eats; even the brand of cigarettes he smokes is more often than not, dictated by the females within his circle.'[76]

But, in private, distinctions were drawn between different groups of women listeners. 2CH in Sydney, which generally advertised itself to potential advertisers as appealing to the 'Better Class of Homes',[77] similarly sought after, and represented itself as attracting, a female listening audience with a clear purchasing power. In September 1935 it established an *Australian Women's League* which charged a membership fee, but more importantly the sporting associations attached to this club charged between one and two shillings a week. The payment of such fees by members was used as evidence to advertisers that 2CH's women listeners enjoyed considerable purchasing power.[78] Similarly, McNair in his book on radio advertising, reported a 1932 Sydney survey (though a fairly unreliable one he admitted) that studied the money habits and listening patterns of women in different socio-economic groups.[79] Though women themselves were addressed as unified, as having a shared orientation, in private the radio business world represented women as differentiated according to their spending power.

While representing women as a large and important section of the listening audience to advertisers, stations initiated campaigns to ensure that they did deliver this audience to advertisers. Clubs such as 2CH's *Australian Women's League* or *2GB's Happiness Club* were one way of materializing the audience for advertisers (by declaring the number of members enjoyed by each club), and at the same time providing a further means of attracting listeners by involving them in club activities. But the major way in which stations attempted to acquire an audience was by developing what they referred to as 'the listening habit' in the radio audience. By ensuring the regularity and predictability of their programmes, stations attempted to develop similar patterns in the listening habits of the audience. In 1940 2GB began a massive publicity campaign (directed both at advertisers and women) for its new day-time programming, an extension and expansion of the sort of strategies used by stations since the mid-1930s. 2GB's tactic was to advertise itself as providing feature programmes throughout the day 'On the Hour'. In their publicity material designed for *Women's Weekly* readers, 2GB claimed itself concerned to make 'radio doubly attractive for women' and to be so simplifying its 'presentation as to make it easy for the housewife to combine her work and her listening interludes'. To the advertisers, 2GB promoted the idea of day-time advertising by selling this new programming idea as capitalizing on the daily habits of women:

> During the day-time hours, in the breaks between her domestic duties, the wife in the home has ample leisure and uninterrupted time to listen to broadcast programmes.
> She can sit down in comfort and absorb completely any advertising message which is presented to her in sufficiently attractive form.[80]

This campaign highlights the more general strategy adopted by stations to promote radio as the constant companion of the housewife. Radio stations adapted their timetables to the imagined pattern of a woman's life, and then set out to ensure that this in fact became the pattern of their lives. Their programmes were designed to encourage listeners to be regular in their habits – to organize their work and their tea-breaks according to the type or nature of the broadcast now to be heard on the radio. The women's sessions were usually promoted as tea-break occasions and were to be heard somewhere between 10 a.m. and 12 noon. The rest of day-time programming was filled with music, serials or variety perhaps, some news or information programmes, and children's sessions in the late afternoon (with a few stations providing sporting information – race broadcasts – during the day).

2GB's scheme was ambitious. 'On the Hour' the GPO chimes would be heard to let the housewife know that she was entitled to sit down for fifteen minutes, entertained by one of 2GB's special features. This campaign was attempting to structure women's work according to very precise time schedules and to increase their consciousness of time. Game and Pringle argue that women in their consumption and production work in the home have little control over their time, being involved in repetitive routines and required to attend to the needs and rhythms of life of others (usually husbands and children).[81] 2GB's campaign was introducing notions of time – of labour processes closely regulated by time – from the outside world of work as relevant to domestic existence, in particular to women's existence. Just as the women's sessions were teaching women that they should be effective managers in the home – of their time – campaigns such as 2GB's were speaking to women as if they had already achieved this goal. The realities of their work meant that their time was not their own, but they were being told that as competent workers they should be in control, efficiently managing that time.

The attempt to structure women's listening patterns, to habituate them to listening to programmes at particular times of day, was part of a more general attempt by broadcasters to establish regular listening habits in the radio audience. For commercial stations the 'listening habit' played an important role in their being able to sell audiences to advertisers: if the listening behaviour of audiences could be timetabled, then advertisers could be informed of their potential audience. But more generally, it was being assumed that the relationship between broadcaster and audience necessarily involved establishing this same listening habit. In 1936, for example, the ABC launched a series of programmes designed to encourage listeners to associate particular hours of the day with specific radio features. This was not confined simply to items such as news, weather reports and sporting information; it included light entertainment, educational and 'serious' programmes: 6.00–7.00 p.m. every night for dinner music; 10.40–11.30 every night, dance music; Monday night, a serial play; Wednesday night, a national talk; and so on.[82]

Similarly, in the move to regulate audience listening behaviour, programmers exhibited an increasing concern for the punctuality of broadcasts. Throughout the 1930s the ABC made much of the need to achieve perfect timing for their programmes, a matter that proved by no means easy to achieve. Speakers had to be trained to time their talks for the exact slot available, a restriction guest speakers in particular found hard to manage; concerts had to be arranged to fit in with specific programme requirements; entertainers had to adjust their art to the clock not to their audience; and the news had to be contained or spread out according to the time available. And then to make it all flow smoothly, producers were required to learn how to use excerpts from recorded music and to ensure that this music was appropriate to its context.

Through the careful timing of programmes and their predictable occurrence, broadcasters set out to timetable their audience, to impose a pattern on their listening activities (and hence, too, on the rhythm of their daily lives). They were seeking to establish a relationship between broadcast and audience that would permit them to place listeners on a grid. For commercial broadcasters, such a grid or table of listener behaviour was necessary to the selling of specified sections of the total listening audience appropriate to advertisers' products. The development of audience surveys and the utilization of the services of industrial psychology, as demonstrated in McNair's 1937 publication on radio advertising, extended and relied on this same process of representing the audience as divisible into sections on a grid, or a table. But the interest in this representation of the radio audience was broader: 'A' and 'B' class stations sought to timetable the radio audience as a means of determining the features of their audience at any one time. Once the relationship between wireless and audience had been established as a matter of one-way communication, the audience became something passive, something to be filled or satisfied, but something also 'unseen'. Placing listeners on a grid, a table, according to their predicted listening behaviour or habits, provided a means of pinning them down, of appearing to have this 'unseen audience' all worked out, their differences understood and established.

Crucial to the timetabling of audiences was the practice of telling listeners the time. The chiming of the GPO's clock had first been heard on radio as part of the stunt broadcasts – these were some of the noises to be transmitted by the marvellous technology of wireless. But soon the telling of the time became part of the service to listeners, ensuring – insisting – that they regulate their patterns of everyday life. The predictability of programme times was meant to regulate listeners' habits; telling them the time suggested that they ought to be conscious of the time. Time became something to be known with precision. Time structured everyday life. An editorial in the *Wireless Weekly* highlighted the way in which radio was setting out to change people's lives, to make time a key dimension of their daily rituals: headed 'A Matter of Time' it declared.

> 'The time is now . . . '
>
> This announcement prefacing the introduction of musical items over the air during the day and at frequent intervals at night has become one of the most commonplace and regular features of the programme.
>
> How this is affecting the mode of thought of hundreds of people who were previously, to a wide degree, uninfluenced by considerations of time is being realised by the very few . . . . For every once that we looked (or guessed!) at the time of our watches or clocks, we are now reminded half a dozen times of the passage of the minutes via broadcasting.
>
> The outcome is an unobserved quickening of our pace, better scheduling of all our movements and actions to a standard and accurate time.[83]

Time was no longer to be guessed at, but repeatedly and accurately told.

Listeners' letters to the radio magazines and stations referred to their family life, particularly in the evening, as organized to listen regularly to specific programmes. Similarly, letters praised radio for providing information about the time, thus allowing the family to schedule their daily rituals: 'the frequently repeated reminders of the time all seem to fit in with the bustle of getting up, shaving, breakfasting and dashing off to work'.[84] Only occasionally were questions asked about the changes radio was seeking to work on everyday life. The *Daily Telegraph* declared that wireless was making 'a fetish' out of time by announcing the correct time every few minutes,[85] but such complaints were not pursued with any seriousness. An image of everyday life as regular, structured and closely textured by an awareness of 'the time' was being constructed as the natural mode of people's daily existence.

The image of time established in this context had much in common with the concept that was central to the techniques of augmenting labour power in the work-place. The increasing rationalization and scientific management of the labour process advocated by F.W. Taylor required the adoption of regulated procedures in large-scale factories and the precise calculation of the time taken to perform rigidly and minutely specified tasks. Though the organization of paid work constituted the major target of these principles, their advocates were soon arguing for their extension to the home by various means. The writings of Christine Frederick in 1912 about the application of scientific management methodology to household work was an important influence on the design of public housing; and infant welfare bodies, with the propagation of theories about the necessity of regular, timed feedings of babies and a rational, scientific approach to child care, sought to spread the influence of ideas about scientific management to all spheres of life.[86]

Though the concept of time promoted by radio derived largely from a different source – the need for broadcasters to construct a particular representation of its audience – its effects were not necessarily different to those intended by the scientific management principles. As a technique for augmenting labour power, the 'Taylorization' of work required the rigid measurement and standardization of time, a 'detailed partitioning of time',[87] so that time increasingly became something to be used. Similarly, radio, with its frequent telling of the time and its representation of time as minutely measured, worked to produce a sense of time as something to be used rationally in the home. For men it suggested that their work and leisure were to be structured similarly – organized with an acute consciousness of the time. For women, it promoted a sense of the time as strictly and precisely measured. In women's sessions they were told how they should be 'making the most of your time',[88] the constant repetition of the precise time suggesting that time was important to women, to their work in the home. Indeed, radio in general seemed guided by the principles of Taylorism in the way in which it addressed women: it promoted a greater consciousness of time and a sense of its being minutely measured; it advocated scientific, efficient methods of housework and child care practices; and it insisted that women should turn to experts rather than relying on the traditional, shared wisdom of their mothers. These principles were not self-consciously adopted by broadcasters, but rather resulted from the variety of factors identified here influencing the organization and content of radio programming.

Although the women's sessions worked to ensure that domestic work was central to the definition of women's identities, they were also attributing a positive value to that work. The housewife's value was guaranteed in this context by a number of factors: advertisers addressed her as controller of the family's purse strings; the new professional groups addressed her as manager of the home and controller of child care practices; and radio more generally addressed her as the heart of the new family turned inwards upon itself, preoccupied with its private consumption activities. The everyday life of the housewife was quite separate from the public social world, but it was nevertheless accorded a dignity and importance by the existence of special broadcasting programmes and by the interest of these various groups in her activities.

In her discussion of the way in which the opposition between domestic and public orientations appear in all societies to differentiate male and female roles, Michelle Rosaldo suggests the 'the very symbolic and social conceptions that appear to set women apart and to circumscribe their activities may be used by women as a basis for female solidarity and worth'.[89] She speaks of the importance of charities, baking contests, and church clubs to American women as a means of creating an alternative basis of social power through which they manage to gain some control over men or establish a society of their own. The radio clubs which flourished in the 1930s in Australia appeared to function in this way for their predominantly female membership.

In the 1920s radio clubs had proliferated, but concerned specifically with the technology of wireless broadcasting. Often exclusively male, these clubs experimented with wireless reception and transmission and facilitated the exchange of information between members about the construction of wireless sets. The radio clubs of the 1930s, however, had emerged as part of the moves made by stations to provide cheering messages to audiences during the depression. By the mid-1930s, these clubs were organized predominantly around women. They ran sporting activities, social occasions and charity work for women, often with club rooms in the city, suburbs and country areas. They were successful. Mrs Stelzer described the formation of her *2GB's Happiness Club* as responding to the difficulty experienced by so many women in forming friendships:[90] in 1937 she claimed to have 14,000 members and sixty branches in NSW; in 1939 she had 16,000 members. Other clubs were smaller (3AW's *Women's Association*, for example, had 4000 members in 1936); but they all appear to have worked in similar ways. The sporting associations – with an emphasis on golf and tennis – seemed to be the basis for their continuity, but the charitable work also provided a secure organizing basis. There were also some clubs that focused almost solely on charity work such as the Melbourne 3UZ's *The Deed's Family* started in 1937.

The activities of these clubs – golf, tennis, charity work – suggest that they set out to attract a largely middle-class membership. The private statements of stations to advertisers, as in the case of 2CH's representation of its audience to readers of *Broadcasting Business*, appear to confirm this picture. But the mode of address employed by the programmes was not directed at a class-specific audience. Though membership fees and the nature of the activities themselves may have excluded a large number of women, the evidence of radio magazines and station brochures suggest that the programmes themselves sought to address all women. They spoke to their audiences as if all women were one and the same. All women were being urged to establish a position of social power in the home and to pursue the possibilities of an alternative public social world.

This feature of radio programming may have been responsive to the requirements of women, or a reflection of the strategies women were already engaged in as a means of dealing with their exclusion from the public social world. However, the extent of interest in actually organizing these strategies for women by commercial bodies and professional experts suggests rather that it was a means of continuing and legitimating that exclusion – the separate world of women – in the interests of these groups. Women, in turn, no doubt used what was organized for them to establish a basis for some sort of social power, but the radio programmes and clubs ensured that, in this context at least, women were directed towards strategies for accentuating differences and forging alternative public social worlds, rather than attempting to have an influence over or make criticisms about the public social world and its dominance by men.

These demands as a fundamental challenge to the separation between the public and the private, would not be formulated for another thirty years. But the examination of radio in the 1920s and 1930s reveals some interesting ironies about the way in which women were being defined in this period. Radio addressed all women as consumers – of the commodities provided by the market and the knowledge provided by the experts that now surrounded the family; and it addressed them as confined to and fulfilled in the domestic sphere. But it also addressed them as thus having a shared orientation, as being a unified group in their interests and experiences. Radio was addressing one section of its audience in a form that would later become a powerful means of political mobilization and action. Women in the late 1960s and 1970s would begin to mobilize around and to re-work the very form in which the new popular media and other forces had been addressing them since the 1920s and 1930s: that is, as women – with a shared orientation and set of experiences as women. Through this politics of a common identity, they would come together as women, insist upon the particularity and the value that the experience of close involvement with domestic responsibilities gave to their view of the social and political reality, and insist upon the politics of the process by which their lives had been so constituted as confined to this sphere.

4
THE WORLD OF RADIO

The listeners' world and the radio had become one and the same. No longer was it a question of communication (via the 'mike') between two worlds. The broadcaster spoke intimately, as a friend, to the listener – sharing together the concerns, the preoccupations, of the everyday-ordinary as they had been defined by radio. In constructing this sense of the world of radio, the publicity language that surrounded broadcasting, the radio programmes themselves, as well as the radio style of performance, addressed listeners as if they already shared that perspective, that this was already how they understood their world – indeed, that this was not a perspective, but the world, the real world of everyone's lives. In this world of radio, the radio personality assumed a central importance.

Popular personalities and programmes

The stars of radio had been pictured in radio magazines since 1925. Magazines such as *Radio in Australia and New Zealand* carried a personalities page with photographs of performers to be heard on 2FC, for example, and perhaps some notes about the activities of radio stations. Similarly, the front covers of the *Listener In* in the late 1920s frequently pictured a performer soon to be heard on radio. The station's microphone was a central feature of these photographs: the stars of the theatre, by now most commonly used on front covers, were always shown with a station microphone (mostly 3LO in the *Listener In*) clearly displayed on their dressing room table. These stars were part of the outside world, the glamorous world of the theatre, brought to listeners by the marvellous technology of wireless. By the early 1930s, the microphone had disappeared and the stars of radio – rather than of other worlds – were being pictured on front covers and throughout the magazines: these were the radio personalities.

The publicity surrounding the idols of the Hollywood screen encouraged audiences to emulate them, to desire to look like their favourite movie star, but to feel socially distanced from them as people in their glamorous life of conspicuous consumption. The stars of radio, on the other hand, were presented as 'you and me'.[1] They were not the mysterious, exotic, larger than life stars of the movie screen, but were precisely just ordinary people, talking in friendly tones to listeners in their everyday, ordinary lives. They were personalities rather than stars, and each one had an individual style and character. The radio magazines fostered this image by a number of processes. Front cover photographs presented the personalities – now without microphone – in studio portraits. They carried stories about personalities, about their domestic lives and their quirks and characteristics (guarantees of their ordinariness). Studio gossip columns, such as the *Listener In*'s 'Both Sides of the Microphone' or the *Wireless Weekly*'s 'Between You and Me and the Microphone', provided listeners with intimate secrets about radio personnel and their lives on and off the air. Cartoon drawings and family photographs provided a sense of familiarity and ordinariness about performers and announcers. Radio stars were now 'real people', not mere voices. Personalities, it was generally assumed by the 1930s, were essential to good radio. Even the *Labor Daily* carried a radio column, 'With the Men of the Mike', telling readers about the idiosyncrasies of various radio performers or announcers, demonstrating the extent to which this image of radio was now rarely questioned.

The 'uncles' and 'aunts' of the past, who 'put on' these radio personas, were seen as suitable for children only. The personas 'put on' by the new-style radio personalities had to be their own. This shift is exemplified in the transformation of 2UE Sydney during 1933–4 from being an old-style station, a family affair run by C.V. Stevenson, to a commercially oriented organization concerned to sell audiences to advertisers. In 1933, Associated Newspapers, who were interested in acquiring a controlling share in the station, asked Frederick Daniell to examine 2UE's total organization and performance (Daniell was later to play a key role in setting up Macquarie Broadcasting Services and the Macquarie Broadcasting Network, major developments in the consolidation and co-ordination of Australian commercial broadcasting). Daniell criticized the 'provincial Radio Uncle gossipy type of atmosphere' of the station and recommended that successful announcers such as Captain Stevens be confined to adult sessions 'and not confuse his personality with listeners by becoming Uncle Steve ... at 5.30'.[2]

Personalities became central to radio station publicity, for audiences and advertisers. 2GB announced in 1939, for example, that listeners would now be able to look forward to hearing their favourite announcers on the air at the same time each night. Charles Cousins, Jack Davey, John Dease and Harry Dearth would provide the central features of 2GB's night programmes.[3] To advertisers, 2GB publicized its personalities as their salesmen. In a brochure titled 'Purely Personal ...', advertisers were told the 'story of 100 Microphone Personalities and Salesmen who guarantee for your product the Audience which it deserves'. With glossy photographs of 100 personalities and a publicity statement about each one's selling power, the brochure insisted on their importance:

> Welcome friends in the homes of their listeners, they can, if they be your salesmen, deliver your sales message personally into the homes of the people who need your products .... If they merely introduce your recorded announcement, their personal prestige can guarantee for your product the audience which it deserves.[4]

McNair, in his book on radio advertising, suggested that all commercial stations were similarly concerned to build up an image of a substantial personal following for each of their announcers and artists to induce advertisers to use their stations.[5] Commercial stations thus promoted the notion that the intimate friendly voice, broadcasting personalities playing themselves, was essential to good radio. But their interest in this mode of performance did not emanate from a concern about the development of radio itself; they were preoccupied rather with persuading advertisers that they understood the potential of radio, what was necessary to its success, and, most importantly, that they had a guaranteed method of insinuating a need for advertisers' products into the lives of listeners-in.

It was not only announcers and popular artists on commercial stations who were appearing in the guise of radio personalities. The front covers of radio magazines, in particular, reveal the way in which classical music performers, 'serious' artists, royalty and political figures were similarly presented as radio personalities, regardless of whether they were to broadcast on 'A' or 'B' class stations. To be able to hear politicians on radio was at first part of the thrill, one of the stunts devised by wireless broadcasting; by the late 1920s they were appearing on the front covers and personality pages of radio magazines. Newspaper feature pages and radio magazines began to discuss the way in which politicians would have to learn to adapt their style to the radio microphone. President Roosevelt's 'fireside chats' on American radio were admiringly referred to as the appropriate style for politicians to adopt when addressing listeners-in. President Roosevelt, said the *Labor Daily*, was 'probably the only great democratic personality on the world stage today who is first rate at political broadcasting'. Politicians, this paper insisted, would have to learn to use the radio technique, to emulate the personal quality of Roosevelt's fireside chats: 'You feel the President is really speaking to you alone .... That he's really standing in your own home, not telling ... but explaining'.[6] Politicians would have to learn to personalize their performance – to play at being themselves, or to put on their own personalities – if they were to conform to the demands of what was now understood as 'good radio'.

Royalty too became radio personalities. The visit by the Duke and Duchess of York in 1927 to open Parliament House in Canberra was welcomed as a great event for radio. The nation would be brought together to hear the Duke and Nellie Melba on this special occasion (but reception was poor and the moment did not live up to predictions). Far more successful and significant for radio were the King's broadcast to the Empire for Christmas 1932 and the 'eye-witness' descriptions of the wedding of the Duke of Kent and Princess Marina in 1934. The *Listener In* carried a photograph of the royal couple on its front cover and declared in its headlines, 'All the World Guests at Wedding'.[7] In 1936 there was no Christmas speech from the King; instead listeners had been 'privileged' to hear the abdication speech of Edward VIII earlier that year, a speech 'full of fairness, restraint and majesty'.[8] At the beginning of the same year, King George V had died and *Broadcasting Business* paid tribute to him as the 'world's most popular broadcaster'.[9] King George, the radio magazines declared, had been able to talk to listeners as if he was in their living rooms, speaking intimately to everyone: royalty became radio personalities, playing themselves – as just ordinary people.

Similarly, classical music performers, conductors and singers, to be heard on ABC stations predominantly but on commercial stations too, were presented as radio personalities in the print media. The *Women's Weekly*, assessing the performance of the ABC during 1938, congratulated it for providing a grand galaxy of 'personalities'; these included Richard Tauber, Lotte Lehmann, Artur Rubinstein, the Budapest String Quartet and the Comedy Harmonists.[10] The world celebrities, famous artists, musical talents, or radio personalities, as these performers were variously called, were presented in studio portraits on the front covers and radio personalities pages of the radio magazines. A drawing of Toscanini conducting appeared on the front cover of the *Wireless Weekly* towards the end of 1938.[11] The publicity language employed by the print media claimed that these artists performed for listeners in the comfort of their own homes; these world celebrities were there to please each listener, to cater for their individual tastes, to play specially for their pleasure.

Adorno condemned the 'commodity listening' thus promoted by radio and other new culture industries, and the political effects he believed would be its consequence. He analysed the processes by which these industries, and radio in particular, set out to make music and its performers familiar and to ensure that music entered 'the sphere of the well-known, thus rendering it more readily comprehensible'. Radio works, Adorno argued, to make it seem to each listener that 'Toscanini is playing for him and him alone'.[12] He criticized the 'standardization of music', classical or jazz, encouraged by the attempt to make music familiar; all music, he claimed, thus becomes more a quotation of itself. The 'commodity listening' promoted by this sense of familiarity and ease of consumption, he claimed, has a soporific effect and deflects listeners from thinking about social conditions and their specific problems. Radio consoles its audience with the message that they are well-served, that the best is now specially brought to them for their selection and ease of consumption.[13]

Yet, apparently cutting across this representation of all radio personalities as familiar was a different set of messages about radio performers that insisted on distinctions and a sense of distance from the ordinary for some. Though the studio portraits used by radio magazines depicted all performers as radio personalities, subtle differentiations occurred in the way in which they were presented. The poses of the different type of stars, their manner of looking at the camera or away from it, and their general mien or style indicated the different worlds of these personalities. Popular stars smiled broadly, straight at the camera; royalty, famous public figures, and classical music performers – all the 'serious stars' – looked quietly at the camera or off-camera, with a slight (if any) smile. The radio world fabricated by the publicity language of the print media set out to create the illusion that all its products, all commodities offered, were equal in the marketplace; but in these subtle differentiations, it also worked to create a sense of distinction. The photographs used in magazines such as the *Listener In* or the *Radio Times* juggled these two messages about radio personalities: by their presentation in this context, all appeared equal – commodities to be selected and consumed by listeners-in; and yet through the different types of images – through the use of specific photographic conventions about the pose required of a subject – differences were asserted. A distinction was being drawn between the world of the 'serious' performer or personality and that of the 'popular' entertainer – between 'art' (and the world of public figures) and entertainment.

Similarly, radio magazines and newspaper radio features at times drew distinctions between radio personalities and artists. In 1936, the *Listener In* devoted a regular page to performers to be heard on 'B' class stations with titles each week such as 'Pertinent Pars about Prominent Personalities' or 'Topical "B" class Tit-Bits'. But it also devoted a page each week to 'artists' engaged by or to be heard on the ABC. Though magazines and newspapers conducted plebiscites to find listeners' most popular personalities, including stars such as the Grand Opera singer Richard Tauber, they also employed in other contexts categories such as 'popular personalities' and 'serious artists' to create distinctions between performers and their art. The distinction between classical music and popular entertainment was a taken-for-granted of programme timetables. Classical music always stood as a separate category in this setting, juxtaposed to other categories of either different types of music (dance, jazz or popular tunes, perhaps), or broader classifications such as variety or light entertainment.

The ABC remained uncertain throughout the 1930s about whether any of its broadcasts should be conducted in the radio personality style, but it took care to differentiate between the manner or voice seen as appropriate for different programmes. In 1944 it produced an announcer's manual that stressed the importance of the announcer's personality: 'the announcer is the Commission's personal contact with

The contrasting styles of the different types of radio personalities: the popular (Photograph: *Listener In*, 10 November 1934)

The contrasting styles of the different types of radio personalities: the serious (Photograph: *Listener In*, 24 November 1934)

the listener'. Except on formal occasions, announcers were instructed, they should think of themselves as 'speaking to a few friends on a subject of common interests'.[14] But these recommendations were made towards the end of the second world war when the ABC had become accustomed to making some significant concessions to the demands of 'popular taste'. By 1946 the ABC would renew its opposition to 'personality building'; referring in particular to talk-type programmes, it declared that the ABC should not follow the commercial stations by allowing listeners to become attached to favourite speakers. Echoing Adorno's concerns, they claimed such programming served to 'standardise public attitudes'.[15]

In the 1930s the ABC was concerned to emulate what it saw as the BBC's style and manner in this area, as well as in others. The BBC was reported as insisting upon their announcers remaining unknown to listeners; their names were kept secret and they were certainly not 'personalities'.[16] The ABC pursued the BBC's authoritative style and distanced manner in many of its programmes. It persisted throughout the 1930s with the rule that all performers and announcers should wear evening dress at night, a symbol of the dignified, formal tone it expected from its personnel (the commercial stations had similarly required their personnel to wear such dress, but had begun to relax the rule even in the early 1930s). Though listeners' letters complained of the ABC adopting the tone of a 'village squire' or 'dogged school master', it continued to prescribe a formal style for its evening announcers and performers.

Yet for specific programmes (and audiences) the ABC required a different manner. In 1936, Charles Moses, new general manager of the ABC, announced a new 'brighter style of programme' for women audiences: day-time sessions were to be infused with 'a friendly, intimate atmosphere'.[17] Similarly, in 1938 the ABC was experimenting with its early morning sessions; the announcer in Victoria was advised to choose 'bright lively records and concentrate on a cheerful naturalness in his approach'.[18] This was the style of morning programme pioneered by broadcasters such as Fred Tupper and 'Nicky' on commercial stations early in the 1930s. (Charles Moses, however, was not entirely happy with this particular ABC experiment and soon instructed the announcer to eliminate all jokes from his programme.) Women and early morning audiences, then, were to be treated to a friendly, human style on the ABC; it was not until the evening that the ABC would assume its full stature as the voice of authority, rationality and formal culture. It was as if the ABC partly relinquished its stance for these specific categories of programmes and conceded that, for early morning audiences and for women, 'everydayness' took over. For these audiences the ABC assumed the same tone of intimate friendliness promoted by commercial stations and the radio magazines as necessary for good radio. For evening audiences, the ABC pursued a different tone – one which spoke of its primary alliance with formal culture and rational thought, not to the demands of radio entertainment or the everyday.

No doubt the line was not so clearly drawn as this in reality and the ABC in practice was more ambivalent about the voice or voices it should use; but the differentiations it was establishing between audiences and how they should be addressed were significant in themselves. Adorno, writing during the 1940s and later of American radio, complained that radio makes classical music performers too familiar and that it produces 'standardized enthusiasm'. These were precisely the trends the ABC claimed to be guarding against when it adopted its stance of formal culture and rational discussion. Though the 'radio personality' style set out to create a friendly atmosphere and a sense of familiarity, the example of Australian broadcasting demonstrates the extent to which some broadcasters at least resisted such notions of good radio. The ABC, in its practice and in its representations about itself, insisted upon and reasserted distinctions between the entertainment provided by radio personalities and the 'serious art' to be heard on many of its programmes. These were precisely the distinctions Adorno assumed to be necessary and immutable, but nevertheless threatened by radio.

This language about the distinctiveness of 'serious art', about its specialness and the necessity of its being presented in a formal rather than familiar manner, suggests an attempt to revive or protect what Benjamin has termed the 'aura' traditionally associated with art. The emphasis on formal tones by the ABC and the reverential attitude evoked for the visiting artists, the 'world celebrities', suggest a desire to stress the uniqueness of each performance and the separation or distance of the craft of these artists from the 'everyday-ordinary'. Of interest here is the connection between the language of Adorno and the representations of radio by those working within the institution itself in the 1930s. Though Adorno raises some important issues, about commodity listening for example, his discussion has also to be seen as confined within the terrain of popular and official discourses about broadcasting in the 1930s and 1940s. Benjamin's position, on the other hand, had more in common with the debates about the potential of new media – broadcasting and films – as technologies, a question eliminated for the most part from popular and official representations of radio, in the Australian context, by the 1930s. Benjamin suggested of film that everyone has the potential to be an expert; he cited as examples the way in which the new film industry in Russia was making powerful use of the masses of people 'playing themselves' and the chance offered by newsreels that a passer-by might be transformed into a movie star. With film, then, Benjamin argued, the masses may be given the opportunity to become experts, critics – of an 'absent-minded' or semi-conscious kind. The Hollywood film industry, on the other hand, seeks to create a cult value for its films. Speaking of commercial movies, Benjamin criticized the publicity machine surrounding Hollywood films as setting out to create an aura around each film by the images of its glamorous stars; this publicity fabricated the '"spell of the personality", the phony spell of a commodity'.[19] Uniqueness, mystery, thereby become characteristic of films, rather than a sense of familiarity and their accessibility.

On the surface radio in the 1930s appeared responsive to what Benjamin argued is the desire of the contemporary masses of people 'to bring things "closer" spatially and humanly'.[20] The radio personality was human, familiar, and spoke as if physically and spiritually close to the listeners. And, it seemed, radio did tend to make everyone something of an expert. Broadcasters and others connected with radio complained of the way in which listeners seemed to see themselves in this role.[21] Listeners' letters suggested that they did still see themselves at times as actively involved in the progress and business of radio – a habit of mind formed perhaps in the previous decade – and they vigorously promoted their suggestions about how broadcasting should be conducted. But the development of various kinds of public participation and 'vox populi' type programmes reveal how effectively radio recruited that image of itself as being human, familiar, to other ends, rather than to facilitate the development of broadcasting as a fully democratic medium.

These shows held out the promise to listeners-in that they too could become radio stars. Many radio programmes in the late 1930s, particularly on commercial stations, worked along similar lines of offering the chance to listeners to be on radio. They included amateur performance programmes like the successful *Amateur Hour* on 2UW Sydney and the *P and A Parade* (Professionals and Amateurs) on 3KZ Melbourne; radio quiz programmes like 3DB's *Information Please*; audience participation programmes with community singing (first pioneered by the 'A' class stations in the 1920s) or 3KZ's *Stumbles*; and street interviews, most successfully run by Norman Banks, with his *The Voice of the People* and the manifold variations on this theme, including *The Voice of the Voyager* and *The Voice of the Shopper*. The publicity surrounding these programmes, as well as their actual formats, worked to suggest that listeners were participants in the world of radio. Spoken of as giving the listeners a voice, or 'their say', or listeners entertaining and communicating directly with each other, these programmes denied or mystified the cultural form that radio had assumed – denied that it was a means of one-way communication – to create an image of listeners actively involved, communicating through the medium of radio. *Information Please* was publicized as a programme that allowed 'ordinary citizens' to turn the tables on 'patronising sage[s]', to ask them the questions; and *Stumbles* was a 'do it yourself' type programme where listeners amused themselves (the studio audience called out mistakes made in a story being read by a radio announcer).[22] Similarly, early versions of talk-back radio, in which Terry Dear on 3AW installed a telephone next to the studio microphone so that listeners could hear his replies to phoned-in comments on his programmes, constructed a self-enclosing world of radio in which listeners and broadcasters appeared one and the same. The sense in which radio could be used as a means of communication between people and groups, as Voigt and others connected with 2KY had discussed in the 1920s, had now been overturned and re-presented as a matter of people communicating within the world of radio. 2KY itself developed such programmes in the 1930s, including 'Argus', the prophet reading the minds of members of a studio audience.

Communicating within the world of radio appeared to break down the barrier between broadcaster and listener – expert and consumer – only to erect a new set of barriers and boundaries. The public participation shows and the 'vox populi' programmes constructed a particular image of the people involved – of listeners-in – and their lives. Their world was a world of fun, entertainment and just 'ordinary' people, people in their everyday-ordinary mode. The everyday-ordinary was made glamorous, exciting, by its being the world of radio. These programmes were presented as responsive to popular demand – to let the people in – only then to establish a powerful definition of what the people and their lives were about and what they would wish to have their say about. They could sing or play music, display their encyclopaedic knowledge, participate in fun, act the fool, make audience noises – and be star for the night. Benjamin's position of the absent-minded or engaged critic was to be surrendered for that moment – or its promise – of participation in the world of radio. Private troubles could be forgotten in this world (or made the subject of laughter and jokes) and the world of public issues remained confined to separate programmes about the outside world.

Further creating a sense of the world of radio as being self-enclosing – of communication, participation, being a matter of participating in the fun and excitement of the world of radio – was the practice of handing out prizes. In quiz shows and amateur competitions, in particular, radio itself became a rewarder, a hander out of success or material wealth. To be a star for the night was reward in itself, but that was open to everyone, everyone was or could be participant in the world of radio. Individual merit or skill was also recognized and rewarded – skill at those things celebrated by the world of radio: entertainment, fun, and knowledge of the everyday-ordinary kind. These rewards or prizes added to the sense of excitement being created for the world of radio, as well as offering guarantees of individuality, of specialness, to its participants.

In the attempt to ensure that listeners were drawn into the world of radio, broadcasters became increasingly preoccupied with programming. They began to look at their programmes as a whole, concerned with the 'flow' of programmes so that listeners, once tuned into their station would stay to hear one programme after another on that same station; and they developed notions of 'composite programmes' to create a sense in which all tastes, all interests, could be satisfied by careful attention to a day's or week's programming. Advances in broadcasting technology in the late 1920s permitted programmers to use mixing and fading devices to blend in noises or sound. This was significant both for programme techniques within one particular session, and for moving from one programme to another or from one item to another (it was also the great delight of broadcasters on the 'B' class stations as they experimented with techniques such as fading out Beethoven's 'Moonlight Sonata' to bring in an advertisement about tooth powders).

To create a sense of unity in programming, short pieces of music became important to fill the gaps. The BBC continued to have silences between its programmed items (breaks in transmission ensured, they believed, that listeners treated broadcast items seriously), but in Australia broadcasters set out to fill the air whenever they were timetabled to be on air, to be broadcasting. This did not mean that all stations broadcast continuously throughout the day: to take Sydney radio in 1938 as an example, stations 2BL, 2KY, 2UW and 2SM all closed for some period during the middle of the day and 2FC broadcast between 10.00 in the morning and 10.30 at night (all other stations in Sydney at this time closed somewhere between 11.00 and midnight and opened between 5.45 and 6.45 in the morning). But for their morning, day-time and evening sessions, the unity of items and the flow of one item to another within a broadcasting period had become important to all stations.

The ABC was careful to ensure that its broadcasters had appropriate 'interlude music' available to them to fill in spaces. Strict instructions were issued at various times to remind announcers that interlude music should be in keeping with the programmes on either side and that it should attract as little attention as possible.[23] The smooth flow of one programme to another and a sense of continuity were seen as means of capturing and holding an audience. Listeners were offered a complete world of entertainment, persuaded that there was no need to switch their dials on the wireless set; their evening was provided for.

The 'B' class or commercial stations similarly were interested in programming the continuity and unity of an evening or day session. One writer in 1937 spoke of contemporary radio as changing from the idea of music recording followed by an advertisement to 'the conception of a well-written, artistically designed and dramatically presented continuity. Programmes today must be interesting, entertaining, and have flow ... that is they must be harmonious or a homogeneous whole.'[24] This may have been the intention of all commercial stations, but some at least encountered difficulties with the integration of programmes and advertisements. The problem was at first one of lack of experience so that advertisements were interspersed too frequently in the programmes, used inappropriately in the middle of pieces of music, or their presentation was poor. But the problem continued throughout the 1930s as the role of advertisers began to change. With the increasing importance of sponsored programmes and the move by advertising agencies such as J. Walter Thompson's into the business of programme production, stations often had little control over their programming. The general manager of the Macquarie Broadcasting Network was to complain bitterly in 1940 of the inability of many Macquarie stations to control the balance of their programming or the blending of various features such as music, comedy and drama.[25] Five years earlier, Frederick Daniell had claimed that the advertising department of 2UE had achieved complete control of programming initiatives so that the quality of the total programmes was destroyed by excessive and blatant advertising.[26] But publicity statements for these stations did not reveal these problems. All stations represented themselves as providing a coherent, well-planned set of programmes for listeners; like the ABC, the commercial stations proclaimed themselves as providing all that listeners could require for the night's or week's entertainment so that they could settle back and relax.

Combined with the notion of programme flow was the attempt by stations to promote themselves as providing a carefully composed set of programmes. At the beginning of the 1930s there had been some debate about whether alternative types of programmes should be provided by some stations. A series of articles in the *Argus* in 1930 suggested that it was ludicrous for a station to offer programmes for all tastes; speaking only of 3LO and 3AR at this time, the *Argus* recommended that one station cater for serious tastes and the other be left to indulge people's tastes in less 'solid fare'.[27] This basic concept of differentiated programming was adopted by the ABC at the end of World War II, but before that time ABC stations and commercial stations preferred mostly to represent their programming as providing for all listeners. In 1929, the Australian Broadcasting Company had declared itself to be arranging 'composite programmes' to please all the listening public. Bernard Heinze, speaking of the company's musical programmes, celebrated their arrangement as being in the 'democratic spirit'.[28]

The attempt to offer a complete world of entertainment and to ensure that one programme flowed into another complemented the message being conveyed by other means of the self-enclosing character of the world of radio. Here all tastes could be satisfied, and here the listener could relax, provided for and pampered. Just as the continuity of a personality was seen quite explicitly by commercial broadcasting stations as a means of drawing listeners into the programmes (and advertisers' messages), so the preoccupation with presentation, programming and flow for all stations was a preoccupation with means, techniques, in the attempt to capture audiences and hold them. T.W. Bearup as manager of Victorian ABC stations, in a 1936 report, spoke of the need for programmers to be concerned not merely with the provision of programmes, but with 'the winning of an audience, and not only winning it, but holding it and continually expanding it'.[29]

Highbrow versus lowbrow

In the 1920s the radio audience had been spoken of as constituted elsewhere, outside the world of radio – as having interests, concerns or cultural preferences derived from other worlds or other spheres of their life. In the mid-1920s, and increasingly in the late 1920s, the radio audience was defined as being made up of 'varied tastes'. This notion suggested a diversity of desires, pleasures and interests to be satisfied by radio, and implied that the sum total of radio programmes could cater for that diversity. But in the 1930s, the terms 'highbrow' and 'lowbrow' emerged as key descriptions of the radio audience. These terms represented the audience as clearly divisible into two sets of cultural preferences, two set of tastes in radio programmes.

In the mid-1920s, the labels highbrow versus lowbrow had been used occasionally to describe different programmes; by the end of the decade they had become terms to describe listeners, and terms used by listeners in their letters to radio magazines and the daily press to identify themselves. For the most part the labels specified particular tastes in music to be heard on radio, but were applied more broadly to mark out orientations to all types of radio programmes. Highbrows loved classical or 'serious' music, 'serious' talks and plays; lowbrows loved jazz, 'light' music (including crooning and dance music), comedy, sport perhaps, and variety. The content of these labels was seldom questioned, and similarly, the distinction or differentiation between them was presented as a taken-for-granted. Additional qualities were at times mentioned – serious versus light, cerebral versus relaxing, heavy versus popular – but again the content of these categories and the distinctions drawn between them were not contested. The debate centred instead on the proportion of the listening audience that was highbrow or lowbrow and the proportion of programming hours that should be devoted to the interests of each group. As part of this debate other issues were raised focusing on the relative merits of highbrows versus lowbrows: highbrows were accused of being snobbish and arrogant; lowbrows were degenerate and ignorant.

Common to all these disputes was the assumption that radio programmes were commodities – cultural goods to be consumed. All participants in the debates and arguments shared the basic premise that broadcast programmes constituted a market of pleasures, a range of amusements, entertainments and edifying treasures to be consumed by listeners in their 'free' hours. The radio audience, it was implied, necessarily adopted a passive role, ready for radio to provide them with relaxation, solace, escape, or perhaps for some, intellectual stimulation, after a hard day's work. This expectation of the passivity of the listener – the consumer attitude – underpinned the view that radio should be an agency of cultural uplift or education of the masses in the same way as it formed the basis of the view of radio as entertainment. Culture and education were commodity goods in the context of the highbrow versus lowbrow debate.

At various times, throughout the 1930s, the debate about the relative merits or value of the claims of highbrows and lowbrows flared in the radio magazines or newspaper columns. Letters to the editor were the most common form of the debate, provoked perhaps by some event: a shift in ABC policy, an editorial, or a random letter (planted possibly by a magazine as its listeners' letters began to dwindle). Often signing themselves 'highbrow' or 'lowbrow', listeners pressed their claims for programmes of their choice. 'Lowbrows' argued for 'bright, pleasure-giving entertainment', for more comedy, 'music of a lively, tuneful and gay character', for 'harmony that is easy to listen to', or 'programmes to soothe the tired man after his day's labors'. They criticized highbrow programmes as 'mournful', 'over our heads', 'not relaxing', 'demanding too much concentration', as 'education crammed down my throat'. One listener in 1931, an 'Irish Australian', called for more 'cheerful' programmes from the 'A' class stations, for 'entertainment rather than "uplift"': 'The English view is that we should be educated (at our own expense) rather than entertained; but I don't see why our stations should be modelled on the BBC.'[30]

The highbrows proclaimed their preference for 'the better class of musical composition', for the 'more uplifting' programmes, for a station that would cater for 'the tastes of the more cultured section of the community', for programmes to please 'people of good taste', or 'for a high class educational service'. They were vehement in their disdain for programmes that catered for 'degraded taste in music', for the 'vulgarities' of jazz, vaudeville and crooning, 'modern trash that has defiled the name of music', for 'moaning crooners and croonettes', or for the 'negroid perversions' of modern jazz or dance music. For the highbrows, their cultural preference was a matter of superior taste or intelligence, but also of moral tone:

> The craving of simple-minded people for novelties at all costs brought about the adoption of the negro dances as their cherished pastime, and thus after the war, jazz, charleston and foxtrot were

favored by a certain class of people. As no composer of standing could be found to instrument those absurdities, certain hidden talents concocted for this purpose hideous noises that have been mistaken by many people, not used to real music, for the genuine article.[31]

Radio magazines and newspapers did not consistently support either highbrow or lowbrow, but when they did advocate the cause of the highbrow they employed terms (and the racist overtones) similar to those of listeners' letters. The *Argus* more often took the part of the highbrow, criticizing in particular the 'A' class stations for their poor standards. When the Commission members for the new ABC were announced, it commended their appointment as people of 'culture and knowledge of affairs' and called on them to ensure that 'the contemptible negroid perversions passed off as dance music' should no longer be allowed to vitiate the public taste. The tunes whistled by boys in the street, the *Argus* leader declared, demonstrated the extent to which this 'unwholesome' music had already 'seized upon Australians'.[32]

Keith Barry, later to work for the ABC, wrote regularly for the *Wireless Weekly* in the early 1930s about the role of broadcasting in elevating the musical tastes of the community. His views supported those of the *Argus*: he insisted that the 'A' class stations must ignore the calls of the masses for low-grade music and give them something culturally uplifting. Commending John Reith of the BBC for his declaration that that institution would provide listeners with something better than they want, Barry characterized 'the voice of the people' as 'the voice of ignorance'. The minority were 'generally right'; the masses, on the other hand, should be treated as children and educated. Broadcasting offered a golden opportunity to begin their education in musical appreciation, to teach them what was authentic music. Jazz or 'negroid tunes' were ephemeral stuff, not true eternal beauty.[33]

The superior tones and moral righteousness of this language stems from two, not unrelated, sources. On the one hand, these statements about good taste, true beauty, moral and cultural uplift, evoked a language formed in the nineteenth century about culture and the education of the masses. Matthew Arnold, responding to the social crisis of his age, wrote of culture as an opposing force to the crassness and anarchy, as he saw it, of 1860s England. Culture as the source of 'right reason', the 'best self' of the nation, and human excellence, was necessary to the progress of humanity. But this culture did not simply stand for tradition, standards or even excellence in its own right; culture, for Arnold, was an ideal and it provided the basis for his social criticism, his vision of a humane future and his call for an extended popular education.[34]

The concern expressed in the language surrounding radio about cultural uplift and the education of the masses drew on this Arnoldian tradition. It was a call for the preservation and extension of 'culture', but as such was seen as an end in itself. The moral tones mobilized in the celebration of culture or the condemnation of the lowbrow were not underscored by a social criticism of a broader kind (of the kind evinced by Arnold), but only by an objection to the 'degeneracy' of the taste of the lowbrow. Excellence, good taste, were ends in themselves, just as was musical appreciation; the masses ought to like the higher class of music. 'People who object to high-class music over the air confess their own lack of taste, refinement, and artistic appreciation.... In fact everything really worthwhile in literature or art would be outside their comprehension.'[35] Much like the argument 'art for art's sake', these statements about the value of classical music or 'serious' programmes assumed society would necessarily be better the more educated the tastes of the masses became, the more they appreciated 'the finer things of life';[36] but this vision rested on notions of good taste rather than the humane values to be elicited and fostered by culture or education.

The second source for the moral righteousness of the language of the highbrow resided in the tension created by the formal equality radio gave to all cultural practices. Piano recitals, horse-racing carnivals and crooners appeared together in the one context and became the same cultural form: the radio broadcast. Radio placed in jeopardy traditional hierarchies of cultural taste; it undermined their apparent naturalness. The highbrow versus lowbrow debate was a popular mode of exploring and playing with this problem and the tensions it created. At the same time it provided the opportunity for distinctions of taste to be vigorously re-drawn. The moral righteousness of the language of the highbrow signalled an anxiety created by the temporary precariousness of the categories. Differences of tastes, the highbrows insisted, were a matter of 'natural' distinction on the part of the highbrow rather than arbitrary difference or individual whim; all other tastes were designated inferior or illegitimate.

Walter Benjamin identified the doctrine of art for art's sake as emerging at the same time as the means of mechanical reproduction –

photography and sound recordings – were emancipating the work of art from 'its parasitical dependence on ritual'. This claim formed part of his argument that mechanical reproduction detaches the artistic object from its tradition, causes its aura to wither and thus makes it possible for 'the beholder or listener [to meet it] in his own particular situation'.[37] 'Art for art's sake', as a theology of art, Benjamin suggested, attempts to resist this change and to reassert the cult value of the work of art, to insist upon uniqueness, 'authenticity', as central to the definition of art. Broadcasting as a means of mechanical reproduction of cultural goods was, in Benjamin's terms, potentially an emancipatory technology. This did not lie in some essential feature of the technology itself, but in the possibility of its exploitation and development in directions appropriate for progressive purposes. But the establishment of the relationship between listener and broadcasting transmissions as one of passive consumer undermined this potential for alternative, democratic social uses of broadcasting technology. The cultural products of radio (whatever their 'brow') became commodities rather than the materials through which listeners could think about their own lives or their social world.[38] The promotion of ideologies of good taste and excellence as an end in itself, like the doctrine art for art's sake, strengthened this resistance to the recruitment of broadcasting to different social ends. The canons of good taste and true aesthetic appreciation were claimed to be incontestable and only understood or appreciated spontaneously by certain sections of the community; for the masses, they had to be imposed. The aura traditionally associated with 'art' could thus be restored and the social distance between art and the masses reasserted.

The ABC provided institutional support and official affirmation of the distinction and superiority of the highbrow taste. Though 'B' class stations did play classical music and provide serious talks at times, the ABC was characterized as highbrow from the outset. Obliged by its parliamentary act to perform the role of public educator, the ABC offered serious, educational, cultural programmes as the dominant feature of its evening broadcasts. Though insisting that the delights of its highbrow culture were open to all, the ABC spoke of the distinction of those who had already acquired its tastes. The formal tones and accent of gentility expected of ABC announcers, and more generally of ABC performers, for its evening programmes in particular, indicated the separateness and distance of its culture from the everyday-ordinary.[39] The ABC adopted this tone in opposition to the 'B' class stations' image of informality and familiarity. It eschewed the personality building and friendly voice pursued by the 'B' class stations for the most part and set out to establish a formal image for its programmes, requiring its listeners to be prepared to – and capable of – leaving aside their everyday lives, the realm of the ordinary, to step into this world of culture.

The public declarations and display of a link between the ABC and the BBC also served to affirm the distinction of those who listened to ABC programmes. In journals, newspapers and parliamentary debates, from the time of its inception, the ABC had been referred to as 'Australia's BBC'. This connection was seen as necessary to and guaranteeing the ABC's image of cultural authority and legitimate culture. As a British institution, the BBC, it was assumed, could draw on and represent a long tradition of superior taste; the ABC was obliged to follow in its footsteps. The adoption of a similar voice and style was seen as ensuring that the ABC played the same cultural role as the BBC; but this mimicry played a symbolic function too in publicly laying a claim to that similarity. Throughout the 1930s various ABC personnel made requests to the BBC for their guidelines and reference notes for announcers. Advice was sought too on instructions to newsreaders and about the presentation of various types of programmes. In 1936 T.W. Bearup, now a senior official for the ABC, visited England to examine the BBC's programme presentation and technical arrangements. The ABC imitated many of the BBC programmes, especially those of an obviously educational or cultural nature: programmes like the *General Knowledge Bee*. And as further testimony to its intimate ties with the BBC, the ABC eagerly sought BBC recorded programmes and in 1937 sent a full-time representative to work with the BBC Empire Service.

Thus, the ABC was anxious that it be seen to have (as well as have) a special relationship with the BBC. In 1936, Charles Moses, general manager of the ABC, became annoyed that various official visitors representing the commercial stations were in London. He wrote to the BBC complaining of their hospitable reception, but was quickly assured by the BBC that the ABC came first. The avowal was genuine; the BBC was keen to sustain close ties with the ABC, but its interest appears to have been determined as much by its desire to establish a secure market for its recorded programmes as by amicable or paternalistic feelings. The BBC sent a representative to various Empire countries in 1932–3, and again in 1933–4, to promote these programmes and saw themselves as competing with the USA.[40] For the

ABC, on the other hand, close ties with the BBC, either by its access to BBC programmes or by clear similarities in style and manner, vouched for the superior culture of its programmes, and hence the distinction of those who consumed them.

The problem for the ABC was how to manage to serve both its select audience and the masses. The ABC's act required it to perform the role of public educator, a demand that sat uneasily with its attempt to protect what was seen as necessarily a minority culture (only a few could fully appreciate or participate in its sensibilities). W. J. Cleary, the second chairman of the ABC, announced that '[m]inorities, especially cultural and spiritual ones, must be nourished'. Yet, at the same time as advocating this preservation of an élite, he committed the ABC to the task of 'creat[ing] a public taste which will tend to lift the intellectual life of the community to a higher plane'.[41] Beyond the rhetoric, however, these two roles did create tensions, particularly about the type of programmes and a mode of presentation appropriate to the ABC. In 1933, Charles Lloyd Jones, the first chairman, excited by the broadcasting innovations that he had observed on a recent visit to the USA, suggested that the ABC should institute a programme similar to the *Amateur Hour* which was popular there. No one within the ABC shared his enthusiasm for following the American lead; a special panel of ABC talks advisers, when asked to comment on this suggestion, all claimed to be horrified. W.G.K. Duncan, Professor of Adult Education at the University of Sydney, declared the proposal 'grotesque'. An 'Amateur Hour' feature would induce only 'boredom, impatience and contempt in our listeners' and 'I, for one', he warned, 'should be tempted to abandon listening-in altogether.'[42] The Commission's report of 1936 indicated that an 'eisteddfod of the air' was eventually found a far more fitting programme for the ABC. While Duncan, and others like him, may have thus been reassured that the ABC was adopting a legitimate cultural stance, the 'Amateur Hour' idea was eagerly embraced by the 'B' class stations and became an important feature of Australian broadcasting in the mid-1930s. In Melbourne, 3KZ's the *P and A Parade* and 3AW's *Amateur Hour* ensured that amateur performance sessions were recorded as the most popular programmes in the *Radio Times* plebiscite of September 1935.

Radio quizzes posed similar problems for the ABC. They were a popular feature of Australian broadcasting in the mid-1930s, but personnel within the ABC were again wary of adopting a programme idea whose cultural style could be judged as insufficiently formal or serious. The BBC had been reluctant to conduct such sessions at first and had confined all competitions to children's programmes. But early in the 1930s, this policy was relaxed and it soon carried quiz contests and competitions of various kinds. The ABC followed, but with some unease. They maintained strict prescriptions about the proper conduct of these programmes, insisting that no prize money be offered for competitions such as *Spelling Bee* or the *General Knowledge Bee*.[43] Some ABC personnel, at least, expressed concern that these programmes might appear to condone inappropriate or irreverent attitudes to the knowledge being tested. A suggestion for a literary quiz programme, 'So You Think You Know Your Literature', was soundly condemned by Keith Barry, by then employed at the ABC:

> the person who knows even most of the answers is apt to be sufficiently interested in literature to have approached it for the serious and satisfying thing it is, and to be possessed, therefore, with a mentality not easily given to patronage of this newest form of old-fashioned parlour game, called the 'Radio Quiz'.[44]

The search for programmes to educate the masses faced the apparently insoluble problem of teaching them a culture that did not come 'naturally', whilst not alienating those for whom it supposedly did. And compounding the problem, the popularizing techniques of programmes such as radio quizzes, or audience participation shows more generally, were seen as endangering the special character of this culture: the programmes threatened to be insufficiently serious, reverent, and formal.

For the highbrows their choice of programmes, and their allegiance for the most part to the ABC, indicated their superior taste, their difference or distinction. For lowbrows, on the other hand, choice was a different matter. In their letters to newspapers and magazines, the lowbrow demanded freedom of choice, to be free of moralizing public officials or the attempt by certain sections of the population to impose their tastes on others. Freedom was symbolized by the turn of the knob on the radio set, the freedom to select from a range of programmes on offer. For these listeners radio provided a market of amusements and pleasures. Claiming themselves to be the majority of listeners, they refused attempts to enlighten or to educate them and declared their desire for programmes that spoke of an ordinary, everyday world in content and style. Community singing, audience participation shows, variety programmes of escapist but homely humour, cosy 'little plays' or serials, talks of a non-patronizing, non-moralizing kind, easy to listen to music, and radio stunts of an extravagant nature constituted the 'popular aesthetic' of radio as it appeared in listeners' letters and in the radio plebiscites conducted by newspapers and magazines. These listeners rejected the distant manner and reserved, formal style of the ABC in favour of the familiar, the everyday – in favour of programmes that conjured up a world that was available and comfortable to them:

> I, as an Australian, object to having education crammed down my throat by supercilious committees and art connoisseurs. In plain Australian, I don't want to be educated. I want the news and wireless features that please me. It will take all the jazz bands in Sydney to make up for the long, horrible years I spent at school.[45]

The ABC, throughout the 1930s, remained uncertain about how much it should bow to this 'popular demand'; the 'B' class stations, on the contrary, obliged. In the early 1930s they began to build an image of themselves as being attractive to listeners, of catering for their wants. The radio magazines assisted in this campaign. The *Wireless Weekly* and the *Listener In* both carried features entitled 'How Doth the Busy B' to draw attention to these stations as alternatives to the 'A' class stations. In the period before market research became essential to the commercial stations, plebiscites and popularity polls for favourite radio personalities served to materialize audiences to potential advertisers and the radio stations themselves; but they served also to represent the 'B' stations as responsive to 'what the public wants'. In the late 1930s, with advertising interests now dominating the conduct of many 'B' stations, audience ratings played this same role. Whilst publicly deploying this latter device to proclaim their commitment to discovering and providing 'what the public wants', privately, audience ratings played a more significant role for the commercial stations: they generated a means of representing (or claiming to represent) the audience attracted by a particular station or programme, in order that the audience could be sold to advertisers as their potential market. Though the popularity (in terms of proportion of the radio audience) of the 'B' class stations was undeniable by the mid-1930s, the promulgation of that image – essential now to their commercial success – became their preoccupation.

'Easy to listen to', 'attractive', 'variety', 'entertaining', 'human', were the terms in which popular programmes were described; if the 'B' stations were to give the public what it wanted – and to be seen to be doing so – then it assumed these parameters would direct their operation. Similarly, when at times the ABC moved to make certain sections of its programmes 'popular' or when it decided to 'bow to the public',[46] these terms appeared in the description of its new programmes or mode of presentation. But when the ABC entered the realm of the popular, it was with a certain air of cautiousness and formality. In 1938 the ABC moved with uncharacteristic haste to introduce the radio quiz *Spelling Bee*, by now a most successful new programme in America and Britain. ABC personnel were suspicious of this new form, insisting that its success was a matter of novelty value; but they wished to pre-empt the commercial stations laying claim to this programme, now given the stamp of legitimacy by the BBC. Specific conditions were set down to ensure that such programmes were conducted in a proper manner. No prizes were given: our 'competing teams', Charles Moses proudly declared, 'have to be content with the honour and glory.'[47] Commentators on the ABC quiz programmes referred to a 'studied politeness', to the ABC's 'very refined spelling bee'.[48] Though indulging the popular taste for entertaining programmes, the ABC retained a distant tone, its air of formality, rather than relaxed friendliness.

In these discussions of what was popular, of what the listening public demanded, the parameters assumed marked out a particular style, voice and mode of presentation. To be friendly and relaxed, to speak in an everyday, familiar voice and to present material as entertainment rather than as something good for you characterized the popular programmes, guaranteed that they would be popular. The demeanour of the programme was assumed to be essential to its popularity, as well as being the basis upon which it was designated as popular. This point was emphasized when occasionally a broadcaster or an editorial of a radio magazine discussed the possibility of highbrow programmes such as classical music concerts being popular. Certain prescriptions were set down, including that the pieces be short, easy to listen to and of a familiar character – items such as Handel's 'Water Music' or opera arias performed by well-known singers were mentioned. No questions were raised about why one piece of music had become popular and not another, why one piece could be removed from the taint of being 'highbrow'; at issue was the general conduct of the programme within which it was to be heard; this determined whether or not the piece was to be considered too highbrow or not.

For the most part, however, highbrow programmes were not regarded as potentially popular. Rather, lowbrow and popular were equated. The terms within which a popular programme was defined generally duplicated the terms used in letters to the editor by listeners describing themselves as 'lowbrow'. Newspapers and magazines made this equation explicit, defining 'lowbrow' and 'popular' in similar ways and using the terms interchangeably when discussing specific programmes or stars. Central to this equation was the assumption behind both terms of the everydayness of the programmes designated by either or both these labels. Listeners writing in favour of lowbrow programmes commended them for their 'homeliness', 'cosiness' or for their 'not being above our heads'. These qualities were similarly referred to in the delineation of what was popular or more generally, in depicting the style of broadcasting pursued by the 'B' stations. Norman Banks of 3KZ, for example, was frequently rated as a popular broadcaster, a judgement based on the radio polls and plebiscites but explained by his ability to speak in a friendly, homely style.[49] Similarly, the popularity of programmes was said to be determined by their palatability, their heartiness, their cheerfulness, their humanness and their focus on everyday happenings. Popular programmes were represented as everyday in style and content, and as speaking to listeners in their everyday lives.

In these particular forms of talking about radio, then, a clear dichotomy was asserted between the lowbrow and the highbrow, between the popular and the cultured. The difference constituted was a matter of speaking to the majority of people in their everyday existence or form versus speaking to the minority in a non-everyday form. All were invited to participate in this latter culture, but most, it was assumed, could not do so with ease – naturally – and would eschew such programmes as not for them. The language of choice, of what the public wants, represented this process as a question of individual decision or choice: radio was a democratic medium, its riches were open to all.

The equation of popular with lowbrow concealed an important difference between the categories. In the context of radio, popular took its initial definition from the number of consumers for a particular item (or claimed for that item). In explaining this popularity, the orientation of the programme was then described in terms of its concern with the everyday-ordinary and its familiar and friendly style. Lowbrow, on the other hand, took its initial definition from what it was not: highbrow. As a taste and as a quality of the commodity to be consumed, lowbrow was not serious, not art, not concerned with being morally or spiritually uplifting, not preoccupied with uniqueness or 'higher' values. Unlike the category of the popular, the notions of highbrow and lowbrow began with the assumption of a hierarchy of taste or cultural preferences.

This difference between the definition of the popular and the lowbrow was not simply a repetition of how they were defined in other contexts. It stemmed from the particular function of the categories of highbrow and lowbrow played in the construction of the radio audience. In the early 1930s, and to a lesser extent in the late 1920s, radio magazines and radio personnel had begun a campaign to teach listeners to be selective in their listening habits, to pick programmes 'suited to their tastes'. Their pleas for 'intelligent listening' assumed that the tastes of listeners could be met by the radio programmes: everyone was catered for. As soon as the public develops 'a system of selective, rather than continuous listening', H.P. Williams, the first general manager of the ABC, insisted, they will find that everyone can be satisfied by the programmes offered.[50] Earlier the Australian Broadcasting Company had called on listeners to learn the art of listening, to exercise discrimination, to choose programmes rather than simply turn on the radio set, expecting to be pleased by every item on the one station throughout the evening.[51] The newspaper columns and radio magazines, with their increasing preoccupation with listing programmes rather than technical information, similarly advised listeners to consult programmes, to choose.

This advice was part of the process of teaching the radio audience how to be listeners-in, teaching the consumer orientation to radio and its programmes. To switch on the wireless set at random and to leave it on that one station was behaviour appropriate to an interest in radio as technical novelty or scientific wonder; selecting programmes was appropriate behaviour for listening-in. But to assure listeners that the choice was there, that they could select programmes and be satisfied, the categorization of programmes and audience according to a specific set of tastes worked to suggest that this was indeed possible, that programmes and consumers could be readily matched. As Adorno and Horkheimer commented about labels, such as A and B films or the different prices for magazines, such differentiations as highbrow and lowbrow suggest that everyone is catered for by the market through a hierarchical range of goods; the customer is shown that all needs are capable of fulfilment by the culture industry.[52] As labels that had quickly been applied to programmes and to consumers, the terms highbrow/lowbrow worked in this way to suggest that all tastes could be known and catered for by the radio stations. Indeed, Australian listeners were deemed particularly fortunate: the dual system of 'A' and 'B' class broadcasting stations ensured that all preferences and desires were served. Competition made for a vitality in Australian broadcasting, T.W. Bearup of the ABC claimed, but, most importantly, he stressed, the alternative systems made certain that programmes of 'the "popular" class' were available while the ABC stations were 'giving programmes which it is altogether right and fitting that they should provide'.[53] The debate between highbrow and lowbrow represented differences in cultural practices as a question of differences in patterns of consumer choice, and listeners were classified according to their 'brow'.

This categorization constituted people's tastes as an object of knowledge and as a means of pinning them down, putting all listeners in their place. Their tastes could be identified and placed on a hierarchical table. Furthermore, the individuals themselves were specified. It was not simply a question of having a taste for something highbrow; it was a matter of being a highbrow or a lowbrow. As highbrows or lowbrows, all individuals could be specified, known, and all individuals could specify or identify themselves. Tastes, consumption patterns, were represented as crucial means of self-definition.

Similarly, radio plebiscites produced a means of specifying individuals, of pinning listeners down. The development of audience research in the late 1930s in Australia elevated this preoccupation to a science as market research set about knowing, and developing, listeners' patterns of consumption. Plebiscites asked listeners to indicate their favoured programme type, their favourite show, station or personality. The first major attempt was the *Argus* plebiscite in 1925, and they were still being conducted in the mid-1930s by journals such as the *Radio Times* and the *Women's Weekly*. They were publicly represented in two ways: either as a kind of box-office check, a means of 'digging out listeners-in',[54] for stations anxious to know they were being listened to, or as a means of allowing listeners to determine the radio programmes provided: 'the public may fashion its programmes'.[55] Occasionally it was admitted that they were a means of allowing advertisers to catch sight of their potential market. Public gatherings of listeners performed this function as well – station picnics such as those frequently organized by 3AW, community singing and radio clubs – served to materialize audiences for potential advertisers.

But the plebiscites performed two additional functions in the construction of the radio audience and its relationship to the radio programme. The first was that of representing radio stations as responsive to listeners' wants. Listeners could 'have their say', they had a means of communicating with the stations and their programmers. Letters to the editor in radio magazines played the same role – the *Listener In* at various times printed listeners' letters under the heading the 'Listeners' Microphone'. These images denied that radio was a means of one-way communication and represented the consumers of its programmes as active participants in the world of radio. The second function was that of generating a means of knowing or specifying individuals – according to their consumption patterns. Listeners could have their say as representatives of specific taste markets, of a particular consumer orientation. This was the form in which individuals existed in the world of radio: as lovers of dance music, as devotees of Nancy Lee, as fans of Gracie Fields, as followers of cricket, as one of the 75 or 80 per cent who prefer to listen to the 'B' stations.

These were the dominant terms in which the audience was discussed in the language about radio in the print media and the statements of radio personnel and officials. Listeners' letters in magazines and newspapers frequently reproduced and extended this mode of representing the position of the listener-in. In signing themselves as 'lowbrow', and generally in their referring to themselves according to their tastes in music or radio programmes, they appeared to embrace these terms as a meaningful identification. However, listeners' letters also elaborated two alternative positions for the listener-in, two alternative forms in which listeners could have their say.

The licence fee charged by the federal government, first as a means of subsidizing the 'A' stations, and later as a means of financing the ABC, was declared by some listeners as being the form in which they should have their say. These letter writers complained that the licence fee did not operate in this way. The 'B' stations succeeded in catering for the popular taste, yet the 'A' stations, for which they as licence-holders paid, ignored their demands. 'A' class stations, wrote one listener, 'receive more of our licence fee and it is to those who receive our money we have the right to look for our entertainments'.[56] Others objected to licence fees as unjustly requiring the majority of listeners to pay for stations that only catered for the tastes of a minority: 'We, the masses, who comprise over eighty per cent of the listeners, supply with our fees the very life blood of the National Broadcasting System, thereby allowing him [the culture enthusiast] ... to breathe in the culture he deems so necessary.'[57]

These statements insisted that the licence system established a market relationship between the radio audience and the 'A' stations; they did not challenge the construction of the radio audience as consumers. The licence fee constituted a form in which listeners suggested they could have a meaningful say. If the market system was allowed to operate as it should, they argued, then they would have a direct influence on radio programmers. As buyers, or 'masters' as one listener characterized the relationship in rather more feudal terms,[58] they should be able to ensure that the 'A' stations heeded their demands and set out to cater for their interests. The simple market relationship envisaged in these arguments was far less abstract than being a vote in a ballot, a tick on a plebiscite question sheet.

The second alternative form in which listeners' letters represented the position of the listener, the form in which they received the radio programmes offered and desired to have their say about them, was as members of a specific class grouping. Referring to themselves as 'workers', 'working people', 'laboring men', 'the working part of the population', 'a working man's wife', or as 'the working class', most of these listeners called for brighter, more relaxing and entertaining programmes. Criticizing the 'A' stations as catering only for a minority of listeners, they pressed their demands as the majority of listeners and the major proportion – the 'working part' – of the population:

> I frankly think that the Commission does not try to please the majority of listeners. The programmes are unbalanced. Take your publication [the *Wireless Weekly*] of any week and compare the time devoted to high-brow items, as compared with other music, plays or humor ... the great bulk of listeners (working men) call for relaxation. In my humble opinion they do not get it. They then turn to B class stations for an enjoyable programme.[59]

For many such letter writers, their claims were made more urgent by the depression. '[W]hat with these dull days of depression',[60] they complained, they did not wish to come home to hours of classical music on the wireless, to dull talks or a surfeit of gramophone records. Many referred to the wireless as the main form of recreation for working people in these times of depression, as the only thing which allowed them to forget their worries. They did not wish to be educated or 'initiated into high-toned music, but asked for 'plays, long or short, good band concerts, more humor, and less of that highly classical or orchestral music which only appeals to the minority'.[61]

Occasionally one of these writers would be explicit about what they saw as the class bias of the ABC in its programme content and general demeanour. A letter in the *Wireless Weekly* spoke of the failure of the 'A' stations to provide for the majority of listeners and added,

> it is a pleasure to know that there are stations like 2MV that listeners-in can tune-in to when they are fed up with 'Talks in French' or 'Talks on cooking' that want a small bank to buy the ingredients, and other talks that can only be of interest to the wealthy class of N.S.W.[62]

They objected to the snobbishness of the ABC and to the snobbishness it encouraged in its listeners. They spoke of the affectation of the ABC announcers, and of the listeners to the ABC who believed themselves to be superior, 'the thinking members of the community'.[63]

Evidence for the validity of these accusations was furnished by the letters from listeners supporting the ABC, in which they designated themselves as 'music lovers' or 'highbrows'. These listeners argued that 'B' stations worked according to the slogan '"music for the ignorant masses"' and that the 'A' stations, on the other hand, should serve 'the well-informed', the 'thinking people', people of 'good taste', the 'civilised minority', the 'refined class'.[64] Although seldom employing an explicit language of class, these letters proclaimed the appreciation of highbrow radio programmes as an affirmation of one's membership of an élite – a naturally superior group of listeners:

> Would it not be unfair to expect factory-hands, laborers, navvies, etc., to understand and enjoy music and speech that are natural to men of professional status? Likewise, we cannot expect B-class enthusiasts to enjoy entertainment provided for thinking people ... [but] we do oppose their criticism of that which is quite beyond their mental scope.[65]

For this latter group of listeners the opposition between highbrow and lowbrow was claimed to be as much a question of taste as class. Their appreciation of highbrow programmes, of high-class music in particular was a sign of their distinction: 'People who object to high-class music over the air confess their own lack of taste, refinement, and artistic appreciation.'[66] Proclaiming taste to be a collectively recognized symbol and measure of difference, the notion of highbrow constructed a means of unification and of separation: a sense of unification with those of shared tastes and refinement, and a sense of separation or distance from those who lacked the sensibility and judgement to appreciate art.[67]

Some critics of the ABC and its highbrow listeners drew attention to the luxury and symbolic value served by the cultivation of these tastes. They criticized the way in which listeners with highbrow tastes sought to display their superiority, to claim publicly their distinction from all other listeners. Similarly, listeners who referred to themselves as working people pointed, explicitly and implicitly, to the material conditions that separated them from those who could claim for themselves cultural legitimacy. Listeners as 'working people' embraced what was defined as the ordinary, the everyday, and commended the 'B' stations for their friendliness, their humanness. They were tired after their day's labours and did not wish to be subjected to a culture that was unfamiliar and demanding. They rejected the language of taste and refinement of the highbrows and drew attention instead to the class position of those who could and would wish to indulge in such concerns. Highbrow programmes were only of interest to the 'wealthier class', the minority who were not part of the working population, 'the privileged' or 'an exclusive number of the community'.

These listeners used a language that spoke of their position or existence outside the world of radio. They identified themselves first and foremost by their membership of a class – the class of working people. Their interest in or preference for particular radio programmes followed from that primary identification. They offered no critique or argument that the position of listener-in could be anything other than that of the consumer of the goods provided; but they rejected the message that they should identify themselves as consumers, that they should see themselves as defined by their cultural tastes.

To speak of oneself as a 'working man' or one of 'the working part of the population' in this context, drew on a language – the language of class – which had been established as an important mode of political and personal identification in specific historical moments. Its repetition here shows the way in which it continued to play such a role in the 1920s and 1930s. But the rhetoric about taste and consumer choice mobilized by the publicity language surrounding radio contributed to the vitiation of this language of class. The capacity to define their own principles of identity for a whole section of the population was being replaced by an orientation to the marketplace and to the means of self-identification being offered there.

Furthermore, unlike the claims associated with the category of highbrow that represented its consumers as a unified group with fundamental characteristics in common, the image of the lowbrow worked only to construct abstract unities such as 'the majority', 'the mass of the people' or 'the unpopular'. Within this framework, lowbrows made their choice of programme not on the basis of shared understandings or experiences, but as a matter of individual choice. What was popular was, then, a question of the massed vote of individual egos, votes in a referendum or a radio plebiscite. The preference for the everyday, the ordinary, celebrated as the basis of popular programmes appeared to respond merely to the convergence or intersection of private, individual concerns and orientations. The concept of the popular thus represented the common interests or cultural preferences of the majority as accidental or spontaneous, rather than as a possible sign of shared material conditions, common experiences of the social world. And the constant link made between the popular and the lowbrow ensured that the desire for art and entertainment to make itself accessible, 'close' to people's lives, remained simply a preference, one set of tastes in a natural hierarchy of tastes.

The problem of the 'B' class stations

In 1928 a special article in the *Listener In* drew attention to the growing use of the 'B' class stations. Other papers and magazines noted that these stations were beginning to compete as broadcasters with the 'A' stations and suggested to listeners that they could turn to 'B' stations for alternative programmes to those offered by the 'As'. These comments reflected a shift in the operation of the 'B' stations from being simply an extension of the amateur licences – for the use of experimenters, radio enthusiasts and radio traders – to their functioning as broadcasters of radio programmes. The article in the *Listener In* portrayed the 'B' class stations as catering for the needs of sections of the listening public and suggested that a certain number of such stations should be retained 'for the purpose of providing services of a character, such as educational or matters of interest to rural listeners'.[68] This interpretation of the role of the 'B' class stations represented the radio audience and the broadcasting stations within the dominant terms of the language about radio of the period: the audience was constituted by their concerns outside the world of radio – as sectional interests – and the broadcasting stations were transmitters of material, rather than producers of radio programmes. But such discussions of the 'B' stations signalled the changing significance of these stations in Australian broadcasting.

There were other signs. The 'B' class broadcasting stations formed an association in 1928 to protect their interests. The first major preoccupation of this association was to lobby the government for a proportion of the licence fee revenue. The association argued that their stations were increasingly attractive to listeners and hence responsible for some part of the licence revenue collected.[69] The 'B' stations did not yet conceive of themselves as an alternative system of broadcasting, but more of an adjunct to the services offered by the 'A' stations. This model was similarly put forward by listeners and the press in their advocacy of the 'B' stations. As broadcasters, they were not yet spoken of as possessing a special character – a character later to be represented as attributable precisely to their non-reliance on financial support from governmental sources.

Perhaps the most important change was the purchase of 3DB by the *Herald* newspapers in 1929. When 3DB Ltd took over this station from the original licensee, Druleigh Business College, in 1927, its financial arrangements shifted to a dependence on advertising revenue.[70] 3DB promoted itself at this time as initiating 'the American idea of making its revenue from advertisements' and advised that 'any person losing a motor car and valuables of any description could have the fact broadcast immediately upon paying a fee'. The station promised to provide a programme that would favourably compare with those of the 'A' class stations.[71] The purchase of 3DB by the *Herald* marked the beginning of newspaper interest in the control of 'B' class stations.

At the beginning of 1930 the PMG was faced with a large backlog of applications for 'B' class licences from individuals, organizations and companies. No new licences had been issued for some years and powerful bodies such as the Council of Churches were lobbying him to obtain a broadcasting licence for their organization. The 'B' class licences, when first issued in 1924, were granted for an initial period of five years, and so by 1930, with a number of licences now up for renewal, the whole position of 'B' class stations appeared in need of urgent review.

The government had failed to clarify the position of the 'B' class stations before it passed over the 'A' class stations to the Australian Broadcasting Company in 1929, but had set up an advisory committee, chaired by the DPT, H.P. Brown. No parliamentary decision was taken about the future of the 'B' stations, but in determining which bodies should receive licences, Brown, in conjunction with Joseph Lyons, PMG at that time, made decisions crucial to the position and future power of these stations. New licences were issued between 1930 and 1932 to bodies such as the Trades Hall Council in Melbourne (3KZ), the Catholic Church in Sydney (2SM), the Council of Churches in Sydney (2CH), the Adelaide *Advertiser*, owned by the *Herald* since 1929 (5AD), and to a number of other newspapers in various states, including the *Age* in Melbourne, in conjunction with the music company, Allan's, and J.C. Williamson Ltd (3AW). These new licensees were far more economically and politically powerful bodies than the old 'B' class licensees.[72] The 'B' class stations were being placed on a firmer footing and the changes occurring in their conception given official sanction.

The PMG confirmed this commitment in 1930 by announcing that the terms 'A' class and 'B' class were to be dropped from official communications. The 'A' class stations were now to be called the National stations and those operating under the old 'B' class licence were to be described as 'licensed broadcasting stations'. Both the *Listener In* and the *Wireless Weekly* pronounced this official change of names as heralding a new era in the development of private broadcasting: it demonstrated that the private stations formed 'a definite and important part of the broadcasting system'.[73] These stations were no longer to be demeaned by the use of terms that suggested their secondary place. Yet the labels stuck in popular and official language. They continued to be used in newspapers and magazines – including the *Listener In* and the *Wireless Weekly* – in listeners' letters, and less frequently, in parliamentary debates. A deputation to the PMG in 1934 from the Federation of Australian Broadcasting Stations (formed in 1930) pressed for, among other things, the elimination of the label 'B' class in references to their stations and proposed that the term Commercial stations be applied to all their members.[74] The terms 'A' and 'B' class stations, however, remained in common usage throughout the 1930s.

In the press reports of the PMG's announcement in 1930 about 'A' and 'B' class stations, he insisted that the 'A' class stations should, above all, be national in their orientation, hence their new designation by this label. He was less clear about the role or orientation of the 'B' stations, though their position was secured. The *Listener In* interpreted the PMG as encouraging 'B' stations to pursue (or continue to pursue) the sectional – that is, the non-national – interests of the radio-listening public. This representation of the role of the 'B' class stations replicated the *Listener In*'s earlier statement of the 'B' stations' contribution to Australian broadcasting. Since the mid-1920s this had been one of the dominant ways of talking about the 'B' stations: the 'A' stations, paid for by the licences of 'the general body of listeners', must 'provide a comprehensive service of general utility', said the *Daily Telegraph* in 1927, but the 'B' stations, 'not under the same obligation', were free to cater for 'a section or sections of the general public'.[75] The 'B' stations filled in the gap left by the 'A' stations. By 1931 similar arguments were being advanced, but with a different edge: the value of the 'B' stations, declared the *Wireless Weekly*, was that they freed the 'A' stations to be more national in spirit, less concerned with the varied tastes of the listening public.[76] This statement shifted the rhetoric of sectional (members of a group) versus general (national) onto new terrain: the rhetoric of the popular was becoming increasingly important so that the opposition now appeared as the popular (individual interests) versus culture (national). A special domain was being marked out for the 'B' stations. They no longer filled in the gaps left by the 'A' stations, but rather, by doing something different, they created a space for the 'A' stations. This argument provided a justification for the 'B' stations' continued existence and their continued operation as non-government, privately funded bodies.

The Australian Broadcasting Commission was formed on 1 July 1932, but the 'B' stations remained a problem. No official decision had been made about what role, if any, they should be allowed to play, though a large number of 'B' stations now existed (forty-six in 1932). The Prime Minister, Joseph Lyons, stated early in 1932, while the ABC's bill was still being debated in parliament, that 'Cabinet had not yet gone into the question of B class stations'.[77] In the course of these debates some politicians argued that both 'A' and 'B' stations should be nationalized, some argued that the 'B' stations should receive a portion of the licence fee, and others argued that the 'B' stations should be permitted to remain independent. The ABC bill was concerned only with the 'A' class stations.

The Lyons government presented the ABC bill to parliament in basically the same form as it had been prepared by the Labor Scullin government in 1931. It included a provision that the ABC could accept advertising in the form of sponsored programmes. Before it was passed this part of the bill was amended so that the ABC was prohibited from all advertising. The government was accused of meekly carrying out the instructions of *Herald* newspapers and of being dominated by press interests. Lyons, according to Walker's analysis of Australian newspapers, enjoyed a 'favourable' relationship with the press, but in the case of Keith Murdoch (the powerful newspaper proprietor in Melbourne) that relationship was much more than a question of good will. In Walker's terms, Lyons and Murdoch were close – friends who lunched with each other when in the same city.[78] As PMG of the Labor government in 1930, Lyons had been instrumental in the *Advertiser*'s receiving a 'B' class licence.[79] Now as Prime Minister and leader of the new United Australian Party (UAP), his government was responsible for changing its own bill to ensure that the ABC could not compete with the 'B' stations in the field of advertising. Intermittently, throughout the 1930s, questions were raised in parliament and in certain sections of the press, about the continued existence of the 'B' stations as private bodies. But by the time the ABC's bill was passed, the 'B' stations were no longer a problem to be solved by legislation. They had become a powerful political force. A BBC official remarked of the position occupied by the 'B' class stations in Australia: 'They are backed by a very powerful section of the Press – a section, incidentally, which put the present Prime Minister into power and maintains him there.'[80]

For the new ABC, the 'B' stations quickly constituted a problem of a different kind. From the beginning people associated with the ABC were uneasy about the existence of these other broadcasting stations. Charles Lloyd Jones, the first chairman of the ABC, and his deputy, Herbert Brookes, were both unhappy that the government had failed to nationalize all stations, though they disagreed about a solution. Brookes argued that the ABC should fight to get rid of the 'B' stations. Jones insisted that these stations were so politically strong as to be almost untouchable. It was the government that had decided to have this dual system of broadcasting and they would have to worry about it, not the

ABC. 'It is a political question,' he declared, and the ABC should get on with its own business.[81] But the 'B' stations did not remain only a political question for the ABC; throughout the 1930s they constituted a problem for the ABC in a variety of ways.

The most straightforward issue was one of competition. Throughout the 1930s the ABC lost staff to the 'B' stations, either because of higher wages or because of dissatisfaction with the ABC. As the 'B' stations became larger concerns, the ABC complained of the amount of money their competitors were able to put into programmes, thus creating expectations in listeners about programme standards. But perhaps the competition that hurt the most, as far as the ABC was concerned, was the 'B' stations' access to BBC programmes. Charles Lloyd Jones wrote to John Reith of the BBC at the end of 1932 complaining that 'the prestige of the National Service in Australia was being damaged' because 'B' stations were being given access to BBC programmes.[82]

Though the BBC wished to secure a reliable market for its programmes by maintaining good relations with the ABC, it continued to have some contact with the commercial stations throughout the 1930s, never quite understanding (or admitting to understand) the ABC's desire to establish an intimate and exclusive relationship between the two national institutions. For the ABC, the BBC stood for cultural legitimacy and was their source of authority for broadcasting innovations. For the BBC, the ABC was to be taken seriously as a reliable market for its programmes and as the national broadcasting institution of an Empire country; but at times personnel within the BBC complained of the ABC. In private, they criticized the ABC's sycophantic attitude and suggested that its interest in BBC programmes was sometimes dubious. In 1936 one BBC official noted the complaints made by Charles Moses, as general manager of the ABC, that the BBC was supplying talks 'largely by unknowns', and commented that 'it has been obvious to me for some time that the Commission is much more interested in personalities of speakers than in subjects'.[83]

Less clear was the question of whether or not the ABC was in competition with the 'B' stations for audiences. The ABC throughout the 1930s remained uncertain whether it was in the business of capturing audiences: for the most part it could not resolve its commitment to culture with its obligations, as a medium of mass communication, to the radio audience. Public statements by ABC officials usually recorded a primary commitment to culture. T.W. Bearup, as manager in Victoria for the ABC, represented the ABC's role as providing 'a bureau of the fine arts'.[84] Such statements considered the ABC's relationship with the radio audience – the general audience – only within the terms of the ABC's education function. But educational objectives also entailed a primary commitment to culture: culture was to be conveyed to a wider group than its traditional participants to raise the standard of taste of the general community. The culture was not to be transformed by this process of dissemination, and indeed it was imperative that it should not be undermined by any attempts to popularize it, to 'sugar the pill'.[85]

The 'B' stations in this instance did not constitute a problem as competitors so much as a threat to the authority of the ABC's cultural stance. Some ABC personnel argued that the 'B' stations freed them from any obligations to please the popular taste in radio programmes, but for the most part they believed that the ABC was placed at some disadvantage, that its status was undermined by the existence of the 'B' stations. The BBC, both the ABC's mentor and measure, could be far more uncompromising, they claimed, than the ABC. John Reith's dictum that the BBC would give its public 'something slightly better than they want' was difficult to emulate because the ABC could not dictate the direction broadcasting would go in Australia, unlike the BBC in Britain. When excluding crooners, various ABC personnel argued that they could not be as ruthless as the BBC. The BBC had ruled that it was banning from its programmes,

> any form of anaemic or debilitated vocal performance by male singers, insincere and over-sentimental performance by women singers, numbers which are slushy in sentiment, or are otherwise not good in taste, and numbers, with or without lyrics, which are based upon tunes borrowed from standard classical works.[86]

The listening public, the BBC decreed, were to hear only 'virile' music. In Australia, some ABC personnel argued, competition from the 'B' stations required that crooners would have to be heard on ABC programmes, though in 'very small doses'. Many people like crooners, they claimed, and the 'B' stations would not follow the ABC's example by excluding them from programmes. Anxious to follow the BBC's lead, the ABC felt itself hampered by the presence of the 'B' stations.

Occasionally at least, the ABC felt forced into the business of capturing audiences by the existence of the 'B' class stations. At other times it reacted vehemently to challenges or criticisms of its operation which employed a market sense of public service: the ABC's primary function was to 'assist a democracy rather than to entertain' said one official statement of the ABC's role.[87] Such a commitment, it declared, ensured that the ABC necessarily could attract only a minority audience when competing with stations whose financial existence depended on attracting 'the mass listening ear' and pandering to the demands of the masses to be entertained. The 'B' stations had now established themselves as catering for the majority of the wireless audience: the listening public. The ABC insisted that its public service obligations, its role as an institution of national culture, precluded it from an orientation to the market.

Yet the ABC remained uneasy about its relationship with the listening public throughout the 1930s. The 'problem of the B stations', as formulated by people connected with the ABC, was a way of talking about that relationship. Whether they adopted the position of defiant insistence that the ABC could not compete with the 'B' stations for audiences or complained about the 'B' stations as placing pressure on them to be more popular, the issue being addressed was how to reconcile the ABC's official position as a 'bureau of culture' with its form as a medium for mass communication. Clearly the ABC as a producer of programmes did operate as a bureau, an academy of sorts: it encouraged Australian artists (through its competition for new plays, through eisteddfods, by paying singers, musicians and actors, and so on); and it acted as an entrepreneur of high culture, in particular through its orchestral concerts. But what had this to do with being radio – with being a medium of mass communication from a central source to listeners or consumers of programmes, the form in which radio was now established?

The language of public service formulated a conception of the ABC's role as serving – encouraging and protecting – the national culture, the 'best self' of the nation. Cleary, as the chairman under whom the ABC had begun to obtain some sense of purpose, insisted that only the ABC as 'an organisation devoted to national service and not to profit can properly be entrusted with the preservation and cultivation of those "finer things of life"'.[88] As such a body or academy, however, the majority of members – the radio audience – were treated as passive eavesdroppers, as non-participants. For those who felt themselves already participants rather than simply recipients of this culture (or who wished to display that they were), this mode of address did not concern them. For this minority audience, the ABC disseminated a culture that was familiar and in which they recognized themselves. For the larger section of the radio audience, on the other hand, this culture was not recognized as familiar, nor as authoritative, and they turned away.

The problem of the 'B' stations for the ABC was a problem of authority. This was the basis of their envy of the BBC's position of monopoly: the ABC with the 'B' stations beside them could not speak with authority to the listening public, nor would the majority of that audience listen to them. The ABC was constituted to speak on behalf of the national culture, but a large part of the nation would not listen to it. This tension was articulated in other terms too: the ABC's yearly report for 1932–3 spoke of the difficulty of not being able to coerce, to 'compel' the radio audience. The masses were taking the ABC at its word, it seemed. The culture of the ABC was produced by a special group of 'artists' and 'intellectuals' and its appreciation came 'naturally' only to a small group of discriminating consumers. Hailed as consumers – who would, however, have to be taught this culture as an acquired taste – the masses responded to the rhetoric of an implied choice and became self-consciously 'lowbrow'.

This alternative, offered by the discourse of 'highbrow versus lowbrow', did not work as a critique of this language of culture, but it did provide a position from which the claims to sacredness and the distance of that highbrow culture could be rejected. The implicit judgements by the ABC of legitimate taste, its 'airs' about itself, were to be ignored. The 'problem of the B stations' for the ABC was that of a cultural body, required as a medium of mass communication to take an educative interest in a broader group than the traditional participants in this culture, but with no means of coercion and no means of insisting upon its legitimacy and authority. Within this framework the only alternatives were either to make some concessions to the 'popular taste' or to talk solely to the 'minority audience'.

For those in the ABC who desired to speak to more than the minority audience, the BBC stood as the model. As a monopoly it could speak with the authority the ABC lacked and to which they aspired. Raymond Williams's analysis of the establishment of the BBC, however, suggests that the BBC's authority, its confidence in its own voice, stemmed from an additional source. He argues that the BBC's establishment and public acceptance as a monopoly until after the second world war depended on a 'pre-existing cultural hegemony'. In Britain, the existence of an 'unusually compact ruling class' had successfully introduced a dominant version of the national culture. There was at least an appearance of consensus about what were legitimate cultural values and who could speak on behalf of that culture. It was this that ensured acceptance of a particular definition of the public service role of the BBC, its monopolistic control of the airwaves as a public service, and the confidence of its voice.[89] John Reith's dictum that the BBC would give its public 'something better' than they wanted was not simply the expression of a forceful man; it reflected the position of the BBC as a cultural institution and the structure of the cultural field in Britain at that time.

The power of newspaper interests, and more generally the 'B' class stations, ensured that the ABC did not acquire a monopoly similar to the BBC's and nor was it to achieve this position in the years to come. But Raymond Williams's analysis of the BBC suggests that it was not this lack of monopoly control – the competition from the commercial radio system – that undermined the status of the ABC or detracted from its ability to speak as a cultural authority. The difference between the ABC and the BBC was a matter of the extent to which a state institution could draw on and speak on behalf of a social group (or groups) whose cultural understandings were represented as general to the society (or symbolizing the 'best self' of that society). In Australia, British culture retained a powerful position in defining legitimate culture, but new social groups without the traditional alliances to Britain were becoming powerful economically, politically and culturally.[90] The ABC, in its looking to the BBC, nourished traditional orientations to things British. Yet the ABC was part too of the thrust away from a colonial, dependent culture. It was required to foster Australian art and intellectual work, and in this way reflected the moves occurring in the field of cultural relations to define an independent Australia or at least a non-British Australia. The ABC's uncertain voice was a product of the shifts taking place in the field of cultural and social relations.

While unable to speak on behalf of the cultural leadership or dominance of a particular social group, the ABC did play a role in constituting cultural links among certain powerful groups in Australia. Occasions like symphony concerts with their rituals and displays of shared understandings provided a context in which connections (both symbolic and physical) among different groups could be forged and affirmed; occasional complaints to newspapers or radio magazines suggest that the concerts organized by the ABC performed this function. Letters spoke of the dominance of 'society people' on the organizing committees for concerts, of the ABC's policy of permitting season ticket-holders to retain their seats indefinitely as favouring 'the privileged' and 'the wealthy people', of the concerts being more 'a fashion parade' than for music-lovers, and of 'the musical-cum-society clique' ensuring that public bookings for tickets closed overnight.[91] Nor was the ABC an unwitting participant in this process of establishing a 'society' atmosphere at its orchestral concerts. When the orchestral concerts in Brisbane continued to be an embarrassing flop in 1939, the general manager recommended a tactic he said had been tried successfully elsewhere: persuade a group of people to form a social committee who were likely, 'by their own attendance' or 'apparent enthusiasm', to be able to make it '"the correct thing" to be seen at orchestral concerts'.[92]

The consumption of culture in such contexts may have different meanings for different groups. For the economically powerful, it can facilitate an opportunity for the display of wealth and leisure, the luxury of being able to distance oneself from the economic world and everyday life. For a professional, educated class, on the other hand, it provides an opportunity to exercise superior and discriminating knowledge, to exhibit the capacity to be able to distance oneself from these worlds at the abstract level.[93] The ABC provided a basis for the establishment of links between these groups, a sense of shared culture, despite possible differences in orientation. Orchestral concerts were occasions for the public display and affirmation of these common understandings, but the ABC more generally, with its culture to be appreciated only by the more 'discriminating' sections of the community, offered a more intangible sense of unity, a sense affirmed by notions of distinction and exclusion. The ABC proffered a public and private certification of the identity, unity and legitimacy of its listeners as a (cultural) élite.

But the ABC's role in the construction of cultural links among ruling social groups was limited. The ABC's culture was not one with which all such groups identified. Some rejected such artistic and intellectual orientations in favour of all that was modern, practical and scientific. People such as Keith Murdoch did not oppose the ABC because his newspaper interests were in competition with this institution, or because its public service role was anathema to his virulent commercialism; he rejected the ABC as a cultural body because it stood for art and not a technocratic science, the traditions of intellectuals, artists and musicians and not practical common sense, for British/Australian ways and not American/Australian ways, for cultural heritage and not modern individualism. Thus the ABC was unable to pursue a cultural stance that would have legitimacy among all sections of the powerful, while it was without authority among those who talked power.

After the second world war, the ABC would change its mode of operation to provide (in any city where there were two stations) a National programme on one station of more 'serious' material 'to cater for the more discriminating section of the community', and an Interstate programme of 'lighter entertainment' for 'those listeners who preferred light and easily assimilated entertainment'.[94] The ABC was now, in part, addressing its listeners as markets, tastes, in much the same way as its commercial competitors. The war had placed new demands on the ABC and expectations that it would be more responsible to the 'popular taste'. But the provision of alternative programmes followed the BBC's lead and like the BBC entailed an implicit streaming of programmes (despite the denials of Richard Boyer, the ABC chairman). The BBC broadcast three programmes, thus making finer distinctions between its listeners' tastes, but both institutions referred to hierarchies – to 'ordinary listeners' versus those of greater 'discrimination', those 'persons of taste, intelligence and education'.[95] Listeners were now clearly defined by what they consumed in the broadcasting field.

The 'B' stations were defined as a political problem in the mid-1930s when they began to form networks or chains of stations. In 1930, 2UW arranged to broadcast reports of the cricket test matches being conducted in England that year, sponsored by advertising, which it then sold to broadcasting stations in several states. This 'hook-up' of broadcasting stations was greeted by various commentators as an important step in the development of the 'B' class stations. The 'chain broadcasts' established a basis for co-operation between these stations and opened up possibilities of a national audience for the 'B' class stations. Such a potential audience promised to place these stations on a different basis: a national audience could be used to attract the interest of big advertisers. The *Wireless Weekly* predicted that 'B' stations would be able to develop sponsored, and hence better, programmes.[96]

In 1933, 2UW again was part of a signficant step in the progress of 'B' class broadcasting. When the ABC was established in 1932, the Australian Broadcasting Company, under the chairmanship of Stuart Doyle, was not disbanded. Doyle (who had not been offered a position on the new Commission) announced in 1932 that his company would secure 'B' class stations in every capital city. In 1933 he took over station

2UW, a move seen as a first step in his plan to run a chain of stations throughout Australia. His intention was clearly to compete with the ABC as a national system of broadcasting stations.[97] To indicate the seriousness of his challenge, Doyle attempted to use the initials 'A.B.C.' to announce and advertise station 2UW, a step the ABC moved to prevent with some haste and anger, claiming sole rights to the title. 2UW became one of the stations in the Commonwealth Broadcasting Network which in 1937 joined up with the *Argus* network to make a chain of twelve stations. Declaring itself 'The Cream of Australian Entertainment', this new Commonwealth Broadcasting Network claimed to cover 80 per cent of all Victorian, New South Wales and Queensland audiences.[98] A national audience for 'B' class stations was beginning to appear a reality.

In 1935, the PMG introduced a regulation limiting the number of stations that could be controlled, directly or indirectly, by any person, company or organization. The maximum number of stations was one in any capital city, four in a state, or eight in the Commonwealth. The regulation was prompted particularly by the activities of AWA. In 1935 this company was advertising itself as having a 'Six Link Chain' in NSW provincial cities and its letterhead in 1936 claimed it to be associated with twenty-three stations.[99] In 1937, the PMG recorded AWA as holding the licences of four stations in Australia and one in Port Moresby, Papua; holding shares in two stations; being responsible for conducting the services of 2CH (its licence was still owned by the Council of Churches); and having interests in four other stations.[100] The PMG's move to regulate station ownership was attacked by such bodies as AWA, but was also bitterly opposed by the Australian Federation of Broadcasting Stations. Voigt, who had been founder of the Federation, resigned from the organization, as did its secretary in protest at the Federation's stand. They supported the government's moves as an attempt to prevent AWA and other large bodies gaining a stranglehold on commercial broadcasting in Australia; but they were minority voices. Powerful bodies, including press interests, ensured that the PMG's regulation was limited to questions of ownership, not with the linking up of stations to form networks or chains.[101]

The Macquarie Broadcasting Network was formed in 1938. Its publicity statement for various radio journals in July 1938 announced that it had fourteen member stations 'from Queensland right round to Perth'.[102] One month after its establishment it was claiming to have stations in every state, including the Australian Capital Territory; and by

1940 it was selling itself to advertisers as reaching 90 per cent of Australian listeners. Member stations of the network were urged to clear a set amount of time in the peak evening period (6.45 p.m. to 9.30 p.m. on weekdays) so that sponsors could be offered standard times on all stations throughout Australia. Advertisers were being sold a national coverage of the Australian population; the Macquarie slogan was 'Make Australia your Market – Use the Macquarie Network'.[103]

The stated purpose of the network was to sell station time to advertisers and to produce and distribute programmes for member stations. Macquarie Broadcasting Services attended to the programme side of transcriptions and the production of programmes in Australia. Artransa, a company owned by Macquarie, imported transcriptions from the USA and England. In Australia, programme production was handled by Frederick Daniell. Macquarie constituted a culture industry by itself with interests in organizations such as a record production company, a company selling transcriptions to New Zealand, the Australian and New Zealand Theatre Company, a number of broadcasting stations, and a World Library transcription agency.[104]

Control over programme production was an important feature of the service offered by Macquarie Network to member stations. Until its formation, the most important trend in programme production for commercial broadcasting had been the role of advertising agencies. Two advertising agencies in particular, George Patterson and J. Walter Thompson, both with intimate connections with American broadcasting, were major producers of programmes, a position they maintained throughout the 1940s (in 1946 these agencies were said to still control 50 per cent of all programmes on peak-time commercial broadcasts).[105] Macquarie constituted itself as a challenge to the advertising agency's dominance: the network idea was sold to stations as returning control over programmes to broadcasters and more generally allowing them once again to determine how their total broadcasting sessions would be conducted. Daniell had been genuinely concerned with this issue as early as 1935 when he complained that the advertising department of 2UE was being allowed to dictate programme initiatives and to overrun all 2UE programmes with blatant and excessive advertising.[106] In his campaign to establish what would eventually become Macquarie Network, Daniell was particularly anxious to prevent the total dominance of advertising agencies, and at the station level advertising departments, in the programme production business.

Daniell's preoccupation was not simply a concern for good radio; he saw it as essential to the commercial success of radio. For the 'B' stations the radio audience was a body of consumers to be sold to advertisers. Programmes of good 'listener appeal' were necessary to the capture of audiences for their sale to advertisers. Similarly, programmes at regular and predictable times of the day and the overall flow of programmes were key factors in acquiring and keeping an audience. Primary obligations were declared to the development of attractive programmes, but the driving force behind these concerns was the acquisition of audiences for each part of the broadcasting day that could be sold to advertisers.

> As far as Macquarie Network Stations are concerned, for years a great deal of money and all our efforts have been directed to producing programmes of a high standard of entertainment, so as to build up our listening audience. Since the standard of entertainment offered by Network stations is the very foundation of the acceptance of the Network with advertisers, we feel that standard must be very jealously guarded.[107]

In public, commercial stations addressed the radio audience as freely choosing consumers of programmes. Commercial broadcasting, they declared, set out to please the majority of listeners all the time. This rhetoric built on the representation of listeners as not simply having tastes, but being tastes in radio programmes. Whether as a particular market (those, for example, for whom 2UW as a racing station catered) or as a member of the general listening public (the popular taste in radio programmes) commercial broadcasting catered for your every need and whim. And it was your choice: 'The austere heights of grand opera or celebrity concerts are not the concern of the commercial stations. "Programming" concentrates on variety and popular appeal.'[108] As the market for commercial broadcasting, the radio audience determined the nature of its programmes: the massed egoistic vote of the listening public. Choice was a matter of the individual's whim, yet the reality of that individuality and choice was to be one anonymous vote in the mass market.

In private, the 'B' stations were concerned primarily with how to represent that mass vote as measurable, something that could be known. A number of discourses were deployed in the attempt to assure advertisers that they were in fact being sold an audience (and a receptive one). The opposition lowbrow versus highbrow facilitated a means of talking about what was popular – an image of the content and style of a programme was linked automatically with its potential consumer interest. When station 2KA (Katoomba, NSW) opened, it assumed a natural connection between a certain programme type and a mass audience in order to sell station time to advertisers: 'We have planned the greatest appeal to the greatest number of listeners by providing only sweet, melodious and bright music. . . . The listeners will be served – results for you *must* follow.'[109] Such publicity statements constructed a popular aesthetic as a means of representing the mass audience – the popular – as known and understood. In the business of selling audiences to advertisers what mattered was the appearance, the unproblematic character of these means of specifying the audience.

Magazines such as *Broadcasting Business* played a role by advising advertisers about the type of programme likely to be useful in selling their product, and in telling success stories about programmes. *Chatterbox Corner*, with Nicky and Nancy Lee, was praised as 'doing a good job in placing new products on the Victorian Market'.[110] Moreover, these magazines, and the publicity material of the stations themselves, produced portraits of the typical listener to particular programmes or to radio in general as a way of conjuring up the listening public for potential advertisers. Images such as radio provides 'a latch key to nearly every home' or the description of listeners as being 'the family group in its moments of relaxation awaiting the advertiser's message'[111] again portrayed the radio audience as known and understood.

Listener surveys were the most powerful technique employed in the representation of the popular, of the listening public as known. These extended the earlier methods of radio plebiscites and public gatherings of listeners as ways of materializing audiences and attracting the interest of advertisers in radio as a means of reaching consumers. But survey methodology evoked the image of science as a means of convincing advertisers that they really were catching a glimpse of this potential market. The development of industrial psychology and the more methodical processes of listener research provided persuasive evidence that listeners were being measured, that their daily habits and tastes in radio programmes were known. McNair's book on radio advertising included a foreword by Dr A.H. Martin, lecturer in psychology at the University of Sydney and honorary director of the Australian Institute of Industrial Psychology, as testimony to the authority of the surveys reported by McNair, and to their science. The use of sampling techniques, McNair claimed, furnished an accurate picture of the radio audience – of the listening habits and preferences of the general audience, as well as of specific sections of that audience. This information, he insisted, was essential to the advertiser: 'No advertising message can attain to its maximum effectiveness, unless it is delivered at the right time and to the right people.'[112]

The radio audience was being measured, pinned down – not primarily, in this instance, according to their preferences for radio programmes, but according to their potential as consumers of other products. While the radio audience was being persuaded that they as the listening public could be totally catered for by the broadcasting stations, their every need identified and provided for within the world of radio, radio advertisers were being persuaded that the radio audience could be fully known as consumers, their patterns of daily life and consumption activities measured. 2CH advertised itself as offering:

> Extensive Coverage of Better Class Homes ... resulting from high quality entertainment appeal makes 2CH the logical choice of advertisers who want immediate sales of reasonably priced products. Sell over 2CH and make your radio advertising really profitable because ... 2CH attracts a Money Spending Public.[113]

To public officials, the commercial stations used a different language again. Justifying their networking activities, they represented the relationship between the 'B' stations and the radio audience as a matter of serving 'the best interests of the listening public'; networking promoted the public interest 'through the development of resources generally beyond the capacity of individual stations'.[114] By the early 1940s the network principle had been established. A few public figures, like John Curtin, Labor leader of the federal opposition, opposed the practice, but it was quickly disappearing from the agenda of broadcasting issues. In 1942 the Gibson Committee, a parliamentary committee established to examine the broadcasting system in Australia, dealt briefly with networking in its final report. The Gibson Committee concluded that there was nothing inherently wrong with the networking system, recommending only that future developments be watched to prevent monopoly control.[115]

The 'B' stations were no longer problems in the political arena. The PMG would be concerned with issues of censorship in the 1940s, but its regulations applied to all stations. In the post-second world war period, monopolies would remain a major issue in relation to the media more generally rather than the commercial stations by themselves. The ABC was to become more of a problem than the commercial stations, though the role of the latter would be considered in general inquiries into broadcasting in Australia. The ABC would remain uncertain of its commitment and relationship to the radio audience. The 'B' stations, on the other hand, had elaborated a number of ways of representing their relationship to the listening audience to suit the various contexts in which they operated.

5

EAVESDROPPING ON THE OUTSIDE WORLD

No country, it was said, had embraced radio so eagerly. Australians listened to their sets for long hours compared to people in other countries and at the beginning of 1940 had twenty-five ABC stations and ninety-eight commercial stations serving them across the continent.[1] The radio told them of a world, a reality, that broadcasters and listeners shared together – the everyday ordinary; this world was presented as their domain, the sum-total of their normal social experiences. But in special programmes radio told them of another world, a world that was separate, distanced, from their daily lives. This was the outside world of public occasions, political wranglings, and unusual events. Radio brought its listeners news of the non-ordinary in the comfort and security of their own homes, their daily lives.

As it happens

In a speech to parliament in 1923, the PMG, W.G. Gibson, had praised wireless broadcasting for its potential 'to play a big part in the transmission of news'.[2] He cast his prediction in terms of radio being akin to the telephone, but not in competition with this service: radio would transmit news and information to a mass audience rather than act as a means of information through point-to-point or individual-to-individual communication. But radio news as a significant feature of broadcast programmes developed slowly. At first, the programmes defined as news on radio had taken the form of a broadcaster reading out information and stories from the daily newspapers. There was no conception among broadcasting personnel that radio required or would benefit from the collection and compilation of its own news and information, nor was radio conceived of as a source of immediate information itself. The service offered and commended as a powerful justification in these early years for the exploitation of broadcasting technology was one of the transmission of information already collected and framed as 'news' by other agencies.

Two factors determined this reliance on newspapers for radio news and information. The first was the lack of any content natural to radio; no notion or ideas of what should be broadcast through the use of wireless technology pre-dated its development as a domestic apparatus. Reading the newspaper to listeners was merely one of the devices used by early broadcasters to fill the on-air time. For some listeners this service was of little value, but it was hailed as a major advance for those listeners living in the country, where metropolitan papers often took days to arrive. They could now receive news long before the newspapers reached them, and for some it was their only means of receiving information about the outside world. Farmers were specially well served with up-to-date market and weather information not previously available to them. The extent to which they could take advantage of this service depended, however, on whether they could afford a receiving set, whether they could be bothered with the difficulties of re-charging the large batteries needed (city listeners who needed to use batteries could take them to their local radio shop to be re-charged), and whether reception was good in their area.

The second factor involved in radio's reliance on newspapers had more long-term effects. The newspaper companies from the beginning had appointed themselves as guardians in the field of news collection and dissemination. In the early 1920s, these companies were concerned only that radio stations acknowledge the newspaper from which they read their news. By 1929, newspapers, and in particular the Australian Newspaper Conference, an affiliation of newspapers including many of the major metropolitan dailies in the eastern states, were moving to restrict the length and timing of radio news. In 1932 the newly formed ABC made arrangements with the Australian Newspaper Conference that were to curtail the development of radio news programmes until after the second world war. It was a 'gentleman's agreement' because the Conference was not a corporate body; nevertheless, attempts by the ABC, beginning in 1935, to introduce modifications to the organization of its news programmes were met with vigorous opposition from the newspapers.

The agreement limited the ABC to five news broadcasts a day each of five minutes' duration. The news session to be taken from the morning papers between 7.50 a.m. and 8.00 a.m. could be repeated some time between 8.00 a.m. and 11.00 a.m., and supplementary information from these papers added for a bulletin between 1.00 p.m. and 2.00 p.m.; a news session could be given between 7.50 p.m. and 8.00 p.m. from the evening papers, and repeated between 10.00 p.m. and 10.30 p.m. In addition, for overseas news, the ABC signed an agreement with Australian Associated Press permitting it to use a total of 200 words of cabled news a day. The ABC was required to acknowledge the source of their news within the allocated time of five minutes, and at one stage the newspapers attempted to require the acknowledgement both before and after the news. Supplementary news information collected by the ABC itself was restricted to the ABC sports programmes and routine information like weather and market reports. A special concession permitted the ABC to broadcast news about events of national importance outside the normal news periods no more than twenty times a year; but the ABC remained free to broadcast 'on the spot' descriptions of events. The ABC's bill had not required that it establish a news-gathering organization, nor had it been provided with the financial facilities to do so. No doubt any such move would have met with complaints of competition from the newspapers, as the proposal to allow the ABC sponsored programmes had. It was nevertheless expected that the ABC would provide news programmes. Thus the newspapers were able to represent the severely restrictive arrangements, to which the ABC initially agreed, as a service for which the ABC was asked to pay only a nominal fee of £200 per annum.[3]

Throughout the 1920s and 1930s various commentators spoke of radio as a 'newspaper of the air'. The reading of newspapers to listeners reinforced this conception of radio news. The technology of broadcasting was not yet thought about as requiring or facilitating anything particular in the field of news collection or dissemination. In the late 1930s, Frank Dixon, who for a short time was to play a key role in the development of ABC news, wrote to Charles Moses pointing out that there was no national daily newspaper in Australia. The ABC, he advocated, could do much to cultivate a national outlook by filling the gap – by providing 'a truly national news service'. But Dixon claimed no special role for radio in this sphere; he characterized its place in the field by the phrase, the 'Spoken Newspaper'.[4]

Until 1936 the ABC news was read directly from the newspapers by an announcer: each state attended to its own news programme, drawing on local, metropolitan papers and compiling their own bulletins from the cable news. Towards the end of 1935, Charles Moses had begun to reorganize the ABC to produce the voice and the image of a national body. The establishment of an authoritative, national news service formed part of his strategy. Moses was concerned both to provide a nationally co-ordinated service, and to change the presentation of the news. He appointed a federal news editor, Frank Dixon, and announced that the news would be specially written for broadcasting – the newspaper items paraphrased rather than simply read. Yet the distinction he made between the needs of newspapers and the needs of radio was only a matter of writing style: 'What we propose to do is to paraphrase, or re-write, the news into spoken English, and to make it a good deal easier to listen to.'[5] Radio news continued to be conceived as sharing the same basic form as newspaper news.

In the late 1930s, however, a number of innovations emerged that began to define a special role for radio news. The first was an American experiment, in which listeners were treated to a dramatic re-creation, presented by professional actors and accompanied by sound effects, of the major items of news for each week. In 1935 the ABC presented such a broadcast: a dramatized account of the conflict between Italy and Abyssinia in the form of a play – with elaborate sound effects of war and crowds cheering as an actor spoke the words of the Emperor Haile Selassie 'in a resonant bass voice'.[6] Letters to the *Argus* from listeners reviled this example of 'hideous realism' and 'bad taste'.[7] But for the most part, the ABC eschewed such experiments, following in the footsteps of the BBC, where such techniques of presentation had been declared appropriate only for special features to review the year's major events or for topics of '"picturesque" value', not for contemporary events.[8]

Commercial stations, on the other hand, eagerly adopted this innovation with programme titles such as *Time Marches On* and *Thrills*, imitating the American programmes. 3DB Melbourne carried the former show, performed by a group of actors, the Time Radio Players. In October 1936, it announced that it would produce another such feature to complement the great success of the first. The latter programme, *Millions in the Making*, would carry the dramatized stories of millionaires like John D. Rockefeller and Cecil Rhodes, and would employ the same 'fast-moving radio technique'. Sound effects, quick changes of scene and brisk dialogue were said to be essential to the excitement and success of such programmes.[9]

These broadcasts explored the notion that radio could take its audience to the actual events, allow them to feel 'as if' present at these 'great moments' of history. This concept was further developed with programmes that used the actual voices of public figures, the real actors in history. Listeners heard the voices of Hitler and the Prime Minister of Great Britain on his return to 10 Downing Street from Munich in 1938.[10] Such uses of broadcasting technology were confined to programmes clearly distinguished from the formal news broadcasts, but they contributed to the extension of radio's activity in the area of news broadcasting.

Developments in the area of descriptive broadcasts also began to extend and define radio's particular role in the field of news collection and dissemination. Again this category of broadcasts was seen, at first, as distinct from news broadcasts but innovations in this arena changed the way in which broadcasting personnel understood the tasks of radio news. The differentiation between news and descriptive broadcasts was enshrined in the agreement between the ABC and the Australian Newspaper Conference; this feature of the agreement reflected established practice, it was not one forced on the ABC. The ABC could provide detailed information and descriptions of events of national importance outside the normal news sessions. When George V died in January 1936 and Edward VIII prepared to succeed him to the throne, broadcasts about these events were treated as descriptive rather than as news.

The development of descriptive broadcasts as a separate category of programmes did not depend on the nature of the events described, but emerged out of radio's earlier preoccupation with stunt broadcasts. Outside broadcasts had been made of a wide variety of events, ordinary and extraordinary, as a means of thrilling listeners. It was in this form that broadcasters began to explore and exploit an image of radio as 'actually being there', permitting listeners to 'eavesdrop', to be present at an event 'as it happens'. They presented these broadcasts as the sphere of broadcast description programmes or 'actuality' broadcasts, not as radio news.

The first occasion on which radio stations dressed up their stunts in the dignified clothes of a description of 'an event of national importance' was the opening of Parliament House in Canberra by the Duke of York. Though the broadcast was marred by bad static, it was greeted with great excitement. Royalty continued to provide such opportunities in the development of descriptive broadcasts, but other events were also eagerly pursued by wireless broadcasters. The adventurous feats of aviators were creating considerable public interest and radio descriptions of their arrival in Australia quickly became an essential feature of the event. The PMG in 1930 went to great lengths to ensure that radio stations could transmit information of Amy Johnson's arrival in Darwin 'as it happens'.[11] To do so the PMG arranged to transmit the message one minute before the landing did actually happen so that stations could broadcast its occurrence at precisely the right moment. Similarly, the opening of the Sydney Harbour Bridge in March 1932 provided an excellent opportunity for radio stations to demonstrate to listeners their capacity to bring them exciting descriptions of major events. Though on this occasion the event proved more thrilling than some stations were prepared for, as some announcers missed the excitement when Captain de Groot, a member of the New Guard, a fascist organization, slashed the ceremonial ribbon before it could be cut by the Labor Premier of NSW, J.T. Lang.

Sporting programmes provided a major area for the development of the techniques of descriptive broadcasts and they shared some important characteristics with the wider category of 'Descriptive Broadcasts'. Detailed accounts of sporting events were exploited throughout the 1920s and 1930s as a means of attracting interest in radio. Throughout the 1930s advertisements for wireless sets became more frequent preceding each cricket season, urging people to buy the latest wireless equipment to facilitate their enjoyment of these great events. Sports broadcasts were announced in terms that emphasized the immediacy of radio, the way in which listeners could be there – hear the cricket balls clicking and the drumming of the horses' hooves, all in the comfort of their own living rooms: 'You follow the race "close up" from start to finish – get every detail vividly clear – free from crowds and discomfort, seated in the luxury of your own armchair.'[12]

The sense of actuality created for sporting broadcasts began as a stunt. It was not at first considered essential to the content of these broadcasts; it was an additional means of creating excitement about radio itself – the thrill was associated with the technology and its miraculous feats. In the late 1920s the sense of actuality became part of the representation of radio as a medium between two worlds: radio brought the outside world to listeners in their private world. The attendant noises of a cricket match created the appropriate atmosphere to allow listeners to believe they had 'the best seat in the house'. By the mid-1930s, the technology of wireless was no longer emphasized; it now appeared as a simple, direct means of communication, so that just as listeners could hear radio personalities speaking intimately to them, they could now hear the outside public event 'as it happens'. 'Broadcasting is the act of distributing sound, of widening the area of audibility for the benefit of those who cannot be within earshot of the point of origin. It enables those who are absent to participate in an event through the media of sound.'[13]

The immediacy or sense of actuality now associated with all descriptive broadcasts represented radio's messages or content as unmediated by the technology or those exploiting it. Listeners were said to be the beneficiaries of a medium of direct communication, to be themselves participants in the events brought to them by radio. Though there were no necessary steps from the broadcast of stunts to this latter representation of the role of broadcasting, the earlier images served to establish it as an apparently straightforward means of communication. Listeners could accompany the diver to the bottom of Sydney Harbour and hear all the associated 'real' noises of this extraordinary occasion. The continuity of this rhetoric served to eliminate questions about what noises, what features of the outside world, were selected and framed or contextualized for the listeners' ears.

In late 1936 one major event formed the basis for combining features of the descriptive broadcast with news broadcasting. The abdication of Edward VIII was an event of 'national importance' and, as such, the ABC could report it independently of newspaper accounts. Arrangements were made for the duration of the crisis for special cables to be sent by the ABC's representative in London. Instead of providing listeners with straightforward descriptions of events, the ABC presented its information in the form of 'immediate news', thus emphasizing radio's capacity for instantaneous communication. This use of broadcasting foreshadowed the change that would take place in the 1940s in the concept of radio news. It formed too the first step in the ABC's formulation of the basis for its own independent news service.

War news further ensured that radio began to represent itself as able to bring immediate information about outside events of world-wide significance – the big news. The invasion of Abyssinia by Italy in October 1935 had been claimed to be 'the first time in history, radio has advised listeners of the outbreak of war'. In this instance it was the commercial stations which provided the news from cabled messages. All

Sydney commercial stations but two, 2KY and 2SM, combined for the purpose to relay the same messages; the ABC also availed themselves of the service.[14]

At the end of 1936 Charles Moses wrote to the director of the BBC's Empire Service: 'We are following with great interest the increase in news broadcasts in Europe generally. This is doubtless provoked by the growing international tension, which here of course, however deceptively, is much less felt.'[15] The ABC's correspondence with the BBC suggests that its growing concern with news broadcasting was partly a result of the international events. At least some personnel within the ABC (Moses and Dixon in particular) indicated that the ABC's public service function obliged them to take a keen interest in such matters. But there were other reasons too: the ABC's anxiety to follow in the footsteps of the BBC and the competition between the two systems of broadcasting stations in Australia. In 1937, newspapers were not interested in providing detailed information about the outbreak of war between China and Japan, and this time the ABC was again arranging for its own cables.[16] On 1 October 1938 the front cover of the *Listener In* carried the headline 'What Will War Mean to Radio?'. The invasion of Czechoslovakia by Germany was reported to listeners by the ABC re-broadcasting each morning short-wave broadcasts received the previous night.[17] Frederick Daniell complained to the manager of station 2UE that the ABC was 'cleaning up the listeners in New South Wales' by its provision of 'an authoritative news service'.[18]

The *Listener In*'s depiction of the role of radio in reporting Germany's invasion of Czechoslovakia illustrates the extent to which radio news was not yet clearly defined. With grandiose flourishes, the journal reported that 'Radio has played a tremendous part in the world-shaking events of the past week'; listeners, it declared, had heard 'history being made'. The re-broadcasts of short-wave transmissions provided a 'vivid dramatization of the highlights of the news'.[19] Instead of a news service that gave listeners the most immediate and authoritative information available, the *Listener In*'s account spoke of the ABC's efforts on this occasion as if they had presented one of the dramatized news-type programmes.

The ABC developed its news programming in other ways apart from its efforts to cover the 'big news' of international war crises. It now provided a Sunday night news service (not covered by the newspaper agreement); it increased its news staff and early in 1939 the PMG directed the ABC to appoint its own representative in Canberra. The Prime Minister, Joseph Lyons, had clashed with the daily press over their refusal to publish a statement of government policy.[20] The ABC became increasingly preoccupied too with its presentation of the news. The extension of its role in news reporting to providing detailed and immediate accounts of world crises meant that radio news presentation could no longer simply be a question of re-writing news items to be appropriate for spoken transmission. These were events of national significance furnishing opportunities for the ABC to speak as a national body. But they were events too that were reported with great haste to listeners, and they were events surrounded by considerable political and ideological manoeuvring, internationally and locally. The ABC was most anxious in this context that it give a voice to its new broadcasts that was authoritative in style, national in resonance, and objective in tone.

Letters were sent to the BBC seeking guidance about the appropriate method of news presentation. In 1935 Dixon began to prepare a style sheet for the instruction of news editors. A request was sent to the BBC for a copy of their style sheet; it was dismissed with the reply that no such set of instructions existed at the BBC, for 'trained journalists are supposed to know'.[21] Yet Asa Briggs's history of the BBC shows the news organization within that institution had similarly been concerned with developing an appropriate radio news style since the early 1930s;[22] it seems they were in an uncharitable mood on this occasion. Undaunted, the ABC persisted with drawing up guidelines for its news presentation. They now maintained that the techniques of print journalism could not be transferred unchanged to radio news. Listeners, they argued, could not re-read a paragraph of a news story, nor could they ask an announcer to repeat it for them: the different requirements of the two media were manifest.

At the beginning of 1938 Moses issued a set of 'Hints for the Guidance of ABC News Compilers'. It included instructions about simple wording and phrasing, about the lead-up sentences to ensure that listeners did not miss the vital point of the story and the 'ABC formula' for the ordering of information provided: 'Where, what, when, how'. In addition, the guide sheet stressed the primary importance of impartiality, factual news, the absence of sensationalism and reliability. The ABC's national status, Moses concluded, 'suggests to the public that we are impartial in our presentation of news'; to ensure and retain this image, he warned, 'reliability needs to dominate everything in the ABC news'.[23]

The ABC stressed simple, plain language for all its reports: a terse style rather than dramatic descriptions. Humour was permitted only if it emanated from 'the facts of the story'. All accounts of murders, accidents and crime of any kind were to be eliminated as far as possible in the interests of 'good taste' except where 'the public interests' demanded it.[24] These restrictions on humour and sensational stories were advocated as necessary to distinguish the ABC news from that of the newspapers and as essential to the dignity required of a national body. To enhance its 'national voice' the ABC decided in 1939 that all references to the states should be eliminated from the news bulletins and an emphasis given to stories of a 'national interest'. With the outbreak of the second world war, the ABC was to stress its national voice and the capacity of ABC radio to speak to all people at the one time thus unifying the nation in this time of crisis (it used this image both in speaking to listeners and in its arguments to the government for greater financial support for the ABC news).

An image of objectivity and authority was difficult to sustain when the news was taken from newspapers, most of which, Moses argued, had a 'political axe to grind'. The restriction on the length of the news broadcasts also created a major problem. In 1938 Dixon recommended that all news sessions be rehearsed so that announcers could read the items clearly and with 'a sense of news values'. He criticized the restriction on news length. Five minutes was too short a period in which to provide a reasonable amount of material and still to read with 'rhythm and clarity' and with 'intelligence'.[25] Four years later, Dixon dismissed the notion that announcers should rehearse the news bulletins: the authority of the ABC news now depended on the ABC appearing to have the latest facts to relay to listeners. An important transformation had taken place in the ABC's thinking about radio news in these four years. Moves by the ABC to make its news service increasingly independent of the newspapers facilitated this change, but also reflected the ABC's beginning to define a special role for radio in the field of news. In 1938 Dixon had been concerned only to push for two more minutes to be added to the news bulletin, time to allow the announcers to read more slowly. The slower pace and careful rehearsal would ensure the proper tone and style of the ABC news. By 1942 Dixon defined radio news as 'live, up-to-the-minute news, which does not wait for people to "prepare" and "rehearse"'. ABC news now stressed its presentation as 'factual news', immediate news, and its readers were trained in 'the

ABC's style' of 'straight presentation' and an absence of 'dramatization and showmanship'.[26]

Other ideas did exist about the format that should be adopted by the ABC. As it began to build up a news organization, proposals about news presentation came from a number of sources. In 1939, H.D. Black, then an economics lecturer at the University of Sydney and not connected with the ABC at the time, wrote suggesting that ABC news bulletins should include recordings of important speeches by public figures, the history of news items rather than simply brief condensed summaries of information, and, where appropriate, a summary of newspaper comment on particular items. A few years later, S.H. Deamer, the editor of the *ABC Weekly*, a journal established at the end of 1939, proposed that the ABC should do more than simply read news and information summaries. Deamer advocated the use of the voices of ABC correspondents around the world and excerpts from the speeches of important public figures.[27] But the ABC remained wary at this stage of using voices in their news broadcasts other than those of their news readers. The inclusion of the voices of public figures, it was argued, could undermine the emphasis on factual news and the lack of sensationalism that the ABC wished to promote as characterizing its news service. The ABC was anxious to distance itself from the dramatization of news-type programmes. The recordings of public speeches were confined to special feature programmes and the question of comments on the news reserved for news commentators, again in special programmes.

Some commercial stations were nervous about the ABC's increased activity in the field of news. By 1939 the listening public, it was said, was becoming more 'news conscious' and the ABC alone was benefiting from this shift. Frederick Daniell wrote early in September 1939:

> I am particularly disturbed as I have made a survey of my own friends outside the broadcasting world, also the butcher, the tramdriver, etc., and it seems to me at the moment, that the majority of people are listening to the National Service for, what they say, 'first information'.[28]

The ABC during 1938 and 1939 had defined a particular category of programmes as important radio; world events, as well as its efforts, were seen to have created an audience for such programmes. During the first few years of the war the ABC was to define further the nature of those programmes and radio's particular tasks in the field of news, while setting limits on the content and style of presentation considered appropriate to radio news.

It would be some time before the commercial stations began to compete on this ground and to challenge the ABC's conception of what was necessary to good radio news. Throughout the 1930s these stations had included news programmes of various kinds: some brief five-minute reports, read from the newspapers like the ABC's; some programmes combining news and comment or news reviews; the dramatized news broadcasts; and later, some more innovatory programmes, like 2GB's *Eye Witness News* and 2UW's *Flash News*. Both of these sought to provide immediate news, drawing on the sense created by the outside or actuality broadcasts that radio could take listeners to the events without delay; 2UW introduced telephone reports to increase the excitement and to promise listeners that they would provide 'instant information'.[29] But the heavy reliance on the daily newspapers for the information content of their programmes in the 1930s curtailed the development of news broadcasting for commercial stations in this period. The news information provided was not the property of the station and thus could not be used to seek advertisers. But advertisers were to prove reluctant to sponsor news broadcasts even after the war. The reason is not clear, although the dominance of the ABC in the field, and for some time its universality during the war (commercial stations were obliged to take three ABC bulletins a day for the duration of the war), seem at least to be part of the reason. The Macquarie Network did consider establishing a news service to compete with the ABC's at this time and stations like 2GB developed feature programmes of news commentary and 'actuality' recordings. But it was not until after the war that these innovations began to be exploited fully and to challenge the image of radio news established by the ABC with its preoccupation with 'straight presentation' and the voice of authority.

In 1940 the ABC transferred its news commentaries to the Talks Department.[30] This now appears to have been part of the ABC's strategy to lessen the status of its news commentator 'The Watchman', E.A. Mann, and to introduce a more diverse set of commentaries on the news than had hitherto been provided. But it served too to set the news clearly apart from comment or opinion on the news: the news could thus be delineated as a factual, information service for listeners. During 1938 and 1939, 'The Watchman' had become an annoying problem for the

ABC as members of parliament and other individuals increasingly complained of the strong views expressed by this commentator. The ABC did begin to place restrictions on 'The Watchman's' broadcasts, though it also made the firm declaration that news commentators should be able to, according to Alan Thomas's analysis, 'advance definite points of view, provided someone had a right of reply'. The news service, the ABC insisted on the other hand, must be impartial.[31]

The distinction was not one that had always been drawn for radio news and information programmes. In 1930 H.P. Williams, who later was to become, briefly, until his death in 1933, the ABC's first general manager, provided a popular news commentary programme for the Australian Broadcasting Company. Broadcasting from his home each morning, he read to listeners from news items cut out from the daily newspapers, but he also made extensive comments on the news in this same programme.[32] Similarly, the commercial stations at times during the 1930s provided programmes that combined both information and comment (though they also followed the ABC's example with comments in separate programmes from regular broadcasters, like 3UZ's 'The Sentinel').

Yet the ABC did draw a distinction between news and comment on the news. It sought to promote its authority and public standing by claiming to be a purveyor of pure facts and the source of public information about events of an epoch-making character. It set out to represent itself as speaking to and on behalf on the nation. It claimed to bring the world into the living room of listeners, but not the world coloured or shaped by political or other interests like the newspapers' news, but *the* world, *the* news. The absence of commercial interests, its independence (though somewhat shaky) from government and its status as a national institution made it possible, the ABC proclaimed, for it to provide this service. Later it would point to its capacity to provide news 'as it happens' to revitalize its claims to this role. The ABC drew on a rhetoric about objectivity and impartiality to create a particular status for its news service, and hence for itself more generally. It would thus also contribute to the dominance of this rhetoric and its role in the definition of the political.

Radio, listeners were told, 'bring[s] the world to you'.[33] The information and 'factual' accounts received by listeners through the news broadcasts and other programmes such as weather reports, descriptive broadcasts and sport, all emanated from a source outside the world of listeners-in: radio would keep listeners 'in touch' with that world, but it was a world represented as separate from them and their everyday lives. And as just one of the many offerings provided by radio, the news appeared on an equal footing with music programmes, plays, serials, talks on a variety of subjects, religious services, and women's sessions. The ABC reports for each year included news (or sometimes the broader description of essential services – news, weather and market reports) as one of eight or more categories of programmes. Music constituted about 50 per cent of programme time and news and essential services 12–13 per cent: information about the outside world thus became just one of the items to be selected and enjoyed by listeners-in, just one of their leisure interests served by radio. Though radio did play an increasingly vital role in keeping people informed about major events, it also ensured that the 'facts' about these events would appear to be simply commodities to be appreciated on the same level as the other goods on offer – heard in between the dinner music, the latest serial, or the evening play, and all without leaving the comfort of your armchair.

The basis of an opinion

Though the ABC took its news from newspapers throughout the 1930s, it insisted that it could bring listeners straightforward information, the facts, about the world. It recognized the strong editorial lines taken by newspapers, yet was adamant that the facts could be gleaned from the news coverage provided, just as the sensational or emotive words and unsavoury items could be eliminated from the stories used. The problem, as it was posed by the ABC, was to establish a neutral or balanced language that would simply report information rather than propagandize as the newspapers did. This stance ignored the extent to which journalistic practices of newspapers ensured that a particular view of the world was integral to the news reported and the items of news selected as news. The ABC's language about its own impartiality and objectivity further denied that its own news was itself, inevitably, a construction of social reality.

Journalistic practices of all news gatherers and writers produce a particular picture of the world through the processes of selecting news as news, the spokespersons identified as appropriate for statements about the news, the contextual details chosen to make sense of the news, and the language employed.[34] Thus the dichotomy insisted upon by the

ABC between the propaganda of newspaper reporting and its own news set up a misleading distinction. Necessarily, all news is framed by these journalistic practices; and to that extent, all news is biased, partial. Indeed, in the 1930s, a number of explicit mechanisms employed by broadcasters and by government officials ensured that a specific and limited set of world views gained access to news and other broadcast programmes. These mechanisms were not peculiar to radio, but they did evolve in particular ways because of the way in which radio's relationship to its audience had been constituted.

The processes of official and self-imposed censorship were the most obvious means by which radio shaped the world it brought into listeners' homes. In part imposed by the PMG, in part brought about by pressure from politicians, and in part self-imposed, censorship established a rigid set of frames around the view of the world conveyed to listeners in news programmes and, more generally, in all radio programmes. In the 1920s the PMG primarily concerned himself with the censorship of political broadcasts; in the 1930s such censorship became more vigorous and it became a powerful means of defining what were the political issues of the day, of defining a sphere of legitimate politics. In addition, the PMG in the 1930s assumed the role of moral guardian of listeners' homes.

Amended wireless regulations in 1930 detailed the powers already held by the PMG to censor broadcasting matters found 'objectionable' or undesirable in the 'interests of the community'. In a letter from H.P. Brown to John Reith a year later, Brown indicated that the PMG saw the major problem as the 'B' stations' ownership and use by a vast range of groups. Radio was not yet clearly conceived as a medium for the transmission of radio programmes and, hence, the PMG preoccupied himself with specifying the types of views that should be excluded from access to listeners via the means of broadcasting. The 'A' stations could maintain a 'reasonable balance' of view, said Brown; but the 'B' stations were exploited 'for the broadcasting of extremist views and severe criticisms of the government'.[35]

The PMG required that all political speeches broadcast from the 'B' stations be submitted to scrutiny in synopsis form before broadcast. Two cases in which the PMG exercised his powers of censorship in 1931 caused some public furore. It prohibited a broadcast by the Citizens' League in Adelaide as a blatant instance of political propaganda. When challenged in parliament, the PMG listed the proposed topics to be covered in the programme. They included attacks on the South Australian Labor government's policies, including a sugar embargo, and an account of the 'menace of communism'. Critics of the PMG's action averred that the Citizens' League could not be described as an extremist organization and that such censorship constituted a suppression of free speech.[36] The banning of a lecture on peace in Sydney attracted fewer expressions of public outrage. The *Labor Daily* took up the issue, objecting to a 'so-called Federal Labor Government' that could permit the suppression of a speech on peace from a member of the International Friendship League.[37] Censorship issues such as these revolved around definitions of propaganda, 'legitimate' versus 'extremist' viewpoints, and freedom of speech.

During the 1930s the PMG's attitude to the 'B' stations changed. The PMG still retained his powers to scrutinize speeches when he so desired, but the relationship became more benign with reminders sent to stations about the need for wise discrimination.[38] The ABC instead became the arena for PMG and governmental intervention. Though the ABC's act permitted it to determine to what extent and in what manner political speeches may be broadcast, the PMG could prohibit the broadcasting of 'matter of any class or character'.[39] Such directions by the PMG to the ABC were required to be in writing, but it was not until 1942 that the ABC was obliged to record these acts of governmental intervention. Similarly, the definition of 'political speeches' remained vague until that time. Thereafter the ABC's control over political broadcasting extended to 'any matter relating to a political subject'; the use of the loose term 'political speeches' in the ABC's act had previously appeared to limit its control to election speeches by politicians.[40]

Undoubtedly instances of direct government intervention in ABC broadcasts occurred in the 1930s, as well as cases of pressure exerted by the PMG or members of parliament.[41] The absence of regulations requiring that such interventions be recorded in this period makes it difficult to determine their extent and frequency; nevertheless, statements by the first two chairmen of the ABC indicate that this issue did concern them. Charles Lloyd Jones and W.J. Cleary issued vigorous declarations about the need for the ABC to preserve an independence from the government of the day and to be impartial in its presentation of political and social issues. A statement directed to the PMG in 1933 averred that: 'The progress of science and the harmonies of art will be hampered by too rigid rules and too constant a supervision by the State.'[42] But it was the ABC's self-censorship that produced its overriding air of staidness and initiated cases of blatant censorship that provoked the most public criticism. Some of these instances were in response to government directives about legitimate viewpoints; some reflected the ABC's own definition of the limits to be placed on public debate.

In 1938 the ABC banned a talk to be given by Judge Foster as the first in its new series of national talks, 'The Viewpoint Changes'. The title of Foster's talk was to have been 'Freedom of Speech' but was not permitted to go on air by the ABC because of its attack on various organizations and individuals. Cleary, as chairman of the ABC, defended its action publicly and privately with vigour and conviction. Foster, like all other speakers, had been instructed to treat his topic 'objectively'; the topics for this series were all 'highly contentious' and it was imperative that they be approached in a 'scholarly and impersonal' way.[43] When Foster refused to change his talk to comply with these requirements, the ABC banned it as unsuitable for broadcasting. Foster had attacked the 'Organized Church', the government for its treatment of Egon Kisch (a Czechoslovakian who had come to Australia in 1934 to address an anti-war and anti-fascist congress but had been treated as an illegal immigrant), the War Precautions Act, 'military officers' and 'censors' for their suppression of the anti-conscription case during the first world war, and the government's persecution of himself and others operating on behalf of this same cause. Such comments, according to the ABC, were not objective or impersonal.

Cleary claimed that newspapers antagonistic to the ABC initiated the public debate that followed. He credited the protests from the Melbourne-based Council of Civil Liberties with sincerity, but in Cleary's estimation their 'rather advanced . . . views as to freedom of speech' marginalized their claims.[44] Certainly the press by this time was on the whole predisposed to grab every opportunity to lambast the ABC. Cleary had on other occasions pointed out the way in which powerful sections of the press were continually on the watch to criticize some aspect of the ABC's activities;[45] and Herbert Brookes as deputy chairman used the occasion of a public speech in 1937 to complain bitterly about the press and its continual obstruction of and belabouring of the ABC.[46]

Cleary's assessment of the comments from the press over the Judge Foster issue and his reference to '"friends and enemies" with axes to grind' (among whom he listed only Labor Party leaders) may have been justified. Yet his dismissal of the civil liberties argument appears to evoke a different set of considerations. Cleary's suggestion that the views of this group were marginal because they were more advanced than those of the general population indicates that he saw censorship as more than simply a question of acceptable content. In another statement of the ABC's response to its critics on this issue, Cleary asserted that the speakers for this series of talks had been asked to give a 'scholarly and impersonal tracing of the change in public opinion' to guarantee that 'listeners would not be befogged or side-tracked by personalities, abuse, and play upon political or religious prejudices'.[47] Judge Foster's error had been to take a stance and to be frankly critical of established institutions. Though Cleary and others associated with the ABC constantly stated their primary commitment to principles of impartiality in cases such as the Judge Foster incident they claimed the primacy of other considerations. Censorship had to be imposed, they argued, when points of view stepped outside the limits defined as rational. Beyond that point, they declared, listeners were unable to judge for themselves. Within the sphere of those opinions deemed legitimate, listeners could be expected to make their own assessments; the ABC's only obligation was to give expression to the different voices speaking about any issue. Beyond that sphere, listeners could no longer be considered active agents making their own decisions and they became the subjects of propaganda.

This notion of listeners, as well as the fear that they might be 'side-tracked' or 'befogged' by personalities, recognized that listeners played a passive role. They were consumers of the opinions delivered rather than participants in a debate. But the passivity only became a problem for the ABC in the case of those opinions or ideas they deemed non-legitimate. Scholarly accounts of the state of public opinion, or the balanced views of 'authoritative and forceful speakers' who examine problems in a 'cool and impersonal manner' forestalled any considerations of the listener's position as consumer. Similarly, debates between opposing points of view on issues of legitimate public concern eliminated the question of the position of the listener-in. The problem arose only in the process of excluding a range of opinions and issues from the field of legitimacy.

Conder, as general manager of the ABC, had articulated the problem in these terms when discussing a proposal by the ABC in Victoria to broadcast an address by an advocate of the Douglas Social Credit system. Conder and Herbert Brookes agreed that such a broadcast would be unwise: the ideas of Douglas Social Credit, said Conder, argued for something 'very closely akin to an economic, if not actual revolution'. Public opinion should not be allowed to depend on the 'oratorical ability' of speakers who wish 'to tear down [rather] than defend existing systems'.[48] The ABC's stance limited the range of views disseminated to those that lay within the bounds of parliamentary politics and that accepted the existing institutions or fundamental structures of the society. It set out to make sure that equal time was allowed for the different viewpoints within that range and defined this practice as constituting impartiality and objectivity.

In another instance of self-censorship by the ABC, the publicly provided arguments claimed a surfeit of talks on international affairs, though private documents concerning the incident reported investigations of the speaker's political affiliations. In July 1938 the ABC management informed Constance Duncan that her talks on international affairs for the women's session were to be terminated. She was told that the daily and weekly commentaries by 'The Watchman', the BBC's commentaries once a week, and the Sunday night talks provided the ABC with adequate coverage of international affairs by experts. A confidential report, however, listed Duncan's membership of organizations and her political sympathies. She had spoken at meetings of organizations affiliated or in some way connected with the Communist Party, such as the Movement against War and Fascism; and the Bureau of International Affairs to which she belonged was dubbed anti-British in its support for the League of Nations Union. The private report described her as not a member of the Communist Party, but believing in some form of 'Christian Communism'.[49]

Constance Duncan represented a vastly different viewpoint from that of 'The Watchman', whom K.S. Inglis has characterized as standing for 'a robust liberal imperialism and Christianity acquired in the time of Queen Victoria'.[50] Though Cleary, in particular, felt uneasy about the freedom given to 'The Watchman', his opinions remained within the boundaries of legitimacy. His strong views, even when delivered in the form of vitriolic criticisms of federal or state government activities, did not challenge the established institutions or structures of society. Indeed, the stridency of his voice, though causing some embarrassment and discomfort to the ABC, served, as Inglis suggests, to symbolize and draw attention to the ABC's independence from newspapers.[51] Thus, although the ABC did have some concerns about the dominance of 'The Watchman' in the field of news commentary, these were readily suppressed in their moves to censor Constance Duncan. Her talks were reinstated after public protests at her removal, but they were limited to one session a month instead of weekly. By the end of the year, the ABC was seeking other viewpoints than that of 'The Watchman' to provide more 'balance' to its news commentaries. His standing within the ABC declined further the following year, when the new Menzies government issued specific directions with the outbreak of war that 'The Watchman' must refrain from attacking British government policy. But neither changes in the international situation nor within the ABC facilitated greater access to radio of the views of people like Duncan. Though her chief preoccupations were with peace and anti-fascism, her viewpoint was considered extreme, rather than the other side of the balance to conservative views like those of 'The Watchman'.

Fears of war increasingly became the rationale for censorship in the second half of the 1930s. In May 1937 Australia acceded to an International Convention on the Use of Broadcasting in the Cause of Peace, a convention drawn up under the auspices of the League of Nations. The convention specified that radio stations should not broadcast programmes on international affairs 'to the detriment of good international understanding', programmes that 'constitute an incitement... to war', or transmissions 'likely to harm good international understandings by statements the incorrectness of which is or ought to be known to the persons responsible for the broadcast'.[52] The ABC indicated that it was in agreement with the convention, and indeed reported that it already operated according to these principles; a number of commercial stations also replied favourably to a PMG circular asking for their co-operation. The press discovered the agreement some months later and the radio stations' compliance with the government's requests to observe its guidelines; they relished their outrage and horror at this censorship. They accused the PMG of being 'a Hitler', 'a Goebbels' and 'a Goering of the air'. Freedom of speech was at peril and the *Sun* editorial warned that the PMG would become 'Editor and Censor over the opinions of distinguished students of foreign affairs'. The president of the Federation of Commercial Broadcasting Stations claimed that this attempt by the government to control foreign affairs broadcasting was 'a blow at democratic institutions'.[53]

The ABC had, however, as it indicated to the PMG, been complying with a similar set of principles of its own accord before this date. Thus, people returning from the Spanish Civil War found themselves banned from broadcasting on the ABC on the grounds that their statements would constitute a criticism of a foreign government.[54]

The ABC's vigorous self-censorship made it unnecessary for the government to intervene in its affairs. But 2KY found the PMG quite willing to take a strong line to ensure that its broadcasts stayed within the boundaries defined as appropriate by the government. 2KY went off the air for a brief period on 21 December 1938 after its licence was withdrawn by the PMG. Specific objections by the PMG to 2KY's broadcasts related to statements by a news commentator about the dispute at Port Kembla in NSW over the export of pig-iron to Japan; but the PMG claimed that he protested previously to 2KY about its news commentaries on international and local affairs. The 2KY news commentator, unrepentant at first, said in a statement to the *Argus* that the trouble had arisen because of his criticisms of the government in the Port Kembla dispute and of the PMG for his 'anthropoid idea of thrusting all women back into the kitchen and making them have children', a proposal, he said, akin to Hitler's dictates to women in Germany.[55]

Despite protests from labour organizations and the Federation of Commercial Broadcasting Stations, the PMG insisted that 2KY had been repeatedly warned about its statements in news commentaries and that he had acted correctly and fairly in withdrawing 2KY's licence. He extracted an apology from 2KY and five days later they were back on air. The incident revealed the lack of tenure of commercial stations' licences and their vulnerability to government control; protests from the stations and the press framed the issue within these terms. They evoked the principle of 'freedom of speech' and linked the incident to the government's willingness to assume the role of a dictator by signing the International Broadcasting Convention. The PMG, on his side, spoke of the need to allow 'both sides of the question' to be heard – the 2KY commentaries, he claimed, allowed those accused no right of reply. He thus called on the same liberal principles as did his critics. The liberal discourse of individual rights and freedom of speech dominated the debate: the issue of censorship appeared a matter of an authoritarian government versus the different claims about whether all opinions were being heard equally.

The government, on the other hand, explained its signing of the international convention and its immediate assumption of the need for strict censorship of the press and radio at the outbreak of war in different terms. These decisions were necessary, they declared, to the collective interest of the population. This position too donned the robes of liberalism, for the common or collective good now being protected, it was claimed, was that of the ensemble of individual interests. The state's role in imposing censorship in normal times was to facilitate the free circulation of ideas, those deemed acceptable. All ideas were equal and should be treated as such, as long as they did not step outside the realm of legitimate politics, as it had been defined. But in the case of war, those restrictions increased as the government identified itself with the collective interest and could claim to be above criticism. Objections to government censorship or the ABC's self-imposed censorship did not challenge the liberal discourse, and nor did the government's or the ABC's justifications of their own censorship activities; participants in the various debates at this time simply drew on different interpretations of its claims.

The willingness to impose self-censorship was by no means exclusive to the ABC. The commercial stations similarly drew sharp distinctions between legitimate and non-legitimate political broadcasts. These processes became evident when a mistake had been made in inviting a particular speaker to broadcast or in permitting access to the station's air time to someone whose views turned out to be outside the boundaries defined as valid. In September 1931 a speaker on 3KZ advocated the value of strikes as a means of uniting workers even in instances where the strikes did not achieve their short-term goals. The speaker urged all workers to unite under the communist banner. 3KZ professed acute embarrassment about this broadcast and claimed no prior knowledge of its content. The offending speaker, a member of the Victorian Labour College, had stood in for someone else at the last minute. The *Argus* reported the incident as probably 'the first time in the history of wireless in Australia [that] the broadcasting of Communist and revolutionary propaganda' had been permitted. Letters to the newspaper declared that such speeches should be confined to the Yarra Bank Sunday afternoon soap-box forum.[56] The PMG accepted 3KZ's explanation of their ignorance of the speaker's intentions and let the matter drop. The 3KZ management vowed that no such incident would occur again and in 1932, when a speaker from the Teachers' Industrial Union advocated the value of strike action, the announcer cut the programme off and substituted a musical interlude.[57]

Members of the Communist Party and affiliated organizations did have limited access to the commercial stations throughout the 1930s, mainly it seems by buying time for their own programmes. At election time they were able to broadcast speeches on commercial stations, again by buying time but their financial resources were limited. On the ABC they could also broadcast election speeches until after the second world war when, under pressure, the ABC changed the rules about election broadcasts in such a way as to exclude them.[58]

In their normal programmes in the 1930s such revolutionary views were rarely heard on the ABC, though it did permit a discussion in 1936 of the factional battles in the NSW Communist Party about Stalinism. Discussions of communism, of alternative political and economic systems, or of the value of strikes did not constitute normal or desirable topics for rational discussion on either the ABC or the commercial stations: valid topics for debate were restricted to the realm of contemporary parliamentary politics and the spectrum of views currently represented in that sphere. The representatives of viewpoints outside these limits achieved even less credibility. Trade unionism did get discussed on the ABC occasionally, but the ABC preferred to provide its own experts to 'ventilate controversial questions of industrial problems', rather than to permit trade unionists to speak directly about their activities.[59] Trade unionism did not constitute a legitimate voice, only a controversial question. And finally, restrictions on the language of broadcasting so that terms like 'bosses' were automatically excluded as not part of rational discourse[60] closed the circle in defining the sphere of legitimate politics.

In the 1930s 2KY, as a station of the labour movement, did little in terms of offering a critique or an alternative to this process (nor did 3KZ, though its establishment as a labour station had not been founded on such a well-developed political and class position as had 2KY's). The critique of the notion of propaganda by people associated with 2KY in the 1920s and their demands for partisan-style education through the media could no longer be heard. Like all other commercial stations, 2KY had adapted to the role of entertaining listeners-in with its daily sessions dominated by music and racing broadcasts. Its talks or information programmes consisted of brief news, a fifteen-minute news review or comment programme each weekday and the occasional speaker on topics not necessarily focused around issues concerning the labour movement. Up until 1936 2KY had always taken its news from the *Labor Daily* and the management had described its news programme as 'given frankly from a Labor point of view'.[61] In 1936, as part of struggles over the control of 2KY, the station briefly took advertising from the *Daily Telegraph* and its news from this same paper. Protests to the station and to the *Labor Daily* expressed disgust that 2KY should promote this blatantly 'anti-labor' newspaper.[62] Though its attitudes to strikes and its interest in the activities of the labour movement may have been different from other stations, 2KY's exploration of and articulation of an alternative range of opinions were confined to a small section of its radio programming. And though it may have told its listeners about a slightly different world than other stations, it did nothing to challenge the notions of propaganda and impartiality now clearly dominant in the field of broadcasting. Thus when it lost its licence briefly at the end of 1938, 2KY exploited the same language of free speech and the free circulation of ideas; it failed to challenge the way in which only certain ideas and certain types of speakers had first to pass the test of 'propaganda' and 'legitimacy' before gaining access to this medium.

Censorship was not simply a repressive discourse: it did not conceal certain aspects of the world from listeners so much as produce a definite view of the world, a particular representation of social reality. Political censorship defined a range of legitimate political views and a range of issues as constituting the domain of rational political and social questions for public debate and public consideration. Other viewpoints and issues were thus simultaneously pushed off the agenda, made marginal and irrational. Moral censorship similarly defined the acceptable limits and understandings of the social world for listeners and produced a specific representation of social reality. It suggested that the social order it depicted was based on natural distinctions between men and women, the different needs and natural inclinations of the two sexes.

Thus advocates of the free circulation of ideas did not necessarily include all people as full participants in this arena. Strong claims existed for some sort of censorship on moral lines for the protection of 'women and children' or 'our homes'. Within the discourse of liberalism this principle indicated that women and children were not fully individuals in their own right. They should be sheltered for they were not suited, or in the case of (male) children not yet ready, for the public sphere of the fully adult citizen – the individual. The formation of a 'rigorous' and 'robust' democracy depended on the free circulation of ideas, but women and children, by their 'nature', it was implied, could not participate fully in this domain. Women had been recognized as adult individuals to the extent of having political suffrage, but this argument for moral censorship suggested they could not participate fully in the formation of democracy. They must be protected in the private sphere of the home, protected from the ideas that circulate freely in the public domain.

A number of witnesses for the 1927 Royal Commission on Wireless had voiced their concern about radio's intrusion into the home.[63] The main complaints at this time referred to the broadcasting of races and betting information and salacious bed-time stories for children. In the 1930s letters to the editor, parliamentary debates and occasional articles by the print media complained of bad language, thrillers in particular that were bad for children's minds, jokes and comedy acts in bad taste, songs of a suggestive kind, and the sexual innuendoes uttered by some announcers. The concern expressed was for the harm done to women and children or the intrusion of such matter into the home. The 'fireside life of the family' was under threat; radio as an intimate medium could take the family by surprise.

The report of the Joint Parliamentary Committee on Wireless Broadcasting gave official sanction to these fears in 1942 and the PMG was given formal powers to censor both radio stations and artists who broadcast 'objectionable items'. The report argued that the problem of radio's influence was unique. It suggested that in going to the theatre people made a deliberate choice about what they saw and heard, whereas the experience of listening to radio required no such effort. In addition the specific content of the broadcast heard often turned out to be unpredictable and unwanted:

> An objectionable broadcaster ... can usurp the power to injure others against their will. He can invade the circle of families and their friends gathered at the meal table or the fireside to hear what they expected to be an enjoyable programme, only to find it marred by the interpellation of embarrassing vulgarity or some salacious joke designed to break down the barriers of modesty between the sexes.[64]

In the public sphere such matters were left to the adult individual; but the private sphere of the home, the sphere of women and children, was to be protected. Radio had been constituted as an intimate medium speaking to the private individual, the consumer, and as such it threatened to bring features of the public world into the home. This understanding of the relationship between the radio and its audience served to reinforce differentiations between men and women and the relegation of all women to a private sphere. Political censorship practices for radio broadcasting had defined a particular set or range of ideas as legitimate and rational. Moral censorship affirmed and legitimated the patriarchal order as natural and rational.[65]

The ABC agreed about the need to protect the home from undesirable intrusions of programmes of bad taste and immorality. In 1933 it banned a popular artist, Dot Brunton, because she refused to eliminate the swear words from the play *Dearest Enemy* in which she was to have been heard. Two years later the ABC eagerly followed in the footsteps of the BBC by adopting its set of dictates to all broadcasters and writers for BBC programmes. The ABC forbade all racist epithets, references to marital infidelity or immorality of any kind, references to physical deformities and painful or fatal diseases, and any emphasis on drunkenness. For its potential playwrights the ABC required that there be no blasphemy, coarse or profane expressions, no suggestive remarks, no homosexuality, no characters afflicted with insanity, impediments of speech or other bodily defects, no sordid tragedies and no controversial questions about politics or religion. A writer for the *Wireless Weekly* pondered the question of what was left in human existence for the aspiring playwright to deal with and suggested that the ABC would be unable to present any of the plays by Shakespeare or G.B. Shaw.[66]

The commercial stations were not so cautious. They were quick to engage artists such as Dot Brunton and Dorothy ('Dilly') Foster for programmes of unseemly songs and risqué humour. The PMG began to warn commercial stations by circular in 1932 of the need to listen to all records before broadcasting them and to be careful in the presentation of their own programmes. In 1936 it began to keep a file of complaints about programmes broadcast from the ABC and commercial stations. Many of the complainants referred to the need to protect their households or women and children. Letters protested about double meanings and sexual innuendoes; a typical joke found objectionable was the veiled reference to the first night after the wedding.

The PMG wrote to stations asking them to withdraw records or censor their artists or announcers. Songs such as 'The Man Who Comes to My House' and 'She Had to Go and Have It at the Astor' caused offence, and both the ABC and commercial stations agreed in 1940 to cease using them. In 1939 the PMG constantly objected to 2GB about the indecent jokes and bad language of Arundel Nixon, one of their popular personalities. 2GB discontinued his programme for a brief period, but in January 1940 he was back on air with a new name for his programme, *Keep It Clean* – a reference, Nixon avowed, to the sponsoring of the programme by a manufacturer of cleaning products.[67]

Programmes of vaudeville comedy and music hall humour did not represent a major proportion of programming time on commercial stations; they were to become more important in the 1940s. But broadcasters such as Jack Davey, Arundel Nixon and Dorothy Foster began to build up a considerable notoriety for themselves in the late 1930s through such programmes and by their taunting the PMG in his efforts to censor them.

Censorship thus constituted the first step to ensure that listeners received a specific representation of social reality and one in which a limited range of opinions and viewpoints constituted rational debate about various aspects of their lives. Concepts of impartiality and objectivity served further to endorse and to extend these practices of censorship. The ABC in particular deployed these concepts to enhance its image as a national institution – as an institution of the liberal state it stood above private interests, non-partisan and adjudicating between the claims of all points of view. Yet a range of views had already been set aside, prevented from gaining access to radio as non-valid, irrational and, simply on the basis of their content, manipulative.

The concept of 'both sides of the question' or 'opposing viewpoints' dominated broadcasts of talks, public speeches, news commentaries and parliamentary politics. It served to constitute all issues as matters of controversy upon which both sides should have equal say, and it excluded from public debate all matters deemed not to be a question for discussion. The latter did not enter the field of controversy for they were characterized as matters of propaganda only – of having only one side. Controversial issues remained within the limits established by parliamentary politics and traditional social practices. The rhetoric, however, worked to construct these issues as *the* issues of contemporary society, and hence, the range of views expressed about the issues as defined, as the full range of opinions existing in the public domain.

Arguments for the necessity of impartiality in radio broadcasts, like those for censorship, took their initial justification from the one-wayness of radio communication. In 1926, the *Listener In* compared radio with the public meeting situation where the audience can argue with the speaker: 'It is ... peculiarly exasperating to have to listen to opinions which disagree with one without having the opportunity to reply.'[68] The article advocated 'a variety of opinions' so that 'partiality' could be corrected. Later radio was compared to newspapers where the reader was said to have far greater control over the news items and opinions to be heard. Radio as a means of one-way communication, over which the listener had no control, must sustain the free circulation and equity of ideas. Both sides of the question must be given equal access to broadcasting time.

In the mid-1930s the focus of this language shifted with the ABC's increasing preoccupation with its national role. Now impartiality became not so much a requirement of radio that stemmed from its relationship to the listening audience, as a requirement of the ABC as a national body. In 1935 the ABC moved to establish a more developed talks orientation, deliberately seeking out a certain level of controversy to promote its role in fostering 'a robust public opinion'.[69] As a national body, an institution of the liberal state, the ABC would sustain the free circulation of ideas by its impartial, non-partisan interest in rational debate. Yet the topics chosen as 'controversial' in 1935 set a cautious tone: they included debates about the uniform railway gauge for Australia, the peopling of tropical Australia, the respective claims of amateurism and professionalism in sport, and freedom of speech (a more successful venture on this occasion, it seems, than the ABC's later attempt to deal with this topic).[70]

The ABC adopted two different programme formats for those issues that it defined as controversial. It set up a debate between two 'experts' or employed a BBC innovation of dramatized conversations. The latter technique appears to have been devised for educational purposes: two people could be 'overheard' debating an issue in a dramatized presentation, including the appropriate background noises of a crowded restaurant or train journey. On the other hand, the ABC continued to provide a number of talks or addresses by 'outstanding speakers' on a variety of matters that it deemed not to require the same 'controversy' treatment. For these programmes and for the formal debates, the ABC pursued a policy of seeking outside speakers or experts. Unlike the BBC, which could draw on a wide range of intellectuals,[71] the ABC relied chiefly on university experts, with people such as Walter Murdoch, W.G.K. Duncan, and G.V. Portus being among the ABC's most favoured speakers (these people also constituted the ABC's Talks Advisory Committees formed in 1935). The status of these speakers as certified by their membership of other intellectual organizations endorsed the ABC's claim to authority and impartiality. The considered opinions of independent experts framed by scholarly judgement and expressed in moderate tones bestowed an air of neutrality and distance from the hurly-burly of sectional interests on these talks and debates. As a national institution the ABC would be non-partisan in content and style.

The ABC recorded complaints from listeners in the late 1930s but a note in these files comments with satisfaction that the ABC received 'as many comments accusing it of using right-wing propaganda as it does from those who accuse it of left-wing propaganda'. This was evidence that the ABC pursued a 'non-partisan practice'.[72] Such evidence was not sufficient, however, if the ABC was to establish an image of itself as a national institution and a legitimate authority on the social and cultural life of the nation. It adopted a number of strategies to display its independence and its impartiality in all matters. It had set out to represent itself in these terms for its news programmes by fostering an image of itself as an authoritative voice, bringing listeners the news, the facts about what was happening in the world outside. Similarly, in making its news commentaries separate from its news programmes, the ABC built on their theme of the authority of its news and its clear distinction from the viewpoints of expert commentators. The ABC found it difficult to represent its news commentaries as serving the principle of impartiality because of the dominance of 'The Watchman's' broadcasts, but when pressed it resorted to claims about his expertise and authority.

The ABC was particularly anxious to exhibit its independence from the government. In 1937 it banned the broadcast of all public speeches given by politicians for a three-month period before the federal elections, its argument being that the government of the day was unduly favoured at election time by the inevitably greater frequency with which its ministers spoke on public occasions. Both the Prime Minister, Lyons, and the leader of the opposition, John Curtin, condemned the ABC's initiative, and it soon relented. Such a concern to appear non-partisan had made the ABC too zealous. In 1939 the ABC again considered employing an obvious measure to demonstrate its impartiality. This time the BBC's example gave the strategy additional credibility. The BBC had decided to allow the three main political parties in Britain access to its microphone for forty-five minutes each once a month; Keith Barry recommended such a move to the general manager as a valuable means of proving 'our non-political outlook as a broadcasting organization'.[73]

These considerations demonstrate the way in which the ABC defined its political impartiality and neutrality. Such impartiality resided in maintaining a formal distance and independence from the arguments and interests of politicians. Their opinions constituted 'both sides of the question', the 'opposing viewpoint', and the ABC as an impartial body allowed them equal access. Thus the definition of legitimate politics of the day produced by censorship practices acquired additional support from these preoccupations of the ABC. They not only confined themselves to parliamentary politics, but went further and focused particularly on the activities and views of politicians. The emphasis on impartiality, on hearing 'both sides of the question', turned issues debated on radio into the issues of the day, excluding from the debate viewpoints that questioned the way in which that debate, those issues, had been framed. The obsession with balancing the viewpoints of politicians, of allowing no party to dominate the airwaves, turned the party-defined politics of the period into the central political issues, into the politics of radio.

The eagerness of Australian politicians to exploit the medium of wireless further contributed to this definition of political issues. Their interest in radio had been cultivated by the willingness of radio stations to broadcast their speeches at any public occasion in the 1920s, as radio stations then were still relying heavily on outside broadcasts to fill their broadcasting hours. In 1927 2KY made a special feature of broadcasting political speeches of the state election campaign in NSW; the power of radio in election battles had begun to be recognized and constructed. Listeners did not always respond favourably to this use of broadcasting by politicians, but by early 1930s radio magazines were vigorously promoting the value of radio at election time. 'It's a Radio Election' announced the *Wireless Weekly* in December 1931 of the election that was to bring Joseph Lyons to power at the head of the UAP (and to have important consequences for the framing of the ABC's act). It was a 'radio election' according to this magazine, not just because listeners would be given election results throughout the night after the ballot boxes closed, but 'because radio offers the swiftest, easiest, and most efficient method of getting straight to the people. Never before has radio played such a big part in public affairs'.[74] Magazines and newspapers began to speak of the need for politicians to learn the 'art of radio speech',[75] to personalize their performance, as politicians began to assume the status of radio personalities. They were advised to deliver their speeches in quieter tones, to deliver their speeches 'as though . . . talking the matter over with a group of friends'.[76]

Radio, it was said, brought political issues into the home so that all members of the family could participate: women, previously excluded from such discussions because they did not go to election meetings, according to the *Women's Weekly*, could now hear the election speeches of all political parties.[77] Undoubtedly radio did have this educative effect by broadening the knowledge of many sections of the community about the election issues and the lines adopted by the political parties. But it also worked to make politics a privatized matter – a matter of making choices between different party leaders, radio speakers, who, by learning to become radio personalities, were packaging themselves as a commodity.

Radio defined the political as the realm of parliamentary politics of the day. It brought that parliamentary politics to listeners in the comfort of their own homes. It was a world separate from them, outside their daily lives, but radio packaged this world for listeners' easy consumption. The politics of parliamentary debates and actions came to listeners in the form of the radio personalities/politicians. The participation of listeners as citizens in the politics of the nation was to make their selection, give their vote to political policies and positions represented in this form.

The world tunes in

Advertisements for wireless sets and broadcasting programmes told listeners that the wonderful medium of radio brought the world into their living rooms. At other times, however, celebratory language about radio programmes or about wireless spoke of listeners themselves as the world. Advertisements or articles about a planned broadcast of the Melbourne Cup, the test cricket matches, or a royal wedding proclaimed 'the world' would 'tune in' to hear these great events. Addressed as the listening public or the radio audience, listeners were constituted as unities which in various contexts were re-presented as the world, the nation or the people.

Early references to radio and the nation did not address listeners in this form; they reflected instead the way in which the audience was at first conceived of as made up of various tastes and interests. Public officials and parliamentarians began to characterize radio as a service to the nation in the mid-1920s. The service consisted of 'convey[ing] to the people in the backblocks, and on remote portions of our coast, the educational and recreational advantages to be derived from hearing the best speakers and entertainers in the continent.'[78] The unity created by radio, according to such rhetoric, grew out of radio's capacity to annihilate distance, to bring to the isolated members of society the same pleasures enjoyed by those less isolated. These pleasures were not radio programmes in themselves, but the pleasures of city living – the resources, recreational and educational, readily available to those living in the major cities. This image continued to be evoked by some public speakers throughout the 1930s, though an opposing viewpoint also began to be important: by the 1940s some speakers were arguing that radio conjured up a seductive picture of city life as being 'a life of gaiety, music, bright lights, entertainment',[79] that threatened to destroy country life. Instead of bringing these advantages to people in remote places, radio now tempted young people in particular to leave the country for the excitement of the city.

The visit to Australia by the Duke and Duchess of York and the opening of Parliament House in Canberra by the Duke evoked many eulogies about radio's power to unify the nation. For a month or so preceding the visit, radio traders advertised their equipment in these terms. Though the Duke's speech could not be heard clearly, this grand occasion in the history of Australia, the newspapers and radio magazines declared, had been brought into the homes of all those fortunate enough to own a wireless set. Comments about the thrill of hearing royalty speak and the capacity of wireless to bring listeners anything of the world out there dominated these celebratory reports about radio's part in this national event.

Descriptions of sporting events on radio were treated in a similar manner in the 1920s. In 1930 the thrill of listening to cricket became even greater as techniques were developed so that listeners could hear reports of the test cricket matches between England and Australia held in England, 'as they happen'. Like the reports of the Duke of York's visit to Australia, the advertisements and print media articles about radio and sport emphasized the thrill and excitement of these broadcasts. These major sporting events or these royal occasions were spoken of as affairs in which the nation, all people, were interested; radio's miracle was to bring them to all listeners.

In the 1930s the emphasis shifted: radio now created the nation, it provided the shared concerns. 'The whole world tunes in' to hear the coronation of George VI; or, according to the *Women's Weekly*'s description of the running of the Melbourne Cup in 1937, 'For a few hours Australia is the most united country in the world.'[80] Through radio and its programmes people were brought together, they became 'the public'; this unity consisted of a shared orientation as individual consumers. By broadcasting these national events, radio brought together the listening public as the nation, the public. They continued to be 'free individuals' but, as consumers of these programmes, they had a common interest – they were a nation.

The BBC, according to Scannell and Cardiff, made major sporting occasions such as Derby Day, the Grand National or the annual Boat Race between Oxford and Cambridge truly national events.[81] These were occasions associated with a particular class upon which the whole national could now eavesdrop with the assistance of radio. They became expressions of a national life without losing their sense of exclusiveness as social events. In Australia, on the other hand, sporting events were depicted in populist terms as activities of the people. Advertisements for wireless sets or articles, such as the one on the Melbourne Cup in *Women's Weekly*, suggested that this interest cut across class and gender lines. Radio indulged this predilection shared by so many people and brought them together around the major events. In Britain radio claimed to make such occasions more accessible; in Australia it was said to be co-ordinating and fostering activities already a national pastime.

In 1932 the chairman of the ABC estimated that it was common for its stations to describe as many as thirty outside sporting events in a week.[82] ABC yearly reports show sporting broadcasts as taking up around 10 per cent of its broadcasting time. Though certain personnel within the ABC, like Keith Barry, complained of an excessive number of sports broadcasts, Charles Moses, in particular, argued that listener interest made it essential that the ABC develop these programmes as an important category of broadcasts.[83] Evidence for this pressure took the form of letters to stations and increases in radio licences around the time of test cricket matches each year. Radio in Australia had been promoted by images of sport as a common preoccupation; it now became a radio programme that claimed to unite, provide a key focus for, the listening public. For the ABC the audience for sport programmes was understood to be a sectional one, a certain proportion of the listening public sharing in common a devotion to sport. Yet, around particular events, the interests of this group were promoted as the general interest by the ABC and a number of commercial stations. In constituting an audience, a public, for the events, radio brought together – created – the nation.

Other programmes too evoked these populist images of the nation: perhaps most obviously community singing, begun in Melbourne in the

1920s. It spread to other states and remained an important feature on ABC and commercial stations in the 1930s. Celebrated as a radio form peculiar to Australia, community singing played a similar function in the early 1930s to the radio clubs like 2GB's *Happiness Club* or the Australian Broadcasting Company's 'Optimist League'. They presented images of the nation as the collectivity of free individuals 'pulling together' in the face of the depression – individuals finding privatized solutions to this problem, brought together by their shared interest in keeping in good spirits. 'Singing', according to Stuart Doyle, chairman of the Australian Broadcasting Company, 'is one of the most bracing means of combating the Depression'.[84] Later in the same decade, explicit references to the depression had disappeared from such discussions of radio programmes and broadcasting in general; but community singing retained its image of unity. Publicity for those programmes spoke of people of all walks of life being drawn together as participants in and listeners to this singing.

A number of types of programmes constituted the listening public as a unity through references to history. The news review programmes, such as *Time Marches On*, presented listeners with a review of the week's news as being a review of their lives, just as did programmes that reviewed the whole year. The ABC produced programmes such as *Do You Remember? – 1938 in Retrospect*, in which listeners heard a review of the activities of royalty, statesmen and Hitler, the dramatic occasions of civil wars, plane crashes, and the centenary celebrations and sport.[85] These were the events of your history brought back to you by radio. In other programmes, such as historical plays, listeners heard accounts of Australian history brought to them as their history, the history of their nation. The ABC in 1937 produced a radio serial *As Ye Sow* in which the fortunes of two families were followed 'against an authentic background of Australian history from the arrival of the First Fleet to the present day'.[86] A year earlier 2KY had provided a historical series 'presented by your local chemist to you – the people of Australia': *Heroes of Civilisation*. In this instance listeners heard stories of the lives of great men – Versalius . . . Lister . . . Pasteur . . . – in a broader look at their history.[87] These programmes represented the activities of 'great men' and the 'great events' in the development of an Australia dominated by white men, as the shared history of all listeners.

Celebratory articles about radio and advertisements for wireless sets provided a further version of listeners' history. Just as radio in the 1920s had stood as an allegory for science and progress, in the 1930s the development of its programming became a symbol of the wonderful pleasures constantly renewed by modern consumer society. The *Women's Weekly* told its readers in 1939 that radio's 'history is a record of constant change' and assured them that the coming of television guaranteed that this progress would continue.[88] The history of radio's progress was an allegory for the history of their world.

But royalty provided the most powerful image of national unity: in paying homage to royalty, in reporting on their activities, and through the broadcasts of speeches by the reigning monarch, radio addressed its audience as nation and Empire. King George V had begun the practice of broadcasting Christmas messages for the Empire and was quickly hailed as a most popular broadcaster, one who had mastered 'the art' of broadcasting. He adopted an intimate style of speaking and like the other radio stars or personalities appeared to be just an ordinary person speaking to each listener in the privacy of his or her home. Reports of these broadcasts represented the listening public as a unity, a family, and the monarch as 'father of us all'. The *Wireless Weekly* commended King George V's speeches as speaking to his '"Children" of the great "family" of the far flung British Empire'.[89]

With the death of King George V, radio 'joined all countries in World's grief'[90] and the familialist themes continued in the presentation of royalty and the Empire throughout the crises of 1936. In March 1936, after his accession to the throne, Edward VIII spoke to an audience said to number 200 million.[91] Within nine months he was telling them of his abdication and there was no Christmas broadcast from the King that year. But the royal occasions continued and the Empire came together as 'a family' to hear royal speeches and descriptions of weddings and coronations. Headlines such as those in popular radio magazines that claimed 'All World Guests at Wedding' constructed this image of familial unity through the sense of a shared focus and the sense of 'as if', in which all 'the world' could seem to be present at this great event by hearing it in the comfort of their homes.

Radio addressed its public as the nation in the form of a collectivity of individuals. As consumers of its programmes, listeners formed a public and their unity consisted of an orientation to the programmes provided. Particular programmes, like the news and the speeches of royalty, represented that unity as more than a shared orientation to the market; the unity became a matter of a common history or memory, a common set of preoccupations, and a common father or paternal head. This rhetoric of 'the nation' at times explicitly worked against or cut across other modes of representing the people – radio, it was sometimes said, brought together 'the cottage' and 'the royal palace', 'all classes and creeds';[92] but for the most part it simply worked as the dominant discourse of radio. Listeners to the radio were the fortunate individual consumers of the programmes provided, brought together as the nation by radio. In 1925 the *Labor Daily* had talked of a rather different unity in which radio would have a role to play: 'Linking up all the Workers'.[93] In the 1930s public discussions of radio constituted listeners as a unity within the world of radio and terms such as workers, working class, unionists or other references to such different, alternative forms of collectivities to 'the nation' or 'the Empire' seldom appeared.

Listeners' letters to the print media, to individual stations, or to the PMG did, however, occasionally utilize the language of class to protest or promote their claims, thus evoking a unity based on shared experiences rather than one that made a claim for a sense of community based on abstract principles only. Three issues provoked listeners to represent their interest in this form. The first arose in the context of opposition to 'highbrow' programmes. As members of 'the working class' or 'the working part of the population', listeners denounced the pretentiousness of highbrow programmes, and in some instances the ABC. The second issue appeared to preoccupy listeners chiefly in the early 1930s: the licence fee of twenty-four shillings per annum, some claimed, would soon mean that only 'an exclusive number of the community' could enjoy the entertainment radio provided. If the PMG did not reduce the radio licence fee, they argued, the slashing of wages for those who were employed and the large numbers of workers unemployed would soon return radio to the status of a luxury.[94]

But the issue that provoked the most vigorous complaints was the question of the broadcast descriptions of horse races and betting information. Racing clubs had begun to lobby in 1930 to have all such broadcasts stopped. To prevent broadcast descriptions of racing events, clubs banned broadcasters from their racecourses. Broadcasters took elaborate steps to continue their descriptions of races, climbing trees, setting up observation posts on the verandahs of nearby homes or erecting high platforms on the back of trucks so that they could observe the racetracks of those courses from which they had been excluded. And race clubs went to considerable trouble to obstruct the efforts of broadcasters, erecting huge canvas sails to prevent observation of the races being run or sounding loud car horns to interfere with broadcasts at crucial moments. In 1937 some resolution of the battle was achieved when 2UW won a high court decision that allowed them to broadcast race descriptions and commentaries from outside the course at Victoria Park, Sydney. Other groups continued to join with the racing clubs to lobby against the broadcasting of betting information and starting prices in particular: church organizations protested that these broadcasts threatened to corrupt the home, women and children, while the police argued that such broadcasts encouraged and facilitated the illegal activities of SP bookmakers. Though the ABC did not provide betting information until after 7.00 p.m., some commercial stations devoted large amounts of their broadcasting hours to providing detailed information and descriptions of races.

All moves to curtail racing broadcasts and the transmission of betting information were met with loud complaints from listeners, some in the form of protests against such attacks on the pleasures and liberty of listeners, but some declaring that these moves would destroy one of the few means of escape enjoyed by the working class:

> As a Labor Party Supporter, I wish to Enter a Protest against The Banning of Broadcasting of Races From Sydney and Melbourne; I may State it is The only Sport That We Miners Enjoy of a Week End up North . . . Surely To heavens We Workers have been getting hit hard Enough Lately Without Taking our only Week End Sport From us.[95]

Signed 'From the Crowd on the Goldfields', the letter was written to Joseph Lyons when he was still PMG in the Scullin Labor government in 1930. But such claims to speak as members of the working class were infrequent. For the most part listeners' letters spoke of themselves as representatives of a particular interest in radio programmes – they adopted the identification of consumer in pressing their claims.

In one other context listeners were identified as a unity constituted outside the world of radio. In newspapers such as the *Labor Daily* that spoke to a readership of labouring men and women, articles and letters to the editor spoke of an interest in radio shared by the paper's readers. The *Labor Call* in Victoria advised its readers to listen to special features of Labor talks on 3KZ, and so did the *Labor Daily* for 2KY. For the most part, however, these papers spoke of listeners as consumers of radio programmes, except when pursuing specific issues about broadcasting.

One issue provoked the *Labor Daily* to speak at some length on behalf of its readers as members of the labour movement. It was, as Inglis shows, the only daily newspaper to criticize the appointment of the first ABC Commissioners.[96] Frequently quoting Jack Beasley's statements in the federal parliament, the newspaper declared all five appointments to be political. Beasley, the leader of the Lang faction of the Labor Party in federal politics, accused the Lyons government of blatant hypocrisy in appointing five people who were explicitly associated with the UAP or, at the least, clearly supportive of the government's policies.[97] The *Labor Daily* purported to speak on behalf of its readers – as members of the labour movement – in making its vigorous criticisms of the Commission. Similarly, a year later, the paper denounced the appointment of Mrs John Moore, as she was always referred to, as director of the ABC's women's programmes in NSW. She was well known for her political work in Nationalist quarters and for her anti-Labor stance. Laborites, said the *Labor Daily*, would not be able to look to the ABC to break the UAP's dominance of radio news and views type programmes while such appointments continued to be made.[98]

These accusations made by Beasley and the *Labor Daily* were either denied or ignored. All other daily newspapers had greeted the appointment of the five Commissioners with high praise; they were people with considerable '[c]ulture and knowledge of affairs', said the *Argus*.[99] But one comment in parliamentary debates during 1932 shed a different light on the issue. Archdale Parkhill, who was to be Lyons's PMG between 1932 and 1934, countered Beasley's complaints in the House on one occasion by claiming,

> I think the honorable members will agree that among the applicants for these important positions there would not be a preponderance of Labor supporters, because those associated with the direction of big enterprises are usually member of the non-Labour party.[100]

All public statements by the Lyons government and by the daily press had agreed that people with 'business acumen' and 'culture' or 'talents' of various kinds needed to be appointed to lead the ABC. Parkhill's statement made explicit what only the *Labor Daily* and Jack Beasley, it seemed, could not understand: that those associated with or in sympathy with the labour movement would not tend to have such characteristics. In 1942 a Commissioner clearly associated with and identified as representing the interests of the trade union movement, P.G.J. Foley, was appointed by the Curtin Labor government. As with news and news commentary broadcasting, such a person was seen to be specifically 'interested', to be appointed for his association with this section of the public, whereas those people connected with conservative politics or social views escaped such labels for the most part. Beasley in his attacks on the ABC in 1932 did attempt to challenge these assumptions and the rhetoric upon which they relied by arguing that the actions of both Labor and non-Labor parties were necessarily biased, that is, interested or partisan; he claimed that had a Labor government been in power then it should have appointed Commissioners for explicit political reasons. But his arguments made little impact in this context. Instead all agreed that the ABC and its early Commissioners were people of great standing and repute and that they represented the best interests of the listening public, the interests of the nation; only Parkhill's comments suggested that there might be more than an incidental connection between political interests, social position and the claim to such qualities.

Though the *Labor Daily* identified a particular section of the community as having an interest in radio as 'Laborites', the dominant discourse of politics made such interests merely partisan, while other interests gained legitimacy by being represented under a different guise as expertise or culture. This closing of the circle thus ensured that identifications such as the labour movement or Labor supporters remained marginal and their capacity to mobilize demands about radio and its programmes constantly undermined. Listeners, it seemed, had much more likelihood of being heard as a 'popular' push for more family serials or less highbrow music. Through plebiscites, and later listener surveys, their voice could be heard and the radio stations (or the commercial stations at least) gave 'the public' what 'they' wanted as consumers, particular tastes in radio programmes. 'Laborites' could have little such power for their interests could only be sectional, biased.

Rarely, then, did another mode of representing the listening public interrupt or challenge the dominance of the identification that made individual listeners privatized consumers. Articles in the print media about radio, advertisements for wireless sets or radio programmes, public and private statements by the broadcasting stations, official statements in parliamentary debates or by the PMG, and the mode of performance now assumed as natural to radio all worked to establish this consensus. Spoken about as the public, and in specific contexts as the nation, listeners were addressed as if this identification formed their primary mode of self-identification: that they were private individuals with a mind of their own about their consumer interests, and, to the extent that they felt any allegiance to anyone, it was in an abstract form to the state or rather the nation.

This major theme in the discourses of radio reveals its central educative function – radio formed a powerful thrust to produce a new form of popular consciousness and pattern of everyday life. Radio addressed its audience as assuming a particular form, as adopting a particular mode of thinking about themselves and their everyday life. It could not coerce its users to adopt this relationship to its programmes, to assume this form of consciousness, but it worked constantly to address its audience *as if* they already operated in this way, *as if* this constituted the natural and the universal way of specifying individuals. Its educative function lay not only in its working to establish this means of identification as the only one in which demands could or would be made about radio; but, further, in its working to eliminate all other forms of identification from the field of legitimacy.

This is most apparent in the case of 2KY – in the gradual erosion of the language that surrounded the establishment of this station and the transformation of its mode of operation. Though this station had been established as a means of class communication and partisan education, by the 1930s it had been transformed into a means of entertainment and, like all other stations, addressed its audience for the most part as individual consumers of the pleasures provided. The language of class had largely disappeared from discussions about this station except as a means of identifying a particular consumer interest in horse races.[101] Only for specific issues were listeners called out to as members of the labour movement, as supporters of the Labor Party, as trade unionists, or as 'Laborites'. For the most part, the language used to discuss 2KY, both by those connected with the station and by others, conformed to the language dominant in the sphere of broadcasting. It thus excluded from such public discussions the discourses of class, the discursive practices that constituted a group of people as having a set of shared identifications and interests formed by common experiences of work and conditions of daily life. The elimination or suppression of these discourses of class from the field, and in particular from the language about and mode of operating station 2KY, diminished their power, their capacity to operate as a means of specifying or identifying individuals in all contexts.

The discourses of radio then established one means of specifying individuals and lessened the effectiveness of others by limiting their ability to operate in this context. The broader political effects of this process can be seen by looking at the way in which radio represented the depression. Only occasionally did the depression get mentioned as a problem and only in so far as it was contained by or limited to references to individual and passive solutions. The calls to 'Stay Home and Be Entertained' or the development of radio clubs and the community singing programmes rendered the depression a private trouble for the individual and a question of personal solutions through escape or solace. With radio, listeners could 'tune out the gloom'.[102] To the extent that individuals joined together in the world of radio, they did so as individuals helping each other, smiling in the face of the economic malady of a world outside their lives, a separate world of the economy and political solutions. Radio brought them news of this outside world, but they as individuals must in the meantime find their own ways of coping, or escaping the troubles, in so far as they were touched in their everyday, private lives. Radio itself also stood as symbol of a society still able to be bountiful, despite 'bad times'. Though many would have to go without or purchase sets by succumbing to the treacherous promises of hire purchase schemes, wireless sets did now seem to be in reach of everyone; and the rhetoric abounded of 'radio is now an everyday necessity, not a luxury'. The radio industry too continued to flourish, according to all reports, and each year the radio and electrical exhibitions declared a definite cause for optimism.[103] In 1947 M. Barnard Eldershaw in her book *Tomorrow and Tomorrow and Tomorrow* attempted to explore why people had not taken to the streets in Australia during the depression as unemployment escalated, why there were so few involved in political action or campaigns around this issue in the 1930s.[104] But an examination of radio in this period suggests that not only did such institutions promote different, privatized solutions, but that radio also was part of a thrust to constitute these solutions as appropriate at all times – in normal and non-normal times. By eliminating from one context a range of identifications that may have mobilized people to search for less privatized, personal solutions – as working men and women or as political citizens for example – radio served to vitiate the power of these identifications to appear unproblematic or effective in all contexts.

This educative function of radio pressed towards the creation of, in

Gramsci's terms, a new type of civilization or humanity. The discourses of radio constituted a new type of citizen: individuals seeking fulfilment in a private, everyday world of domesticity and consumption, brought together only as an abstract collectivity – as a nation or the Empire – by major sporting events or by royalty as the paternal figurehead of the state. But radio's educative work extended further than this and entailed some contradictory pressures. Through a number of processes, radio programmes diffused a type of education that Gramsci characterized in his time as seeking 'to deepen and to broaden the "intellectuality" of each individual'.[105] Most radio programmes contributed to this 'intellectualization' by offering listeners a broader knowledge of music, of the policies of the major political parties, of the scientific changes of the age, and generally, of the worlds outside their immediate experience.

In opening up these new vistas, radio no doubt did contribute to a new level of civilization and intellectuality. Celebratory statements about radio, including listeners' letters, often referred to radio in this way, claiming that radio was turning Australia into 'a vast school room' or that it was 'the greatest invention for the raising of democratic culture'.[106] Articles in radio magazines advised women of their good fortune that they were now 'free to delve into politics, literature, the world of business in our leisure hours'. Previously excluded from or unable to attend many political occasions, the *Listener In* argued, women could now make their own political judgements.[107] With the development of school broadcasts in the 1930s, radio too contributed to the more traditional processes of education. In the late 1930s the ABC introduced listening groups, a BBC innovation, extending the work of adult education previously conducted in that specific form by university extension lectures and the talks programmes. A considerable proportion of broadcasting programmes sustained this educative thrust of radio, whether directly or indirectly.

But this broadening of knowledge and information and the increased access to cultural pursuits previously available only to a minority of the population took a specific form. These new worlds came into listeners' homes as commodities to be consumed, as worlds separate from their daily lives and controlled or produced by others. As in the case of women's sessions, housewives were addressed as consumers of politics, of literature, and of 'public' affairs, just as they were addressed as consumers of the knowledge required to carry out their private tasks in the home. The worlds of politics and social change were worlds 'out there'; radio permitted the listener-in to eavesdrop only on these worlds. Though more interest in parliamentary and party politics may have been created by radio, it set up a limited definition of politics that was confined to these institutions and those who controlled them; and it represented their activities as a world to be consumed by listeners, but over which they had no control except to vote at elections or referendums – or they could exercise their ultimate power and switch to another station. Politics appeared to be the activities of politicians who began to learn to present themselves as radio stars – as personalities to be consumed, rather than to be judged according to their policies. Radio severed all connections between everyday life and the political, to join them up again as different worlds brought together by radio – a means of one-way communication.

A profound contradiction did lie, however, in radio's call to women and the way in which it constituted this group as a unity on the basis of shared characteristics. Rather than functioning at an abstract level only, this notion did provide a means of giving expression to the experiences of women. In depicting all women as the same, as having interests in common, radio had ironically contributed to the production of a public form of consciousness that would become politically powerful thirty years later. Subsequently, in the 1980s women would begin to question the politics of a common identity and look for other ways of articulating and acknowledging differences as well as the shared experiences of women. Nevertheless, the political activities of women in the 1970s and 1980s have been one significant force that has set out to reforge the connections between everyday life and the political that radio in the 1920s and 1930s represented so consistently as separate and distinct worlds.

There was nothing necessary about the way in which broadcasting developed in Australia. Specific decisions were taken and pushed for which led to the emergence of a notion of good radio with its intimate and polished style of presentation dominating the practices of broadcasting. Nor did listeners automatically accept the relationship between the audience and broadcast message assumed in this notion of good radio. Yet the optimism that Brecht and Benjamin expressed about this new technology would be harder to sustain today. Both broadcasters and listeners have become accustomed to its current social use, one which in these critics' terms has negated the progressive, democratic potential uses of this technology.

Nevertheless the story of radio's early development has some significant lessons for today. It shows how decisions are taken that fundamentally shape not only the use of new technology but its political and cultural consequences. With rapid changes now occurring in the fields of information and communications technology, including broadcasting, this history demonstrates the fundamental importance of having the political will to make clear decisions about what sort of broadcasting systems we want, but decisions that also take into consideration their broader implications.

NOTES

Abbreviations

AA	Australian Archives
ABC	Australian Broadcasting Commission
APRA	Australian Performing Rights Association
ARM	Associated Record Manufacturers
AWA	Amalgamated Wireless [Australasia] Ltd.
BBC	British Broadcasting Corporation
BBCWA	British Broadcasting Corporation Written Archives
DPT	Director of Post and Telegraphs
NLA	National Library of Australia
NSW	New South Wales
PMG	Postmaster General
SP	Starting Price
UAP	United Australia Party
USA	United States of America

Introduction

1 *Listener In*, 16 July 1932.
2 *Radio, 1985*, a publication of the Radio Marketing Bureau, Division of Federation of Australian Radio Broadcasters, Milsons Point, NSW, 1985.
3 Jean Baudrillard, *The Political Economy of the Sign*, trans. Charles Levin, St Louis, Mo, Telos Press, 1981, 172.
4 Pierre Bourdieu, *Distinction*, trans. Richard Nice, London, Routledge & Kegan Paul, 1985.
5 Such a view may be attributed, for example to Max Horkheimer and Theodor Adorno, *Dialectic of Enlightenment*, trans. John Cumming, London, Allen Lane, 1972.
6 Keith Windschuttle, *The Media. A New Analysis of the Press, Television, Radio and Advertising in Australia*, Melbourne, Penguin, 1984, 170. See also John Docker, 'Popular Culture and Its Marxist Critics', *Arena*, 65, 1983, 109–21.
7 A selection of the theoretical questions pursued in this study are outlined here: those that provide the central organizing themes or starting points. Other issues will be addressed in the body of the text.
8 Raymond Williams, *Television, Technology, and Cultural Form*, Glasgow, Fontana, 1974, 9 ff.
9 Bertolt Brecht, 'Radio as a means of communication. A talk on the function of radio', trans. Stuart Hood, *Screen*, 20 (3/4), 1979/80, 24–8.
10 Phil Slater, *Origin and Significance of the Frankfurt School*, London, Routledge & Kegan Paul, 1977, 138–42.
11 John Berger, *Ways of Seeing*, Harmondsworth, Penguin, 1972, 7.
12. Walter Benjamin, 'The work of art in the age of mechanical reproduction', *Illuminations*, trans. Harry Zohn, Glasgow, Fontana, 1970, 223–6.
13 ibid., 233.
14 Horkheimer and Adorno, op. cit., 159.
15 Theodor Adorno, 'A social critique of radio music', *Kenyon Review*, VII (2), Spring 1945, 211–14.
16 Horkheimer and Adorno, op. cit., 135.
17 See Docker, op. cit. and Windschuttle, op. cit. For a critique of such uses of the Adorno versus Benjamin argument, see: Pauline Johnson, 'Picturing reality. Essay review', *Arena*, 65, 1983, 121–31.
18 Stuart Hall, 'Notes on deconstructing the "Popular"', in Raphael Samuel (ed.), *People's History and Socialist Theory*, London, Routledge & Kegan Paul, 1981, 239.
19 The reference to the separation of private troubles and public issues in contemporary society is drawn from C. Wright Mills, *The Sociological Imagination*, New York, Oxford University Press, 1959, 186.
20 See Tony Bennett, *Popular Culture: Politics, Ideology and Popular Culture*, Open University course book, Milton Keynes, 1982.

Chapter 1 A gift of science

1. *Daily Telegraph*, 4 December 1923; *Daily Mail*, 4 December 1923.
2. *Age*, 31 March 1923.
3. Ian Bedford and Ross Curnow, *Initiative and Organisation*, Melbourne, Cheshire, 1963, 66–7.
4. *Daily Telegraph*, 19 April 1923.
5. *Labor Daily*, 15 September 1924.
6. *Daily Telegraph*, 9 November 1923.
7. *Age*, 26 July 1923.
8. *Daily Telegraph*, 26 July 1923.
9. Michael S. Counihan, 'The construction of Australian broadcasting: aspects of radio in Australia in the 1920s', MA thesis, Monash Unviersity, 1981, 8.
10. *Daily Telegraph*, 5 February 1924.
11. *Age*, 7 June 1924.
12. Australia, House of Representatives, *Debates* 1924, vol. 107, 2066.
13. *Age*, 21 October 1924.
14. *Labor Daily*, 15 April 1924.
15. ibid., 20 October 1924.
16. Australia, House of Representatives, *Debates* 1926, vol. 113, 3523.
17. *Daily Telegraph*, 16 October 1924.
18. *Radio in Australia and New Zealand*, 23 January 1924.
19. Stuart Ewen, *Captains of Consciousness*, New York, McGraw Hill, 1976, 107.
20. In 1926 AWA was employing 800 people in its Sydney factory.
21. *Daily Telegraph*, 13 May 1936.
22. *Labor Daily*, 12 September 1924.
23. ibid., 3 May 1926.
24. I am grateful to Pauline Johnson for her formulation of this point.
25. Raymond Williams, *Television, Technology and Cultural Form*, Glasgow, Fontana, 1974, 23–6.
26. See Counihan, op. cit., 212–3.
27. Bedford and Curnow, op. cit., 101.
28. *Smith's Weekly*, 22 September 1923.
29. *Daily Telegraph*, 3 September 1926.
30. ibid., 30 April 1926.
31. *Listener In*, 10 October 1925.
32. *Radio in Australia and New Zealand*, 19 March 1924.
33. *Labor Daily*, 3 May 1926.
34. See Beverley Kingston, *My Wife, My Daughter, My Poor Mary Ann*, Melbourne, Nelson, 1975, 110; see also Kerreen Reiger, 'Women's labour redefined: child-bearing and rearing advice in Australia, 1880–1930s', in

Margaret Bevege *et al.* (eds) *Worth Her Salt*, Sydney, Hale & Iremonger, 1982.
35 Harry Braverman, *Labor and Monopoly Capital*, New York, Monthly Review Press, 1974, 276.
36 Peter Spearritt, *Sydney Since the Twenties*, Sydney, Hale and Iremonger, 1978, 54. At first radios were run off batteries; by 1927–8 it was possible to run the set off the household electricity supply.
37 Ewen, op. cit., 109.
38 *Radio in Australia and New Zealand*, 1 April 1925.
39 *Listener In*, 21 November 1925.
40 Nevertheless, a writer for the *Age* (28 October 1924) complained that 3LO was doing little to popularize radio by its relying on children's programmes and cinema orchestral items for day-time programming.
41 *Labor Daily*, 7 December 1925.
42 See Counihan, op. cit., 175 for a detailed and insightful discussion of these points.
43 *Labor Daily*, 16 October 1925 and 20 August 1926. Raymond Williams, *Television, Technology and Cultural Form*, Glasgow, Fontana, 1974, 24, suggests that the only developed use of broadcasting as a mass, public medium occurred in Nazi Germany. Under Goebbels' orders the party organized compulsory public listening groups and wireless receiving sets were put up in the streets.
44 Referred to in these terms in a number of contexts. The theme continued to be used in this manner in 1927. For example: Royal Commission on Wireless, 1927, transcripts, vol. 8, 2310, Australian Archives (AA) CP 657/1.
45 *Labor Daily*, 15 June 1925.
46 *Daily Telegraph*, 9 April 1923.
47 A fascinating example of the resurrection of this conception of broadcasting occurred during the 'Ash Wednesday' fires of 1983 in Victoria, Australia. Local radio stations opened 'their air waves' to people trying to get in touch with friends and relatives, or giving information on the direction of the fires. Barry Hill, radio critic for the *Age*, has made this point in a number of contexts, see for example, 'Oz Radio Now', *Media Information Australia*, 41, 1986, 6–10.
48 As Counihan, op. cit., 122–3 shows; nor were these stations central to the agenda of the 1924 conference about alternatives to the sealed set system.
49 *Labor Daily*, 19 August 1925.
50 *Listener In*, 17 October 1925.
51 *Age*, 8 December 1925.
52 *Daily Telegraph*, 8 February 1924.
53 See, for example: Australia, House of Representatives, *Debates* 1924, vol. 109, 4275.
54 See, for example: *Radio in Australia and New Zealand*, 24 April 1925.

55 *Smith's Weekly*, 13 January 1923 and 29 December 1923.
56 *Daily Mail*, 25 December 1923.
57 ibid., 7 July 1923.
58 This point is also formulated along similar lines by Counihan, op. cit.
59 *Labor Daily*, 20 February 1925.
60 *Age*, 24 March 1925.
61 *Radio in Australia and New Zealand*, 5 March 1924.
62 *Labor Daily*, 7 November 1925.
63 ibid., 20 February 1925 and 22 June 1925.
64 *Daily Telegraph*, 17 October 1924; *Listener In*, 17 October 1925.
65 *Daily Telegraph*, 17 October 1924.
66 ibid., 2 June 1923 and 21 February 1925; *Age*, 6 January 1925; *Listener In*, 4 July 1925; and Amalgamated Wireless [Australasia] Ltd., Letterbook, letter to Mr L. Hooke, 24 October 1924, Ms 9934, La Trobe Library Manuscripts.
67 *Daily Telegraph*, 21 February 1925.
68 *Labor Daily*, 1 April 1925 and 28 July 1925.
69 Stuart Hood, 'Brecht on radio', *Screen*, 20, Winter 1979/80, 25. Brecht went further in his critique of radio, arguing, for example, for the need to develop different programme forms.
70 *Labor Daily*, 24 October 1924.
71 ibid., 5 March 1925.
72 Quoted in Murray Goot, 'Radio Lang', in Heather Radi and Peter Spearritt (eds), *Jack Lang*, Sydney, Hale & Iremonger, 1977, 123–4.
73 *Labor Daily*, 14 July 1925.
74 Royal Commission on Wireless, 1927, transcripts, 2661, E.R. Voigt, witness, AA CP 657/1; see also *Labor Daily*, 18 May 1925.
75 In August 1925, Willis had Voigt appointed his private secretary. Willis was general secretary of the Miners' Federation and vice-president of the executive council of the Trades Hall. Willis was also said to be largely responsible for the establishment of the *Labor Daily*.
76 *Labor Daily*, 9 March 1925, 14 April 1925 and 4 November 1925. Only one newspaper went out the day after the New York pressmen's strike was called, a labour paper keeping strikers informed about the progress of the strike. But eventually a wireless station was used to break their stranglehold on the news and the strike was defeated.
77 *Labor Daily*, 3 June 1925 and 5 June 1925.
78 ibid., 28 November 1925.
79 *Wireless Weekly*, 12 January 1934.
80 Executive Committee Minutes, Labor Council Records of NSW, 24 May 1924, 3 September 1924 and 10 November 1925, A 3843, Mitchell Library; and Records, General Meetings, Labor Council Records of NSW, 20 November 1924, A 3843, Mitchell Library.

Chapter 2 The best seat in the house

1 Bertolt Brecht, 'Radio as a means of communication. A talk on the function of radio', trans. Stuart Hood, *Screen*, 20 (3/4), 24.
2 *Labor Daily*, 7 December 1925.
3 In July 1925, AWA reported that 174¼ hours of outside broadcasts had been made so far that year, AWA Ltd Letterbook, 11 July 1925, Ms 9934, La Trobe Library manuscripts.
4 The *Age* ran an article headed in these terms, 20 October 1925, as did the *Daily Telegraph*, 9 April 1926, using virtually the same text as the first article.
5 Royal Commission on Wireless, 1927, transcripts, vol. 10, 2921–2, S.E. Wilson witness, AA CP 657/1.
6 See the next section of this chapter and chapter 5 for further discussion of news broadcasts.
7 *Labor Daily*, 9 January 1926; 3 November 1926.
8 ibid., 1 December 1928.
9 Royal Commission on Wireless, 1927, transcripts, vol. 10, 3022–3, S.E. Wilson witness, AA CP 657/1.
10 Australia, House of Representatives, *Debates* 1928, vol. 118, 5268–9; *Daily Telegraph*, 29 November 1928.
11 *Daily Telegraph*, 3 September 1926.
12 ibid., 30 September 1927.
13 ibid., 3 September 1929.
14 Australia, House of Representatives, *Debates* 1926, vol. 112, 597.
15 *Radio in Australia and New Zealand*, 1 April 1925.
16 Articles such as 'What chance has broadcasting of influencing language', *Radio in Australia and New Zealand*, 15 November 1927, argued for formal, correct English.
17 *Radio in Australia and New Zealand*, 15 July 1927.
18 Australia, House of Representatives, *Debates* 1927, vol. 117, 2889–97.
19 The *Daily Telegraph* spoke of wireless 'overcoming' distance, but by 1927 the phrase 'annihilating distance' was frequently used.
20 *Daily Telegraph*, 18 March 1927.
21 *Listener In*, 11 October 1930.
22 *Labor Daily*, 5 June 1925.
23 *Listener In*, 4 July 1928.
24 Australia, House of Representatives, *Debates* 1927, vol. 116, Stanley Bruce (Prime Minister), 1555–64.
25 ibid., vol. 117, 2849–89.
26 *Labor Daily*, 5 May 1925.
27 *Age*, 18 November 1927.

28 ibid., 23 November 1926.
29 Royal Commission on Wireless, 1927, transcripts, vol. 10, 2901–16, AA CP 657/1.
30 *Daily Telegraph*, 26 May 1923.
31 Australia, Senate, *Debates* 1927, vol. 117, 1830–5.
32 *Wireless Weekly*, 8 August 1930.
33 ibid., 27 November 1931.
34 ibid., 8 August 1930.
35 Michael S. Counihan, 'The construction of Australian broadcasting: aspects of radio in Australia', MA thesis, Monash University, 1981, 216.
36 Australia, House of Representatives, *Debates* 1924, vol. 109, 4275.
37 Alan Barnard, 'Ruling Australia's airwaves in the 1920s', unpublished paper, 1982 Conference of the Economic History Society of Australia and New Zealand, 4.
38 Royal Commission on Wireless, 1927, transcripts, vol. 1, 109 and vol. 8, 2310–11, AA CP 657/1.
39 ibid., vol. 10, 3060 f.
40 *Age*, 14 September 1927.
41 *Labor Daily*, 16 September 1927.
42 Barnard, op. cit., 28.
43 Copy of tender form, National Broadcasting Service, Schedule No. C451 A, Australian Broadcasting Company, E1/315/1, BBC Written Archives (BBCWA).
44 Broadcasting Tender, Fullers Theatres Ltd, Albert and Son, Union Theatres Ltd, 15 May 1929, file 27/1053, AA MP 341/1.
45 *Wireless Weekly*, 10 May 1929.
46 Stuart Hood, 'Brecht on radio', *Screen*, 20, Winter 1979/80, 18.
47 *Age*, 23 August 1928.
48 Royal Commission on Wireless, *Report* (presented 5 October 1927), Commonwealth Parliamentary Papers, 1926–8, vol. 4, 1565–603.
49 Counihan, op. cit., 233. See also his discussion of the position of the 'B' stations in the 1920s and the PMG changes made in 1930, 213–32.
50 Royal Commission on Wireless, 1927, transcripts, vol. 9, 2514, A.E. Bennett, witness, AA CP 657/1.
51 Theosophical Society booklet and report on broadcasting, 30 June 1935, F.W. Daniell Papers, National Library of Australia (NLA) Ms 1634/365.
52 *Listener In*, 1 August 1928, reported the PMG as stating that he had received over fifty applications for additional 'B' class licences. See also Counihan, op. cit., 218–24.
53 *Listener In*, 18 December 1929.
54 Royal Commission on Wireless, 1927, transcripts, vol. 1, 19, AA CP 657/1.
55 *Argus*, 12 May 1925 to 30 May 1925.
56 Royal Commission on Wireless, 1927, transcripts, vol. 2, 354, AA CP 657/1.
57 *Daily Telegraph*, 20 May 1927.

58 *Age*, 31 August 1926.
59 *Listener In*, 26 September 1928.
60 ibid., 5 September 1928.
61 *New Idea*, 25 April 1930.
62 *Listener In*, 20 March 1926.
63 *Wireless Weekly*, 19 April 1929.

Chapter 3 The intimate voice

1 *Labor Daily*, 26 June 1933.
2 *Daily Telegraph*, 21 February 1925.
3 *Listener In*, 12 July 1930.
4 *Labor Daily*, 19 November 1934.
5 Richard Dyer, *Stars*, London, British Film Institute, 1979, 156–8, argues that this particular mode of performance is quite specific to radio: it is a style of performance in which broadcasters appear to be playing themselves as plain ordinary people.
6 *Daily Telegraph*, 12 June 1933.
7 Nancy Lee, *Being a Chum Was Fun*, Melbourne, Listen & Learn Productions, 1979.
8 *Listener In*, 21 August 1937.
9 ibid., 18 January 1936.
10 *Labor Daily*, 16 September 1935.
11 Paddy Scannell, 'The social eye of television, 1946–1955', *Media, Culture and Society*, 1 (1), 1979.
12 *Wireless Weekly*, 14 July 1933.
13 ibid., 26 May 1933.
14 C.C. Faulkner and J.D. Corbet (eds), *The Broadcast Year Book and Radio Listeners' Annual of Australia*, 1934.
15 *Listener In*, 22 October 1932.
16 *Australian Women's Weekly*, 15 April 1939.
17 *Daily Telegraph*, 12 March 1926.
18 *Wireless Weekly*, 10 April 1931.
19 *Women's Weekly*, 17 November 1934.
20 *Daily Telegraph*, 14 August 1937.
21 *Age*, 12 August 1937.
22 *Listener In*, 30 April 1930.
23 PMG Files, 14 June 1938, File BP 19/1, AA MP 1170/3. These figures were based only on those who had taken out licences. It is not possible to determine how many unlicensed sets there were.
24 Australian Broadcasting System, n.d., F.W. Daniell Papers, NLA Ms 1634/373.
25 W.A. McNair, *Radio Advertising in Australia*, Sydney, Angus & Robertson, 1937, 292.

26 *Wireless Weekly*, 11 November 1932.
27 *Daily Telegraph*, 30 April 1926; 24 March 1936.
28 *New Idea*, 25 April 1930.
29 *Daily Telegraph*, 9 November 1932.
30 Stuart Ewen, *Captains of Consciousness*, New York, McGraw Hill, 1976, 107.
31 *Labor Daily*, 3 April 1933.
32 Ewen, op. cit., 108.
33 *Wireless Weekly*, 13 February 1931.
34 ibid.
35 *Listener In*, 1 January 1930.
36 ibid., 25 July 1931.
37 *Wireless Weekly*, 18 July 1930.
38 ibid., 11 November 1939.
39 ibid., 20 June 1930.
40 *Listener In*, 30 April 1930.
41 Michèle Barrett and Mary McIntosh, *The Anti-Social Family*, London, Verso, 1982, 27.
42 *Wireless Weekly*, 15 July 1932.
43 *Labor Daily*, 16 May 1936.
44 *Daily Telegraph*, 12 June 1934.
45 *Labor Daily*, 17 November 1925.
46 *Truth*, 30 October 1932.
47 See Chapter 5.
48 *Listener In*, 27 September 1930.
49 *Women's Weekly*, 5 September 1936.
50 *Age*, 31 May 1927.
51 That is, in the photographs and drawings used by the print media, as well as in written language.
52 Henri Lefebvre, *Everyday Life in the Modern World*, trans. Sacha Rabinovitch, New York, Harper Torchbooks, 1971, 86.
53 See Athol Tier Papers, NLA Ms 5582.
54 *Radio Times*, 10 July 1943. A number of witnesses before the Royal Commission on Wireless, 1927, declared that serials would never be successful: transcripts, vol. 8, 2076–83, AA CP 657/1.
55 *Wireless Weekly*, 4 October 1939.
56 *Listener In*, 18 July 1936 and 9 October 1937.
57 ibid., 18 July 1936.
58 *Daily Telegraph*, 24 March 1936.
59 *Radio Times*, 28 September 1935.
60 ibid., 6 June 1936.
61 C.L. Moses to C.A.L. Cliff, 25 October 1937, Countries, Australia: Propaganda A–Z, 1936–43, E1/385, BBCWA.
62 *Wireless Weekly*, 1 April 1938.
63 John Potts, 'The function of advertising in the 1930s: Wrigley's *Dad and*

216 THE UNSEEN VOICE

Dave, . . . "Solving the Problem"', draft chapter 1, MA thesis NSW Institute of Technology, on loan to the author.
64 Ewen, op. cit., 113–38.
65 Theodor Adorno, 'A social critique of radio music', *Kenyon Review*, VII (2), Spring 1945, 214.
66 Letters in: *Radio Times*, 10 April 1937; *Wireless Weekly*, 27 May 1938; *Listener In*, 15 January 1938.
67 Lefebvre, op. cit., 73.
68 Ewen, op. cit., 184.
69 *Listener In*, 19 July 1930.
70 ibid., 3 May 1930.
71 *Radio Times*, 4 July 1936.
72 *Listener In*, 18 September 1929.
73 *Women's Weekly*, 13 September 1939.
74 Ann Game and Rosemary Pringle, *Gender at Work*, Sydney, Allen & Unwin, 1983, 119 ff.
75 The Macquarie Broadcasting Catalogue (1940), F.W. Daniell Papers, NLA Ms 1634/386–8.
76 *Broadcasting Business*, 6 February 1936.
77 ibid., 12 December 1935.
78 ibid., 6 February 1936.
79 McNair, op. cit., 318.
80 'On the Hour . . . In Day Time', F.W. Daniell Papers, NLA Ms 1634/126.
81 Game and Pringle, op. cit., 133.
82 *Wireless Weekly*, 25 May 1936.
83 ibid., 26 June 1931.
84 ibid., 31 August 1934.
85 *Daily Telegraph*, 31 August 1934.
86 John Heskelt, *Industrial Design*, London, Thames & Hudson, 1980, 81–4.
87 Michel Foucault, *Discipline and Punish*, trans. Alan Sheridan, London, Allen Lane, 1977, 150.
88 *Wireless Weekly*, 13 March 1931.
89 M.Z. Rosaldo, 'Woman, culture and society: a theoretical overview', in M.Z. Rosaldo and L. Lamphere (eds), *Woman, Culture and Society*, Stanford University Press, 1974, 39.
90 K. Barrett to F.W. Daniell, 23 November 1937, Report of the 2GB Happiness Club, F.W. Daniell Papers, NLA Ms 1634/308/1.

Chapter 4 The world of radio

1 Richard Dyer, *Stars*, London, British Film Institute, 1979, 38 f.
2 Notes for Programme Committee Meetings, 26 June 1934; Points for 2UE Programme Report, F.W. Daniell Papers, NLA Ms 1634/123.

3 *Wireless Weekly*, 5 April 1939.
4 F.W. Daniell Papers, NLA, Ms 1634/315.
5 W.A. McNair, *Radio Advertising in Australia*, Sydney, Angus & Robertson, 1937, 338.
6 *Labor Daily*, 2 July 1938. The implications of this personalizing of politicians and royalty are examined further in Chapter 5.
7 *Listener In*, 24 November 1934.
8 *Wireless Weekly*, 25 December 1936.
9 *Broadcasting Business*, 23 January 1936.
10 *Women's Weekly*, 27 November 1937.
11 *Wireless Weekly*, 18 November 1938.
12 Theodor Adorno, 'A social critique of radio music', *Kenyon Review*, VII (2), Spring 1945, 212; see also T.W. Adorno, *Prisms*, New York, Columbia University Press, 1976, 131.
13 Adorno, 'A social critique of radio music', op. cit.
14 'The Voice of the ABC', 22 December 1944, File: Announcer's Manual, AA MP 237/1, Box 57A.
15 Commission Minutes, 5–7 June 1946, ABC Archives.
16 *Listener In*, 12 March 1932.
17 *Daily Telegraph*, 16 June 1936.
18 Moses to Victorian Manager, 20 December 1938; and telegram, 10 March 1939, File: Early Morning Sessions, Box 11A, AA MP 237/1.
19 Walter Benjamin, 'The work of art in the age of mechanical reproduction', *Illuminations*, trans. Harry Zohn, Glasgow, Fontana, 1970, 233.
20 ibid., 225.
21 For example: W.J. Cleary to H. Brookes, 5 October 1938, Herbert Brookes Papers, NLA Ms 1924/26/710.
22 *Listener In*, 12 November 1938 and 11 March 1939.
23 Memo: Moses to all States, 15 July 1939, Box 59, AA MP 237/1.
24 *Wireless Weekly*, 2 April 1937.
25 General Manager's Report, 7 November 1940, Macquarie Network Convention, F.W. Daniell Papers, NLA Ms 1634/345.
26 Memo, 4 July 1935, F.W. Daniell Papers, NLA Ms 1634/300/1.
27 *Argus*, 3 June 1930 and 4 June 1930.
28 *Argus*, 18 November 1929.
29 T.W. Bearup, Report on trip overseas, 1936, Box 45, AA MP 237/1.
30 *Wireless Weekly*, 8 May 1931.
31 *Listener In*, 26 August 1933.
32 *Argus*, 1 June 1932.
33 For example: *Wireless Weekly*, 29 August 1930; 29 January 1932; 15 April 1932; 29 April 1932.
34 For useful comments on this feature of Arnold's argument, see: Raymond Williams, 'A hundred years of culture and anarchy', *Problems in Materialism and Culture*, London, Verso, 1980, 7.

35 *Wireles Weekly*, 5 February 1931.
36 Chairman's Talk (W.J. Cleary), Legacy Club Luncheon, 'Why National Broadcasting?', 8 August 1940, item 1.1, CA 251, Australian Broadcasting Commission, Head Office Programme Department, General Programme Policies, File No. 1, 1936–42, AA SP 341/1.
37 Benjamin, op. cit., 223, 226.
38 A trend upon which Benjamin himself remarked, quoted in Susan Buck-Morss, 'Walter Benjamin – revolutionary writer' (1), *New Left Review*, 128, July/August 1981, 55.
39 See Pierre Bourdieu, 'The aristocracy of culture', *Media, Culture and Society*, 2 (3), 1980, 238 f.
40 M.A. Frost tour, Empire Services, E4/4, BBCWA. Much of this discussion of the relationship between the ABC and BBC draws on BBC archival material.
41 W.J. Cleary quoting J. Beasley, Chairman's Talk, Legacy Club Luncheon, op. cit.
42 W.G.K. Duncan to Sir Charles Lloyd Jones, ABC Head Office, Correspondence Files, Mrs C. Couchman File, AA SP 1489/1.
43 McGregory to Moses, 16 June 1939, ABC Programmes, S–Z, 1939–46, E1/321/2, BBCWA.
44 Memo: Keith Barry to Victorian Manager, 16 August 1941, File: 'So You Think You Know Your Literature', Box 69, AA MP 237/1.
45 *Wireless Weekly*, 11 January 1929.
46 *Age*, 9 March 1938.
47 C.J.A. Moses to J.C.S. MacGregor, 11 July 1939, ABC Programmes, S–Z, 1939–46, E1/321/2, BBCWA; see also, Keith Barry to Victorian Manager, 31 March 1938, File: 'Spelling Bees', Box 68, AA MP 237/1.
48 *Listener In*, 8 April 1938 and 23 April 1938.
49 ibid., 22 August 1936.
50 *Daily Telegraph*, 12 August 1932.
51 *Listener In*, 1 January 1930.
52 Theodor Adorno and Max Horkheimer, 'The culture industry: enlightenment as mass deception', in James Curran *et al.* (eds) *Mass Communication and Society*, London, Edward Arnold, 1977, 351.
53 T.W. Bearup, Report on Broadcasting Conditions Overseas, April–October 1936, 2, Box 45, AA MP 237/1.
54 *Daily Telegraph*, 24 March 1936.
55 ibid., 29 March 1933.
56 *Wireless Weekly*, 10 February 1933.
57 ibid., 1 November 1935.
58 *Argus*, 1 February 1928.
59 *Wireless Weekly*, 19 April 1934.
60 ibid., 31 July 1931.
61 *Listener In*, 10 June 1933.

NOTES 219

62 *Wireless Weekly*, 26 June 1931.
63 ibid., 25 October 1935.
64 ibid., 21 August 1931, 23 November 1934, 2 August 1935, 15 November 1935.
65 ibid., 11 October 1935.
66 ibid., 5 February 1931.
67 See Bourdieu, op. cit., 253.
68 *Listener In*, 1 August 1928.
69 ibid., 13 June 1928 and 4 July 1928.
70 For further discussion of this and other changes to the 'B' class stations, see Michael Counihan, 'The construction of Australian broadcasting: aspects of radio in Australia in the 1920s', MA thesis, Monash University, 1981, 212 ff.
71 *Argus*, 22 February 1927.
72 Counihan, op. cit., 228.
73 *Listener In*, 2 August 1930; and see *Wireless Weekly*, 14 November 1930.
74 Counihan, op. cit., 211.
75 *Daily Telegraph*, 28 October 1927; *Listener In*, 2 August 1930.
76 *Wireless Weekly*, 9 October 1931.
77 *Daily Telegraph*, 10 February 1932.
78 R.B. Walker, *Yesterday's News*, Sydney University Press, 1980, 128.
79 Counihan, op. cit., 227.
80 Empire Press Representative to A/DES, 3 June 1937, Countries Australia: Empire Programmes, 1937, E1/353, BBCWA.
81 C. Lloyd Jones to Herbert Brookes, 21 August 1933, Herbert Brookes Papers, NLA Ms 1924/26/81-2.
82 C. Lloyd Jones to Sir John Reith, 23 December 1932, E1/315/1, BBCWA.
83 J.A. Clark to C(P), BBC Internal Memo, 1 December 1936, Empire Broadcasting Australia, E2/162, BBCWA.
84 *Argus*, 16 July 1935.
85 At first there was some disagreement about this approach. W.T. Conder, as general manager, brought with him the values of the entertainment business, which Commissioners such as Herbert Brookes opposed. In 1935 W.J. Cleary appointed Charles Moses as general manager; both men were opposed to popularizing techniques and the ABC's policy became clearer on this matter from this point on.
86 No author, 'Crooners News', Box 1/1, 1, File 1, AA SP 341/1.
87 No author, Statement of Commission's View on Item 3, File: Parliamentary Standing Committee, Box 3, AA SP 1489.
88 Chairman's Talk (W.J. Cleary), Legacy Club Luncheon, op. cit.
89 Raymond Williams, 'Institutions of technology', in Armand Mattelart and Seth Siegelaub (eds) *Communications and Class Struggle*, 1, New York, International General, 1979, 265.
90 Richard White, *Inventing Australia*, Sydney, Allen & Unwin, 1981, 148 f.

White discusses the development of large-scale industrial concerns such as BHP and the accompanying shift away from the dominance of British culture (and markets).
91 *Age*, 8 July 1937; *Radio Times*, 29 January 1944; and see also a newspaper cutting date unmarked but approximately June 1939, Herbert Brookes Papers, NLA Ms 1924/26/802.
92 Extract of a letter, General Manager to Manager for Queensland, Memorandum in connection with visit to Brisbane by the Hon. R.B. Orchard, 25 January 1939, Box 1, File: State Visits, AA SP 1489.
93 Bourdieu, op. cit., 251.
94 Press Statement, 1 September 1946, Box 1/1.1, File No. 11, AA SP 341/1.
95 The BBC introduced three sets of programmes: the 'home programme', the 'light', and the 'cultural'. See Programme C, Terms of Reference (approved 14 January 1946), Policy, Third Programme, 1945–54, R34/890/1, BBCWA.
96 *Wireless Weekly*, 18 July 1930.
97 *Listener In*, 1 July 1933.
98 ibid., 31 March 1937.
99 Record of Interview with E.R. Voigt, from J.M. Clark, 30 March 1936, Countries: Australia, Personal, A–Z, 1935–52, E1/378, BBCWA.
100 Australia, House of Representatives, *Debates* 1937, vol. 154, 141.
101 Record of Interview with E.R. Voigt, op. cit.
102 Press Release for *Radio Pictorial*, 14 July 1938, F.W. Daniell Papers, NLA Ms 1634/302/2.
103 Ian MacKay, 'Macquarie – the Story of a Network', unpublished manuscript, Broadcasting Tribunal Library, Melbourne, 32.
104 R.A. Irish, Treasurer, to Acting Executive Director, Macquarie Broadcasting Services, 4 March 1939, F.W. Daniell Papers, NLA Ms 1634/362.
105 MacKay, op. cit., 2.
106 Memo: F.W. Daniell, 4 July 1935, F.W. Daniell Papers, NLA Ms 1634/300/1.
107 Memo Re: Youth Speaks (no author, no date), ibid., NLA Ms 1634/341/1.
108 *Daily Telegraph*, 24 March 1936.
109 Brochure: Announcing 2KA Katoomba, F.W. Daniell Papers, NLA 1634/320.
110 *Broadcasting Business*, 29 October 1936.
111 Document re the formation of Radio Katoomba Ltd (no author), F.W. Daniell Papers, NLA Ms 1634/384/3.
112 McNair, op. cit., 247.
113 *Broadcasting Business*, 12 December 1935.
114 R. Denison (Macquarie Broadcasting Services) to Acting Director, General Posts and Telegraphs, 9 July 1947, 34, BN/2/2, 4, AA MP 1170/3.
115 Joint Committee on Wireless Broadcasting (W.J. Gibson, Chairman),

Report, Canberra, AGPS, 1942. In the conclusion of this report three of the six-member committee recorded their commitment to the Labor Party's policy that all broadcasting should be nationalized.

Chapter 5 Eavesdropping on the outside world

1. See File BP/9/1, AA MP 1170/3; and Box 5 (PMG Files), AA MP 544/1.
2. Australia, House of Representatives, *Debates* 1923, vol. 5, 2582.
3. R.B. Walker, *Yesterday's News*, Sydney University Press, 1980, 117 f. Frank Dixon, *Inside the ABC*, Melbourne, Hamilton Press, 1975, 21 f; Australia, House of Representatives, *Debates* 1935, vol. 148, 2164–5; 'News Organisation', ABC Head Office, Correspondence File, Item 1, CA 251, AA SP 314/1.
4. Memo: M.F.D. to General Manager, 5 July 1938, ABC Head Office, Correspondence File, News Organisation, 1940–43, Item 1, CA 251, AA SP 314/1.
5. *Wireless Weekly*, 16 October 1935.
6. *Argus*, 5 October 1935.
7. ibid., 7 October 1935.
8. J.B. Clark to C. Moses, 22 April 1938, File E1/383, Countries. Australia. Programme Details, 1935–41, BBCWA.
9. *Broadcasting Business*, 8 October 1936.
10. *Listener In*, 8 October 1938.
11. Memo from Chief Inspector (Telegraphs), E.H. Bourne, 21 May 1930, File: 33/4752, AA MP 341/1, 174/s.
12. *Argus*, 12 June 1929.
13. Newspaper cutting from the *Radio Times*, 7 September (no year – approximately 1934 or 5), F.W. Daniell Papers, NLA Ms 1634/380/2.
14. War news broadcast (no date or author), ibid., NLA Ms 1634/125.
15. Moses to J.B. Clark, 8 December 1936, News, 1936–46, E1/371, BBCWA.
16. Dixon, op. cit., 26–7.
17. *Listener In*, 8 October 1938.
18. F. Daniell to A.G. Horner, 28 September 1938, F.W. Daniell Papers, NLA Ms 1634/320.
19. *Listener In*, 8 October 1938.
20. Dixon, op. cit., 32.
21. J.B. Clark to Moses, 26 January 1937, News 1938–48, E1/341, BBCWA.
22. Asa Briggs, *The Golden Age of Wireless. The History of Broadcasting in the United Kingdom*, Vol. II, Oxford University Press, 1965, 154–7.
23. Hints for the Guidance of ABC News Compilers, signed C.J.A. Moses, 1 December 1938, File Ess/9, AA, MP 237.
24. L.R. Thomas to T.W. Bearup, 8 May 1942 (Document to News Staff, 1 May 1942), ABC Files re News Department and News Contract, News

Miscellaneous, 1940–42, M3, AA SP 314/1.
25 Memo to General Manager from MCD, 5 July 1938, ABC Head Office, Correspondence File: News Organisation, Item 1, CA 251, AA SP 314/1.
26 Dixon to Acting General Manager, 16 March 1942, ABC Head Office, Central Files: News, Miscellaneous, 1940–42, Item MB, AA SP 314/1.
27 H.D. Black to C.V.A. Moses, 31 January 1939, ABC Head Office, Correspondence File: News Organisation, 1940–43, Item 1, CA 251, AA SP 314/1; News Organisation, Draft, S.H. Deamer, 9 February 1942, Item 1, Box 3, AA SP 341.
28 Memo to R.E. Denison, 5 September 1939, F.W. Daniell Papers, NLA Ms 1634/301/1.
29 Internal memos from F. Daniell, 19 October 1938 and 22 October 1938, ibid., 322/1.
30 Document (no author, date handwritten) dated 5 March 1943, ABC Head Office, Correspondence File: News Organisation: 1940–43, Item 2, CA 251, AA SP 314/1.
31 Alan Thomas, *Broadcast and Be Damned*, Melbourne University Press, 1980, 88.
32 *Wireless Weekly*, 5 December 1930.
33 *Listener In*, 23 July 1938.
34 There is now a considerable body of literature that discusses the social construction of the news. See for example: Glasgow Media Group, *Bad News*, London, Routledge & Kegan Paul, 1976, and *More Bad News*, London, Routledge & Kegan Paul, 1980; Stuart Hall *et al.*, *Policing the Crisis*, London, Macmillan, 1978; Philip Schlesinger, *Putting 'Reality' Together*, London, Constable, 1978.
35 H.P. Brown to John Reith, 16 September 1931, File 1A, Broadcasting in Australia, 1929–31, E1/341/1, BBCWA.
36 Australia, House of Representatives, *Debates* 1931, vol. 131, 4207–9, 4494–5.
37 *Labor Daily*, 8 August 1931.
38 See for example Circular No. 15 to all commercial stations, 20 September 1935, F.W. Daniell Papers, NLA Ms 1634/125.
39 Australia, *Australian Broadcasting Commission Act.* 1932 (No. 14).
40 Thomas, op. cit., 78.
41 K.S. Inglis, *This is the ABC. The Australian Broadcasting Commission 1932–1983*, Melbourne University Press, 1983, 61.
42 'Status of the ABC', 1932–4, Head Office, Correspondence File, AA SP 1489/1.
43 W.J. Cleary to H. Brookes, 11 May 1938, Herbert Brookes Papers, NLA Ms 1924/26/659.
44 ibid.
45 For example, see *Argus*, 16 October 1935.
46 Dixon, op. cit., 29.

47 Chairman's Statement, 9 May 1938, ABC Head Office, Correspondence File: J.W. Kitto, Box 19, CA 1726, AA SP 1489/1.
48 W.T. Conder to Herbert Brookes, 17 December 1933, File: Herbert Brookes, Box 19, AA SP 1489.
49 File: Talks, General (Women's), Box 75, AA MP 237/1. Nettie Palmer's book reviews for the women's session were also terminated at the same time.
50 Inglis, op. cit., 63.
51 ibid.
52 See Broadcasting and Peace File, Box 3, AA MP 544/1.
53 *Sun*, 29 April 1938.
54 Interview with May Pennefather quoted in *Red Matildas*, an oral history documentary film made by Sharon Connolly and Trevor Graham, shown on ABC television, 16 August 1986.
55 *Argus*, 22 December 1938.
56 ibid., 15 September 1931, 16 September 1931, 17 September 1931.
57 ibid., 16 June 1932.
58 Inglis, op. cit., 171–2.
59 ABC Commission Minutes, 20–21 April 1939, ABC Archives. Comments were made in these terms when considering a request from the *Worker* in South Australia to do some of their own programmes.
60 See, for example, General Manager [Moses] to Mr McCall, 11 December 1944, File: M3, 1942–4, Box 2, AA SP 314/1.
61 *Wireless Weekly*, 12 January 1934.
62 See, for example, *Labor Daily*, 20 March 1936, 21 March 1936; also newspaper cuttings and notes, F.W. Daniell Papers, NLA 1634/384/2.
63 Royal Commission on Wireless, 1927, vol. 8, 2310–11, AA CP 657/1.
64 Australia, Parliament, *Wireless Broadcasting: Report from the Joint Parliamentary Committee* (W.G. Gibson, Chairman), Canberra, 1942, 53.
65 This does not suggest, however, that only men advocated censorship on moral grounds. Women were among the many letter writers (for example, to the *Women's Weekly*) calling for the protection of women and children. One of the major organizations advocating censorship began as a women's organization: the Good Film and Radio Vigilance League of NSW began as a sub-committee of the National Council of Women. The League began in 1922 and its membership widened to include men; in 1928 its activities extended to include radio as well as films.
66 *Wireless Weekly*, 10 May 1935. See also: Memo (no date, no author), Programming of Plays, Box 18, AA MP 237/1.
67 Objectionable Broadcasts, PMG Files, Box 5, AA MP 544/1.
68 *Listener In*, 30 October 1926.
69 Federal Talks Advisory Committee, 1937–46, ABC Head Office, Correspondence File, Item 14.15, CA 251, AA SP 341/1.
70 *ABC Third Annual Report*, 30 June 1935.

71 Paddy Scannell and David Cardiff, 'The social foundation of British broadcasting', a paper prepared for the Open University, 10.
72 Censorship, Questions of Taste, etc. File: Counter Propaganda: PPR 23.21, Box 57, AA MP 237/1.
73 Keith Barry to the General Manager, 24 February 1939, File No. 1, General Programme Policy, AA SP 341/B5/922, D/8.
74 *Wireless Weekly*, 11 December 1931.
75 *Labor Daily*, 2 July 1938.
76 *Wireless Weekly*, 11 December 1931.
77 *Women's Weekly*, 16 October 1937.
78 Australia, House of Representatives, *Debates* 1926, vol. 114, 4430.
79 C.P. Stoneham (Minister of State Development and Decentralization) to ABC General Manager, 6 November 1946, File: Tours by Concert Parties, Box 10, AA MP 237/1.
80 *Women's Weekly*, 30 October 1937.
81 Scannell and Cardiff, op. cit.
82 C. Lloyd Jones to J. Reith, 10 August 1932, Broadcasting in Australia, File 1B, 1932, E1/341/2, BBCWA.
83 K. Barry to General Manager, 22 June 1938, ABC Head Office, Programme Department, Programme File, General Programme Policy, File No. 1, 1936–42, item 1.1, CA 251; and C. Moses to PMG, 13 April 1938, 1.1, Box 1, AA SP 341/1.
84 *Wireless Weekly*, 10 October 1930.
85 '1938 in Retrospect'. Script of Programmes, Box 18, AA MP 237/1.
86 *ABC Fifth Annual Report*, 30 June 1937, 29.
87 *Women's Weekly*, 5 September 1936.
88 ibid., 23 August 1939.
89 *Wireless Weekly*, 31 January 1936.
90 ibid.
91 *Daily Telegraph*, 2 March 1936.
92 *Listener In*, 29 September 1934.
93 *Labor Daily*, 5 June 1925.
94 ibid., 13 October 1932.
95 Letter to Mr Lyons from The Crowd on the Goldfield (received 31 July 1930), PMG Correspondence File, 1901–1939, File 33/4752, AA MP 341. There are a number of documents relevant to this issue in this file.
96 Inglis, op. cit., 20.
97 Australia, House of Representatives, *Debates* 1932, vol. 135, 559–61. Beasley claimed Lloyd Jones to be explicitly anti-Labor; Brookes, Couchman and Wallace were associated with the UAP and Orchard was a member of the UAP.
98 *Labor Daily*, 6 May 1933.
99 *Argus*, 1 June 1932.
100 Australia, House of Representatives, *Debates* 1932, vol. 136, 1735.

101 Memo, Keith Barry, 1 April 1940, File 1, Listener Research A, Box 5/1.10A, AA SP 341/1.
102 *Listener In*, 1 January 1930.
103 *Argus*, 9 May 1935.
104 Now republished by Virago Press, 1983.
105 Antonio Gramsci, *Selections from the Prison Notebooks*, trans and ed. Quintin Hoare and Geoffrey Nowell Smith, New York, International Publishers, 1971, 242 f.
106 Australia, House of Representatives, *Debates* 1932, vol. 136, 1714; *Wireless Weekly*, 18 September 1936.
107 *Listener In*, 28 November 1928.

BIBLIOGRAPHY

Archival sources for this study consisted of material held in the Australian Archives in Sydney, Melbourne and Canberra; some material still held at the ABC itself in their document archives; material held at the British Broadcasting Written Archives at Caversham, England; and sound recordings held at the time of doing this research in the Sound Archives in the basement of the National Library of Australia in Canberra. Detailed references to this material are provided in the notes to this book and are not listed here again. Nor are the parlimentary debates listed here. I list here other primary sources drawn on in this study: private papers; newspapers and magazines; parliamentary reports and commissions of inquiry; and contemporary publications. I have also included the biographies and autobiographies of broadcasters and other personnel connected with early radio that I found useful, though I have given few specific references to this material in my notes. Finally, I have listed books, articles and unpublished material that have formed my thinking about this project; this is not a comprehensive list, but includes those references I found most useful.

Private papers of individuals and organizations

Amalgamated Wireless [Australasia] Ltd., Letterbook, Ms 9934 (La Trobe Library Manuscripts).
Keith Barry Papers, Ms 5076 (National Library of Australia).
Herbert Brookes Papers, Ms 1924 (National Library of Australia).
W.T. Conder Papers, uncatalogued (National Library of Australia).
F.W. Daniell Papers, Ms 1634 (National Library of Australia).
John Hickling Papers, Ms 4890 (National Library of Australia).
Labor Council Records of NSW, A3843 (Mitchell Library).
E.A. Mann Papers, Ms 1955 (National Library of Australia).
Harry Pringle Papers, Ms 5029 (National Library of Australia).
Athol Tier Papers, Ms 5582 (National Library of Australia).

Newspapers and magazines

Age
Argus
Australian Women's Weekly
Broadcasting Business
Daily Mail
Daily Telegraph
Labor Daily
Listener In
New Idea
Radio in Australia and New Zealand
Radio Times
Smith's Weekly
Truth
Wireless Weekly

Commissions of inquiry and parliamentary reports

Report of the Royal Commission on Wireless (J.H. Hammond, Chairman), October 1927.

Report of the Joint Parliamentary Committee on Wireless Broadcasting (W.J. Gibson, Chairman), and *Minutes of Evidence*, March 1942.

Contemporary publications

Australian Broadcasting Commission, *Annual Reports*, 1932–45.

Brown, H.P., 'Broadcasting in Australia', Proceedings of the World Radio Convention, Sydney, 1938.

Faulkner, C.C. and J.D. Corbet (eds), *The Broadcast Year Book and Radio Listeners' Annual of Australia*, 1934.

McNair, W.A., *Radio Advertising in Australia*, Sydney, Angus & Robertson, 1937.

Autobiographies, biographies and reminiscences

Blain, Ellis, *Life with Aunty. 40 years with the ABC*, Sydney, Methuen of Australia, 1977.

Coulton, Barbara, *Louis MacNeice in the BBC*, London, Faber & Faber, 1980.

Dixon, Frank, *Inside the ABC*, Melbourne, Hamilton Press, 1975.

Faulkner, Trader, *Peter Finch. A Biography*, London, Pan Books, 1979.

Lee, Nancy, *Being a Chum Was Fun*, Melbourne, Listen & Learn Productions, 1979.

Manning, Arthur, *Larger than Life. The Story of Eric Baume*, Sydney, A.H. &

A.W. Reed, 1967.

Moloney, Billy, *Memoirs of an Abominable Showman*, Adelaide, Rigby Ltd, 1968.

Patterson, George, *Life Has Been Wonderful. Fifty Years of Adventures in Advertising at Home and Abroad*, Sydney, Ure Smith, 1956.

Pickles, Wilfed, *Between You and Me*, London, Werner Laurie, 1949.

Reith, J.C.W., *Into the Wind*, London, Hodder & Soughton, 1949.

Wright, Lew, *The Jack Davey Story*, Sydney, Ure Smith, 1961.

Books and articles

Adorno, Theodor, 'A social critique of radio music', *Kenyon Review*, VII (2), Spring 1945, 208–17.

Adorno, T.W., *Prisms*, New York, Columbia University Press, 1976.

Adorno, Theodor and Max Horkheimer, 'The culture industry: enlightenment as mass deception', in James Curran *et al.* (eds) *Mass Communication and Society*, London, Edward Arnold, 1977, 349–383.

Allen, Robert C., *Speaking of Soap Operas*, University of North Carolina Press, 1985.

Ashbolt, Allan, 'The role of the ABC', in Brendan O'Dwyer (ed.) *Broadcasting in Australia*, Proceedings of the National Conference held in July 1980 at the Australian National University.

Barnard Eldershaw, M., *Tomorrow and Tomorrow and Tomorrow*, London, Virago, 1983.

Barnouw, Eric, *A Tower of Babel*, New York, Oxford University Press, 1966.

Barrett, Michèle and Mary McIntosh, *The Anti-Social Family*, London, Verso, 1982.

Baudrillard, Jean, *The Political Economy of the Sign*, trans. Charles Levin, St Louis, Mo, Telos Press, 1981.

Bedford, Ian and Ross Curnow, *Initiative and Organisation*, Melbourne, Cheshire, 1963.

Benjamin, Walter, *Illuminations*, trans. Harry Zohn, Glasgow, Fontana, 1970.

Bennett, Tony, *Popular Culture: Politics, Ideology and Popular Culture*, Open University course book, Milton Keynes, 1982.

Berger, John, *Ways of Seeing*, Harmondsworth, Penguin, 1972.

Bertrand, Ina, *Film Censorship in Australia*, University of Queensland Press, 1978.

Boddy, William, 'The rhetoric and economic roots of the American broadcasting industry', *Cinetracts*, 2 (2), 1979, 37–54.

Bourdieu, Pierre, 'The aristocracy of culture', trans. Richard Nice, *Media, Culture and Society*, 2, 1980, 225–54.

Bourdieu, Pierre, *Distinction*, trans. Richard Nice, London, Routledge & Kegan Paul, 1985.

Braverman, Harry, *Labor and Monopoly Capital*, New York, Monthly Review

Press, 1974.
Brecht, Bertolt, 'Radio as a means of communication. A talk on the function of radio', trans. Stuart Hood, *Screen*, 20 (3/4), 1979/80, 24–8.
Briggs, Asa, *The Golden Age of Wireless. The History of Broadcasting in the United Kingdom*, vol. 2, Oxford University Press, 1965.
Brunsdon, Charlotte and David Morley, *Everyday Television: 'Nationwide'*, London, British Film Institute, 1978.
Buck-Morss, Susan, 'Walter Benjamin – revolutionary writer' (1), *New Left Review*, 128, July/August, 1981, 50–75.
Burns, Tom, *The BBC. Public Institution and Private World*, London, Macmillan, 1977.
Campbell, Deborah, 'From theatre to radio: the popular career of Mary Marlowe', in Peter Spearritt and David Walker (eds) *Australian Popular Culture*, Sydney, Allen & Unwin, 1979, 81–101.
Cardiff, David, 'The serious and the popular: aspects of the evolution of style in the radio talk 1928–1939', *Media, Culture and Society*, 2, 1980, 29–47.
Constable, Anthony, *Early Wireless*, Tunbridge Wells, Kent, Midas Books, 1980.
Curran, James and Jean Seaton, *Power without Responsibility. The Press and Broadcasting in Britain*, 2nd edition, London, Methuen, 1985.
Dermody, Susan, Docker, John, and Modjeska, Drusilla (eds) *Nellie Melba, Ginger Meggs and Friends*, Malmsbury, Kibble Books, 1982.
Docker, John, 'Popular culture and its Marxist critics', *Arena*, 65, 1983, 109–21.
Dyer, Richard, *Stars*, London, British Film Institute, 1979.
Ewen, Stuart, *Captains of Consciousness*, New York, McGraw Hill, 1976.
Foucault, Michel, *Discipline and Punish*, trans. Alan Sheridan, London, Allen Lane, 1977.
Frith, Simon, 'The pleasure of the hearth: The making of the BBC light entertainment', *Formations of Pleasure*, London, Routledge & Kegan Paul, 1983, 101–23.
Game, Ann and Rosemary, Pringle, *Gender at Work*, Sydney, Allen & Unwin, 1983.
Glasgow Media Group, *Bad News*, London, Routledge & Kegan Paul, 1976.
Glasgow Media Group, *More Bad News*, London, Routledge & Kegan Paul, 1980.
Goot, Murray, 'Radio Lang', in Heather Radi and Peter Spearritt (eds), *Jack Lang*, Sydney, Hale & Iremonger, 1977, 119–37.
Gramsci, Antonio, *Selections from the Prison Notebooks*, trans. and ed. Quintin Hoare and Geoffrey Nowell Smith, New York International Publishers, 1971.
Hall, Stuart, 'Notes on deconstructing the "popular"', in Raphael Samuel (ed.) *People's History and Socialist Theory*, London, Routledge & Kegan Paul, 1981, 227–40.

Hall, Stuart, Critcher, Chas, Jefferson, Tony, Clarke, John, and Roberts, Brian (eds) *Policing the Crisis. Mugging, the State and Law and Order*, London, Macmillan, 1978.
Harding, Richard, *Outside Interference. The Politics of Australian Broadcasting*, Melbourne, Sun Books, 1979.
Hardy, Frank, *The Four Legged Lottery*, London, T. Werner Laurie, 1958.
Heath, Stephen and Gillian Skirrow, 'Television: a world in action', *Screen*, 18 (2), 1977, 7–59.
Heskelt, John, *Industrial Design*, London, Thames & Hudson, 1980.
Higgins, C.S. and P.D. Moss, *Sounds Real. Radio in Everyday Life*, University of Queensland Press, 1982.
Hill, Jonathan, *The Cat's Whisker. 50 Years of Wireless Design*, London, Oresko Books, 1978.
Hood, Stuart, 'Brecht on radio', *Screen*, 20, Winter 1979/80, 16–23.
Horkheimer, Max and Theodor, Adorno, *Dialectic of Enlightenment*, trans. John Cumming, London, Allen & Lane, 1972.
Inglis, K.S., *This Is the ABC. The Australian Broadcasting Commission 1932–1983*, Melbourne University Press, 1983.
Johnson, Lesley, 'Radio and everyday life. The early years of broadcasting in Australia, 1922–1945', *Media, Culture and Society*, 3, 1981, 167–78.
Johnson, Lesley, '"Sing 'em muck, Clara". The higbrow versus lowbrow debate on early Australian radio', *Meanjin*, 41, 1982, 210–22.
Johnson, Lesley, 'Images of radio. The construction of the radio audience by popular radio magazines', *Melbourne Working Papers*, 4, 1982/3, 34–54.
Johnson, Lesley, 'Radio as popular education', *Labour History*, 45, 1983, 68–79.
Johnson, Lesley, 'The intimate voice of Australian radio', *Historical Journal of Film, Radio and Television*, 3, 1983, 43–50.
Johnson, Lesley, 'Wireless and women. The definition of the modern woman by Australian radio in the 1920s and 30s', *Cultural Politics. Papers in Contemporary Culture, Education and Politics*, Melbourne Working Papers, 5, 1984, 74–94.
Johnson, Lesley, 'The ABC and multiculturalism', *Island*, 21, 1984, 14–16.
Johnson, Lesley, 'The wireless', in Bill Gammage and Peter Spearritt (eds), *The Australians*, 1938 volume, bicentennial history project, forthcoming.
Johnson, Lesley, 'Defining the political. Early Australian radio', in K. Buckley and E.L. Wheelwright (eds), *Communications and the Media: Australia*, Sydney, Allen & Unwin, 1987.
Johnson, Pauline, *Marxist Aesthetics. The Foundations within Everyday Life for an Emancipated Consciousness*, London, Routledge & Kegan Paul, 1983.
Johnson, Pauline, 'Picturing reality. Essay review', *Arena*, 65, 1983, 121–31.
Johnson, Richard, McLennan, Gregor, Schwarz, Bill, and Sutton, David *Making Histories. Studies in History Writing and Politics* London, Hutchinson, 1982.
Kent, Jacqueline, *Out of the Bakelite Box. The Heyday of Australian Radio*, Sydney, Angus & Robertson, 1983.
Kingston, Beverley, *My Wife, My Daughter, My Poor Mary Ann*, Melbourne,

Nelson, 1975.
Lazerfield, Paul F. and Frank N. Stanton, *Radio Research 1941*, New York, Duel, Sloan & Pearce, 1941.
Lefebvre, Henri, *Everyday Life in the Modern World*, trans. Sacha Rabinovitich, New York, Harper Torchbooks, 1971.
Lewis, Peter (ed.) *Radio Drama*, New York, Longman, 1981.
Lowenstein, Wendy, *Weevils in the Flour. An Oral Record of the 1930s Depression in Australia*, Melbourne, Scribe Publications, 1978.
McCoy, Al, 'Sport as modern mythology: SP bookmaking in New South Wales 1920–1979', in Richard Cashman and Michael McKernan (eds) *Sport, Money, Morality and the Media*, New South Wales University Press (no date), 34–67.
MacIntyre, Stuart, *A Proletarian Science. Marxism in Britain 1917–1933*, Cambridge University Press, 1980.
Murray, Robert, *The Confident Years. Australia in the Twenties*, London, Allen Lane, 1978.
O'Brien, Denis, *The Weekly*, Melbourne, Penguin Books, 1982.
Pegg, Mark, *Broadcasting and Society, 1918–1939*, London, Croom Helm, 1983.
Radio, 1985, a publication of the Radio Marketing Bureau, Division of Federation of Australian Radio Broadcasters, Milsons Point, NSW, 1985.
Reiger, Kerreen, 'Women's labour redefined: child-bearing and rearing advice in Australia, 1880–1930s', in Margaret Bevege, Margaret James, and Carmel Shute (eds) *Worth Her Salt*, Sydney, Hale & Iremonger, 1982, 72–83.
Reiger, Kerreen, *The Disenchantment of the Home, Modernizing the Australian Family 1880–1940*, Melbourne, Oxford University Press, 1985.
Rosaldo, M.Z., 'Woman, culture and society. A theoretical overview', in M.Z Rosaldo and L. Lamphere (eds) *Woman, Culture and Society*, Stanford University Press, 1974, 17–42.
Scannell, Paddy, 'The social eye of television, 1946–1955', *Media, Culture and Society*, 1 (1), 1979, 97–106.
Scannell, Paddy, 'Broadcasting and the politics of unemployment 1930–1935', *Media, Culture and Society*, 2, 1980, 15–28.
Scannell, Paddy, '"A Conspiracy of Silence". The state, the BBC and public opinion in the formative years of British broadcasting', in Gregor McLennan, David Held, and Stuart Hall (eds) *State and Society in Contemporary Britain*, Cambridge, Polity Press, 1984, 150–75.
Schlesinger, Philip, *Putting 'Reality' Together, BBC News*, London, Constable, 1978.
Slater, Phil, *Origin and Significance of the Frankfurt School*, London, Routledge & Kegan Paul, 1977.
Smith, Anthony, *The Shadow in the Cave. A Study of the Relationship between the Broadcaster, His Audience and the State*, London, Quartet Books, 1976.
Smythe, Dallas W., 'Communications: blindspot of western Marxism', *Canadian Journal of Political and Social Theory*, 1 (3), 1977, 1–27.

Spearritt, Peter, *Sydney since the Twenties*, Sydney, Hale & Iremonger, 1978.

Stedman Jones, Gareth, *Languages of Class. Studies in English Working Class History 1832-1982*, Cambridge University Press, 1983.

Stephen, Ann, 'Agents of consumerism: the organisation of the Australian advertising industry, 1918-1938', in Judith Allen *et al.* (eds) *Media Interventions*, Sydney, Intervention Publications, 1981, 78-96.

Thomas, Alan, *Broadcast and Be Damned. The ABC's First Two Decades*, Melbourne University Press, 1980.

Thompson, E.P., 'Time, work-discipline and industrial capitalism', *Past and Present*, 38, 1967, 56-97.

Walker, R.B., *Yesterday's News*, Sydney University Press, 1980.

Walker, R.R., *The Magic Spark. The Story of Radio in Australia*, Melbourne, Hawthorn Press, 1973.

Walker, R.R., *Dial 1179. The 3KZ Story*, South Yarra, Currey O'Neill, 1984.

White, Richard, *Inventing Australia*, Sydney, Allen & Unwin, 1981.

Williams, Raymond, *Television. Technology and Cultural Form*, Glasgow, Fontana,
1974.

Williams, Raymond, 'Institutions of technology', in Armand Mattelart and Seth Siegelaub (eds) *Communications and Class Struggle: 1, Capitalism, Imperialism*, New York, International General, 1979, 265-7.

Williams, Raymond, *Problems in Materialism and Culture*, London, Verso, 1980.

Windschuttle, Keith, *The Media. A New Analysis of the Press, Television, Radio and Advertising in Australia*, Melbourne, Penguin, 1984.

Wright Mills, C., *The Sociological Imagination*, New York, Oxford University Press, 1959.

Unpublished material

Barnard, Alan, 'Ruling Australia's airwaves in the 1920s', unpublished paper, 1982, Conference of the Economic History Society.

Centre for Contemporary Cultural Studies, Media Group Presentation (for 1978-9).

Counihan, Michael, S., 'The construction of Australian broadcasting: aspects of radio in Australia in the 1920s', MA thesis, Monash University, 1981.

MacKay, Ian, 'Macquarie – the story of a network', unpublished manuscript, Broadcasting Tribunal Library, Melbourne (no date).

Potts, John, 'The function of advertising in the 1930s: Wrigley's *Dad and Dave* ... "Solving the problem"', draft chapter, MA thesis, New South Wales Institute of Technology.

Potts, John, '"The Price You Pay": radio advertising in Australia, 1934-1945', MA thesis, New South Wales Institute of Technology, 1984.

Reiger, Kerreen, '"All But the Kitchen Sink". On the significance of domestic science and the silence of social theory', unpublished paper, SAANZ Conference, Melbourne, 1983.

Scannell, Paddy and David Cardiff, 'The social foundations of British broadcasting', a paper prepared for the Open University.

Watts, Frank, 'Broadcasts to schools in Victoria. An account of their origin and development', Bachelor of Education investigation, University of Melbourne, 1949.

INDEX

'A' class stations 35, 72, 177
  advertising on 13, 44, 55, 59; 'B' station problem and 145–9; licence revenue 9, 13–14, 27, 61, 141–2; licences 17, 34, 57, 61; programmes 44, 57–9, 62–3, 129–30, 136, 140, 142–3
ABC Weekly 173
Abyssinia 166, 169–70
actuality (sense of) 167, 168–9, 174
ad-libbing 22, 72, 73–4
  'gaffs' 46, 47, 68
Adorno, T. 5, 7–8, 99, 117, 121–2, 139
'Advance Australia Radio Club' 103
Advertiser 147, 149
advertising 56, 115, 174
  on 'A' stations 13, 44, 55, 59; on 'B' stations 9, 13, 59, 61, 81, 115, 126–7, 136, 146, 159–61; children as targets 22–4, 29; family life focus 89–91; market research 82, 140–1; networking 156–9, 161; radio equipment 14–15, 17, 83–7; women as targets 9, 19–23, 64–8, 83, 104–6, 111–12
Age 14, 28, 31, 58–9, 62, 81, 147
Airzone's radios 84
Albert, J. and Son 57
Allan and Company 53, 147
AM broadcasting 2
Amalgamated Wireless (Australia) Ltd (AWA) 13, 15, 17, 35, 90
  government intervention 56–7; monopoly power 50–1, 55, 157; Radiola 84, 85, 86

Amateur Hour 123, 134
amateur shows 123, 125, 134
amateur wireless clubs 12
Amos and Andy 97
'Answer Man' 103
'Argus' 124
Argus 62–3, 67, 127, 130, 140, 157, 183, 200
Arnold Matthew 130–1
art 6–8 118, 121–2
art for art's sake 131–2
Artransa 158
As Ye Sow 196
Associated Newspapers 114
Associated Record Manufacturers 53–4
Association for the Development of Wireless 51
Astor radios 84, 86
audience
  characteristics and needs 1–2, 29–32, 150–6; collectivity of individuals 193–205; commodity listening 6–7, 117–18, 122–3, 128–9, 132; communication with, *see* communication; as consumers, *see main entry*; cultural preferences 128–45; as individuals 60, 63–4, 74, 76, 81; letters from 99–100, 121, 129, 141–5, 198, 199; mass, *see* mass audience; participation 123–5, 135–6; passivity 5, 25, 29, 30, 36–7, 78–82, 128–9, 132, 180; ratings 136–7; self-definition 140–5; social relations of radio 43–9,

54, 70–82; tastes 29, 62–9, 127–45; timetabling of 106–9; *see also* children; family life; men; women
Australian Associated Press 165
Australian Broadcasting Commission 9, 23, 96, 97, 117, 163
'B' station problems 148–57, 162; BBC as model 72, 76, 121, 129, 133–5, 137, 151, 153, 156, 166, 181, 188, 190, 204; competitors 150–2, 154, 156–7; cultural authority 1, 3, 7, 82, 129–30, 132–7, 139–40, 143–4, 150–6; impartiality 176–8, 180, 189–92; national unity image 195–6, 198, 200–1, 204; news 52, 164–7, 169–85 *Optimist's League* 88, 196; programmes 106–7, 126–7, 129, 132–7, 139–40, 143, 144; self-censorship 177–85, 188, 189; sponsorship 2, 52, 58; style 72–3, 76–8, 82, 118, 121–2; viability/value 2, 3; *see also* 'A' class stations
Australian Broadcasting Company 57–8, 72, 88, 127, 139, 147, 156, 175, 196
Australian Child Psychology Society 103
Australian Newspaper Conference 164, 167
Australian Performing Rights Association (APRA) 53
Australian Wireless Committee 57
Australian Women's League 104–5
aviators 168

'B' class stations 3
advertising on 9, 13, 59, 61, 81, 115, 126–7, 136, 146, 159–61; censorship 177–8, 188–9; government intervention 148–50; licences 10, 27, 34, 35, 52, 59–60, 141–2, 146–9; news 173–4, 183–6; personalities 115, 117–18, 121–2; programmes 96, 123–4, 126, 132–4, 136, 138, 140, 143–4, 188–9; style 73, 76, 78
'Babble Machines' 32–7
'background listening' 80–1
Banks, Norman 73, 95, 124, 138
Barnard Eldershaw, M. 203
Barrett, M. 89

Barry, Keith 130, 135, 191, 195
Baudrillard, Jean 3
Bearup, T.W. 28, 127, 133, 140, 150
Beasley, Jack 200–1
beauty (sexual identity) 103–4
bed-time stories 93, 94, 187
Benjamin, W. 5, 6–7, 8, 122–3, 125, 131–2, 205
Bennett, A.E. 60
Berger, John 6
Black, H.D. 173
Blue Hills 97
Boyer, Richard 156
Braverman, Harry 21
Brecht, B. 5–6, 7, 8, 33, 38, 42, 205
Bremner, Marie 40
Brennan, Frank 46, 50
Briggs, Asa 171
Britain 14, 16, 137, 182
theatrical interests 51, 53; *see also* British Broadcasting Corporation; royalty
British Broadcasting Company 22
British Broadcasting Corporation 22, 125, 195
'B' stations' access to 150, 151; Empire Service 39, 50, 133, 170; model for ABC 72, 76, 121, 129, 133–5, 137, 151, 153, 156, 166, 181, 188, 190, 204; monopolistic control 59, 153–4; news 170, 171, 181, 191
Broadcasting Business 69, 104, 111, 116, 160
Brookes, Herbert 149, 179, 180
Brown, H.P. 34, 147, 177
Bruce, Stanley 54–5
Brunton, Dot 188
Budapest String Quartet 117
Bureau of International Affairs 181
Butt, Dame Clara 32

capitalist propaganda 32, 33–4, 37, 52
Cardiff, David 195
Catholic Church 147
celebrities 116–17, 118, 122
censorship 56, 91; moral 186–8; PMG's powers 161, 177–8, 182–3, 187, 188–9; political 177–8, 186,

187–8, 191–2; self- 177, 178–85, 188, 189
'chain broadcasts' 156–9, 161
Chamberlain, Neville 167
charitable work 110, 111
Charlton, Matthew 26, 35
Chatterbox Corner 74, 95, 160
children 135
    in advertisements 68, 91; advertisements aimed at 22–4, 29; bed-time stories 93, 94, 187; care of 101, 104, 106, 109, 110; presenters for 22–3, 36, 46, 47, 71, 114–15; and moral censorship 186–8; as radio enthusiasts 12, 19
Children's Hour 23
'chums' 73, 74
Citizen's League (Adelaide) 177–8
classical music 8, 128, 131, 132, 137
    performers 116, 117, 118, 122
Cleary, W.J. 134, 178–80, 181
Cochrane, A.S. 22, 32, 71
Comedy Harmonists 117
comedy shows 128, 136, 188, 189
commercial radio stations, *see* 'B' class stations
'commodity listening' 6–7, 117–18, 122–3, 128–9, 132
Commonwealth Broadcasting Network 157
communication
    audience participation 123–5, 135–6; mass, *see* mass communication; national unity image 193–205; 'talk back' radio 25–32
communism 178, 181, 184, 185
community links 26, 28, 48–9, 54, 194
community singing 124, 136, 141, 195–6, 203
competition (for ABC) 150–2, 154, 156–7
competitions 31, 135
    see also quiz programmes
'composite programmes' 125, 127
Conder, W.T. 55, 63, 180
consumer goods 21, 87
consumers, audience as 7–10, 15
    choices 78–82, 139–42, 144–5, 159–61; family as 18–19, 98, 102–4, 106, 110, 112, 141; passivity concept 5, 25, 29, 30, 36–7, 78–82, 128–9, 132, 180; unity concept 195, 197–9, 201–2, 204–5; women as 9, 19–23, 102, 104, 112, 204–5
controversial issues (format) 190–3
copyright 50, 51, 53–4, 55, 56
Council of Churches 146, 157
Council of Civil Liberties 179
Counihan, M. 59
Cousins, Charles 115
cricket 43, 53, 71, 156, 194
crooning 128, 129, 151
crystal sets 12, 14, 19
culture
    ABC's commitment 1, 3, 7, 82, 129–30, 132–7, 139–40, 143–4, 150–6; industries 7, 11, 37, 54, 69, 77, 117, 158; mechanical reproduction 6, 131–2; preferences 128–45; products 6–9, 82, 128–9; radio as popular 1–10, 49, 54, 63
Curtin, John 161, 191, 201
Czechoslovakia 170

Dad and Dave 77, 96, 97–8, 100
Daily Mail 30
Daily Telegraph 12, 14, 15, 19, 45, 55, 63, 78–81, 83, 108, 148, 185
dance music 128, 129–30
Daniell, F. 114, 127, 158–9, 170, 173
Davey, Jack 115, 189
Deamer, S.H. 173
Dear, Terry 124
Dearest Enemy 188
Dearth, Harry 115
Dease, John 115
Deed's Family, The 111
de Groot, Captain 168
department stores 17
Depression 87–9, 94, 142–3, 196, 203
descriptive broadcasts 167–70
Digger Hale's Daughter 77, 96
'direct contact' modes 43
division of labour, sexual 90
    see also housework

Dixon, Frank 165–6, 170, 171, 172
Docker, John 4
domestic
  commodity image 11–19, 25, 28–9, 66–8, 87; image (audience) 1–2, 100, 101–2; role (of radio) 19–24; work 19–22, 29, 65, 101–6, 109, 110
Douglas Social Credit system 180–1
Doyle, Stuart 62, 156–7, 196
Do You Remember? – 1938 in Retrospect 196
dramatized recreations 166, 190
Druleigh Business College 146
Duncan, Constance 181–2
Duncan, W.G.K. 134, 190

education function 1, 59–60, 70, 202–3; ABC 58, 133, 151; of masses 33, 36, 128–9, 130–1, 132, 134–6; school broadcasts 56, 204
Edward VIII 116, 167, 169, 197
Edwards, George 97–8
election campaigns 35–6, 184–5, 191–3
Elizabeth, Queen (Duchess of York) 42, 116, 194
elocutionary techniques 47, 71
Empire Service 39, 50, 133, 170
entertainment, art and 118, 121–2
Evening News 52
'everyday' role (radio) 82–100, 203
Ewen, Stuart 15, 21–2, 84, 87, 91, 102
Eye Witness News 174

family life
  ideology of 89–91, 94; radio (role) 18, 82–100; radio as threat 55–6, 91–4, 186–8; *see also* children; men; women
Farmer and Company 14, 17, 33, 42, 43, 51, 61
farmers (information for) 164
Federation of Broadcasting Stations 147, 157
Federation of Commercial Broadcasting Stations 183
film industry 6, 114, 123
Fisk, E.T. 13, 17, 50, 90

Flash News 174
'flesh and blood' radio 71–82
FM broadcasting 2
Foley, P.G.J. 201
Foster, Dorothy ('Dilly') 188, 189
Foster, Judge 179–80
Foys, Mark 14, 17
Frankfurt School 7, 8
Fred and Maggie Everybody 96, 98
Frederick, Christine 109
Fuller's Theatres 57

'gaffs' 46, 47, 68
Game, Ann 104, 106
gender identity 19, 186, 187–8
  female (defined) 90, 100–2, 103–4, 110–12; male (defined) 100–1; *see also* men; women
General Knowledge Bee 133, 135
George V 116, 167, 197
George VI 42, 116, 167, 194
George, Prince (Duke of Kent) 116
Gibson, W.G. 13, 14, 57, 163
Gibson Committee 161, 187
government intervention 50–2, 54–61, 68
  'B' stations 148–50; news 178–9, 182, 183–4
Gramsci, Antonio 204
Grant, Senator 52
Green Diamond Mystery, The 31
Grey, Mrs 36
Grocer and Madam 95

Haile Selassie 166
Hammond, J.H. 56
Happiness Club 88, 105, 110–11, 196
Hazell, Rupert 49
Heinze, Bernard 55, 127
'Hello Man' 22, 32, 46, 71
Help Thy Neighbour 73
Herald 61, 146–7, 149
Heroes of Civilisation 196
'highbrows' 128–38, 153
  self-definition 140–5, 198
Hitler, A. 167, 196
Hollywood film industry 114, 123
Hood, Stuart 58

Hordern, Anthony 17
Horkheimer, Max 5, 7–8, 139
housework 19–22, 29, 65, 101–6, 109, 110
Hughes, Billy 48
Husbands and Wives 73

impartiality, *see* news broadcasts
industrial psychology 160
Information Please 123, 124
Inglis, K.S. 181
international affairs 181–3
International Broadcasting Convention 182, 183
International Friendship League 178
interviews 76, 124
Inverell Municipal Council 26

jazz 8, 128, 129–30
Johnson, Amy 168
Jordan, Dorothy 55, 66

Keep it Clean 188
Kisch, Egon 179

Labor Call 199
Labor Councils 33, 37
Labor Daily 12, 14, 25, 27, 29–30, 32–3, 35–7, 49–50, 72, 91, 114, 116, 178, 185, 198–201
Labor Party 50, 54–5, 179, 200–2
Labor's Education League 36
labour movement 5, 7, 54
 political propaganda and 32–7, 184–6; trade unions 185, 198, 201, 202; unity of 199–201, 202
labour process 109
labour-saving devices 102
Lang, J.T. 168, 200
language (of radio) 202
 as domestic commodity 18–19, 28–9; everyday (definition) 94–6; listener's use 99–100, 141–5; of news 176–7, 185; as popular science 11–12; on 'serious art' 122, 128–32, 153; as social relation 43–9, 54
Lawson Family, The (later *Blue Hills*) 97

League of Nations 182
League of Nations Union 181
Lee, Nancy (Kathleen Whitta) 74, 95, 160
Lefebvre, Henri 94–5, 100
Lehmann, Lotte 117
liberalism 183–4, 186, 189–90
licence revenue 9, 13–14, 27, 59, 61, 141–2
licences 2, 62–3, 89
 'A' class stations 17, 34, 57, 61
 'B' class stations 10, 27, 34, 35, 52, 59–60, 141–2, 146–9; fees 12–14, 36, 50–1, 55, 57, 198; market relations and 141–2, 157; withdrawal of 183, 186
light entertainment 8, 128–30, 136, 156
Lindrum, Walter 40
Listener In 49, 96, 170
 audience 19–20, 24, 62, 64–5, 141, 189, 204; on 'B' class stations 145, 147–8; on personalities 71, 75, 113–14, 116, 118–20; radio advertisements 83, 88, 89, 136; on stunt broadcasts 39–40, 41, 46; on technology 17–18, 68
listeners, *see* audience
'listening habit' 106–7
Lloyd Jones, C. 1, 73, 134, 149–50, 178
London Stores Limited 103
'lowbrows' 128–9, 137, 153
 education of 130–1, 132, 134–6; popular programmes 138–40; self-definition 140–5, 198
Lyons, Joseph 147, 148–9, 171, 191, 192, 199–200

McIntosh, M. 89
McNair, W.A. 82, 105, 107, 115, 160–1
Macquarie Broadcasting Network 114, 126, 157–9, 174
Macquarie Broadcasting Services 114, 158
Mann, E.A. 174
Marconi Company 50, 51
Marina, Princess (Duchess of Kent) 116

market reports 164, 165, 176
market research 82, 136, 140–1
Martin, Dr A.H. 160
Martin's Corner 96, 98
mass audience 2, 3–4, 70, 123
  education of, *see* education function
  manipulation theory 7–8, 159–61
mass communication 4–5, 25–31
  ABC's role 150–4; 'Babble Machines' 32–7
Melba, Dame Nellie 116
Melbourne Concert Orchestra 46
Melbourne Cup 43, 98, 194, 195
Melbourne Trades Hall Council 147
men 93
  in advertisements 68, 91, 99; advertisements aimed at 69; gender identity 19, 90, 100–1, 186; patriarchical order 186, 187–8; social power of women and 110, 111; *see also* family life
Menzies, R.G. 56, 182
Meredith, Gwen 97
microphone
  mike fright 38–49; stunt broadcasts 39–41, 45–8, 113–14; technique 71, 73–4
migrants (as audience) 29
'Mike' stunt 47
mike fright 38–49
Militant Women's Group 36
Millions in the Making 166
monopolies 50–2, 54–6, 161–2
  BBC 59, 153–4
Moore, Mrs John 200
moral censorship 186–8
moral values 129–31
Moses, Charles 97, 121, 133, 137, 150, 165–6, 170, 171–2, 195
Mothercraft Society 103
Movement against War and Fascism 181
Mrs 'Arris and Mrs 'Iggs 95
Murdoch, Keith 149, 155, 190
music 8
  classical, *see* classical music; community singing 124, 136, 141, 195–6, 203; companies 51, 53, 147; highbrow/lowbrow 128–32, 136–8, 151; interludes 125–6

National Party 51
national unity image 193–205
nationalization proposals 148, 149
'negroid tunes' 129, 130
neighbourhood entertainment 26
networking 156–9, 161
New Idea 27, 66, 83
news broadcasts
  ABC 52, 164–7, 169–85; censorship 177–89, 192; commentary 176–86; commentators 133, 167, 171–5; descriptive broadcasts 167–70; development of 163, 166–7, 196; impartiality 35, 36, 37, 176–8, 180–1, 186, 189–92; read from newspapers 42–3, 163–6, 172, 176–7
newspapers 179
  in broadcasting business 51–2, 146, 147, 149, 154, 155; propaganda 176, 177; radio promotion 12, 14–15, 16; read on radio news 42–3, 163–6, 172, 176–7
Nixon, Arundel 60, 188–9
'novel broadcasts' 40, 47
NSW Trades and Labor Council 33, 35, 37, 52
nuclear family image 89–91, 94

One Man's Family 96–7, 98, 100
'open set' scheme 13–14
Optimist's League 88, 196
outside broadcasts 39–40, 42–3, 167
ownership 60, 146, 156–7, 177
  property rights 50–4

P and A Parade 123, 134
Page, Dr Earle 11, 15
Palings (music company) 61
Palmer, Eric 44–5
Parkhill, Archdale 200, 201
Parliament House (Canberra) 194
Patterson, George 158
People Like Us 96
performers 51, 116, 117, 118, 122
personal radio sets 3
plays 81, 128, 136, 166–7

and playwrights 77–8, 188
political
  censorship 177–8, 186–8, 191–2; propaganda 32–7, 177–8, 180, 184–6, 189
politicians 116, 117, 118, 192–3, 205
politics 60, 112
  elections 35–6, 184–5, 191–3; in news 171, 175, 181; of radio 68, 156–61
polls 31, 136, 138
popular culture 1–10, 49, 54, 63
'popular' personalities 113–27
'popular' programmes 9, 136–40, 156
popular science image 11–19, 25, 28, 84, 87
Port Kembla dispute 183
Port Moresby Papua 157
Portus, G.V. 190
Postmaster General 9, 13, 14, 52, 82, 170
  on 'B' stations 147–8, 149, 157, 161, 177–8; censorship powers 161, 177–8, 182–3, 187, 188–9; complaints to 198, 199; regulations 12, 25, 28, 34, 49, 55, 57–60, 157
Potts, John 97
Pringle, Rosemary 104, 106
programmes 31
  audience choices 78–82, 139–42, 144–5, 158–61; content/services 44–5, 55; flow 125–7; government intervention 55–61; popularity 9, 136–40, 156; stunt broadcasts 38–47, 53, 77, 113–14, 136, 167; techniques style 76–8; timing 106–9; variety in 40, 42; women's 55, 76, 100–12, 200
propaganda
  capitalist 32, 33–4, 37, 52; newspaper 176, 177; political 32–7, 177–8, 180, 184–8, 189
public attendance (at broadcasts) 31–2, 43, 124, 141, 154–5
  see also radio clubs
public speeches 26, 173, 177–81, 189, 190, 191–3

quiz programmes 123, 124, 125, 134–5, 137

racing broadcasts 26, 52–3, 55, 106, 187, 198–9
racing clubs 52–3, 198, 199
radio
  annihilates distance theme 26, 28, 48, 194; announcers, *see* radio personalities; audience, *see* audience; content, *see* programmes; domestic commodity image 11–19, 25, 28–9, 66–8, 87; enthusiasts 12, 25, 68–9, 79, 145; equipment 14–17, 19, 31, 66–9, 80, 83–7; 'everyday' role 82–100, 203; form 5, 8, 76–7; language *see* language (of radio); plebiscites 31, 43, 63, 97, 118, 134, 136, 140–2, 160, 201; as popular culture 1–10, 49, 54, 63; popular science image 11–19, 25, 28, 84, 87; as public institutions 63–4; rivals 49–61; social relations of 43–9, 54, 70–82; social use, *see* social use (of radio); stunts, *see* stunt broadcasts; technology of, *see* technology; as threat 55–6, 91–4, 186–8; traders 16–17, 25–6, 28, 31, 38, 52, 53, 58
radio (world of)
  'B' class stations (problem) 145–62; cultural preferences 128–45; personalities (importance) 113–27
Radio in Australia and New Zealand 14–15, 20, 30, 31, 113
'radio catcher' 79
radio clubs 43, 141, 203
  'Advance Australia Radio Club' 103; *Australian Women's League* 104–5; *Happiness Club* 88, 105, 110–11, 196; *Optimist's League* 88, 196; *'Smile Away' Club* 88
radio and electrical exhibitions 11, 15–16, 18, 19, 66, 89, 203
radio magazines
  for enthusiasts 12, 68–9, 79, 145; highbrow/lowbrow debate 129–31 135–6, 138, 141; letters to 99–100, 121, 129, 141–5, 198, 199; on personalities 46–7, 113–14; on stunt broadcasts 39–41, 45; on technology 14–18 *passim*; women's pages 64–8, 101

radio personalities 40
  announcers 46–7, 71–6, 95, 132–3; children's radio 22–3, 36, 46, 47, 71, 114–15; performers as 116–17; personality style 1, 70–6, 95, 117–22; politicians as 116, 117, 118, 192–3, 205; popular (importance) 113–27; 'radio voice' 32, 71, 118, 121–2, 132–3, 137; royalty as 116, 118, 167–8, 197
radio stations
  ABC, *see* Australian Broadcasting Commission; BBC, *see* British Broadcasting Corporation; 2BL 13, 14, 16, 22, 25, 31, 66, 71, 126; 2CH 90, 104–5, 147, 157, 161; 2FC 14, 17, 22, 31, 32, 39, 42–3, 47, 51, 56, 71, 113, 126; 2GB 27, 60–1, 76, 78, 88, 103, 105–6, 110–11, 115, 174, 196; 2KA 160; 2KY 27, 32–7, 52, 60–1, 124, 126, 183, 185–6, 192, 196, 199, 202; 2MV 143; 2SM 126, 147; 2UE 16, 61, 114, 127, 158; 2UW 16, 61, 123, 126, 156–7, 159, 174, 199; 3AR 40, 46, 58–9, 127; 3AW 23, 74, 103, 111, 124, 134, 141, 147; 3DB 52, 60–1, 71, 88, 123, 146; 3KZ 73, 123–4, 134, 138, 147, 184–5, 199; 3LO 23, 28, 46, 51, 55, 58–9, 63, 113, 127; 3UZ 16, 175; 4QG 34; 5AD 147; 5CL 49; 6WF 13; *see also* 'A' class stations; 'B' class stations
radio style/techniques
  announcers 71–6, 95; distinctions (serious/popular) 117–19; listener's role 78–82; programme mode 76–8
Radio Times 69, 97, 134, 140
Radiola 17, 84, 85, 86
realism (in radio plays) 77–8
record companies 53
Reith, John 72, 130, 150, 151, 154, 177
religion 60, 63
Rhodes, Cecil 166
Robinson, Heath 18
Rockefeller, J.D 166
Roosevelt, President 116
Rosaldo, Michelle 110
Royal Commission on Performing Rights 54

Royal Commission on Wireless 25, 27, 34, 37, 43, 51, 54–7, 59–61, 63, 187
Royal Society 42
royalties 50, 53, 57
royalty
  image of national unity 197–8; as radio personalities 116, 118, 167–8, 197; *see also individual members*
Rubinstein, A. 117
Russell, Frank 71
Russian film industry 123

Saunders, George (Uncle George) 22, 46, 71
Scannell, Paddy 195
school broadcasts 56, 204
science (of broadcasting) 160
  popular science image 11–19, 25, 28, 84, 87
scientific management 109
Scullin, James 88–9, 149, 199
sealed set scheme 12–13, 28
Sellars, Vernon 72
serials 76–7, 95, 96–100
'serious' artists 118, 120, 121–2
'serious' music 128, 129, 143–4
'serious' programmes 9, 131, 156
'serious' talks 128, 132
'Smile Away' Club 88
Smith's Weekly 30
social class 62, 104–5, 153–5, 202
  self-definition 142–5; social power and 110, 111; *see also* working class
social reality, construction of (news) 176, 186, 189
social relation (of radio) 43–9, 54
  announcer techniques 70–82
social use (of radio) 4–9, 81–2, 205–6
  political propaganda 32–7; 'talk-back' 2, 25–32, 124; *see also* education function
sound effects 77–8, 166
Spanish Civil War 182
Spearritt, Peter 21
Spelling Bee 135, 137
sponsorship 2, 52, 58, 126, 149, 156
sport 128, 165

British events 195; cricket 43, 53, 71, 156, 194; descriptive broadcasts 168; Melbourne Cup 43, 98, 194, 195; racing 26, 52–3, 55, 106, 187, 198–9; radio club activities 104, 110, 111
Stalinism 185
starting price (SP) betting, 52, 53, 199
Stelzer, Mrs 88, 110–11
Stevenson, C.V. 114
strike activity 35, 184, 185, 186
Stromberg-Carlson radios 84
Stumbles 124
stunt broadcasts 38–47, 53, 77, 113–14, 136
 in descriptive broadcasts 167, 169
Sun 61
surveys (listener) 160–1, 201
Sydney Harbour Bridge 168
Sydney Labor Research Bureau 32
Sydney Morning Herald 52
symphony concerts 154–5

Tait, J. and N. 51
talent shows 123, 125, 134
'talk back' radio 2, 25–32, 124
talk shows 136
Talks Advisory Committees (ABC) 190
Talks Department (ABC) 174
tastes 29, 62–9; *see also* 'highbrows'; 'lowbrows'
Tauber, Richard 117, 118
Taylor, F.W. 109
technology 55
 in advertisements 66, 68–9, 84; of broadcasting 4–8, 14–18, 68–9, 205–6; of dramatized news 166–7; mechanical reproduction 6, 131–2; stunt broadcasts 38–47
Telefunken 50
television 2
Television, Technology and Cultural Form (Williams) 4
theatre stars 40, 113–14
theatrical companies 51, 53
Theosophical Society 60
Thomas, Alan 175

Thompson, J. Walter 126, 158
Those Happy Gilmans 77, 98
Those We Love 96
Thrills 166
Tier, Athol 40, 95
Time Marches On 166, 196
Time Radio Players 166
Tomorrow and Tomorrow and Tomorrow (Barnard Eldershaw) 203
Toscanini 117
Toti dal Monte 43
trade unionism 185, 198, 201, 202
Tupper, Fred 74, 121
Turnby, Gertrude 22

unemployment (in Depression) 88, 203
Union Theatres Limited 57
United Australian Party 149, 192, 200
United States 31, 35, 96–7, 133, 137, 166

valve sets 14, 15
variety shows 95
Varley, Gwen 103
vaudeville 95, 129, 189
Vautier, Dorothy 76
Voice of the People, The 124
Voigt, E.R. 25, 27, 32–5, 36–7, 49, 56–7, 157
'vox populi' programmes 123, 124
 see also audience: pariticipation

Walker, R. 149
war news 166, 169–70, 172, 173, 182–4
War Precautions Act 179
'Watchman, The' 174–5, 181–2, 191
wavelengths 13, 27, 61
Ways of Seeing (Berger) 6
weather reports 164, 165, 176
Wells, H.G. 32
When the Sleeper Wakes (Wells) 32
Whitta, C.N. (Nicky) 46, 73–4, 95, 121, 160
Whitta, Kathleen 74, 95, 160
Williams, H.P. 139, 175
Williams, Raymond 4, 16, 153, 154

Williamson, J.C. 51, 147
Willis, A.C. 35
Wilson, S.E. 42, 43, 56
Windschuttle, Keith 4
Wireless Telegraph Act (1905) 55
Wireless Weekly 96, 97, 108, 192
  on audience 53, 58, 79, 130, 188; on 'B' stations 136, 142–3, 147–8, 156; on personalities 114, 117, 197; radio advertisements 83, 87; on technology 68, 79
women
  advertisements aimed at 9, 19–23, 64–8, 83, 104–6, 111–12; in advertisements 68, 91; audience 8–9, 29, 36, 121–2; as consumers 9, 19–23, 102, 104, 112, 204–5; domestic role 19–22, 29, 65, 90, 101–6, 109, 110; gender identity 90, 100–2, 103–4, 110–12, 186; political interests 193, 204–5; programmes 55, 76, 100–12, 200; protection of (moral censorship) 186–8; radio clubs for 88, 103, 104–5, 110–11; tastes and needs 64–8, 69; *see also* family life
Women's Association 111
Women's Weekly 93, 104–5, 117, 140, 193, 194–5, 197
Workers' Education Association 42
working class 33–7, 49, 142, 144
  unity image 198, 199
Wrigley Company 97–8

For Product Safety Concerns and Information please contact our EU
representative GPSR@taylorandfrancis.com
Taylor & Francis Verlag GmbH, Kaufingerstraße 24, 80331 München, Germany

www.ingramcontent.com/pod-product-compliance
Lightning Source LLC
Chambersburg PA
CBHW070600300426
44113CB00010B/1328